THE C-WORD

A STORY ABOUT THE EFFECTS OF CANCER

Jean Taylor

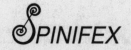

Spinifex Press Pty Ltd
504 Queensberry Street
North Melbourne, Vic. 3051
Australia
women@spinifexpress.com.au
http://www.spinifexpress.com.au

First published by Spinifex Press, 2000

Edited by Janet Mackenzie and Kath Knapsey
Typeset in Stone Serif by Claire Warren
Cover design by Wingrove Wingrove Design
Made and printed in Australia by Australian Print Group

National Library of Australia
Cataloguing-in-Publication data:

 Taylor, Jean, 1944– .
 The C word.

 ISBN 1 875559 99 X.

 1. Ovaries – Cancer – Patients – Australia – Biography.
 2. Lesbians – Australia – Biography. I. Title.

 616.99465092

This project has been assisted by the Commonwealth Government
through the Australia Council, its arts funding and advisory body.

Acknowledgements

I acknowledge and pay my respects to the Wurundjeri tribe of the Woiworung language group of the Kulin nation who are the traditional owners of the land I live on. And thank them for their generosity in allowing us to be here at all.

There were many more people who supported both Maurs and myself than are named in this book and, much as I would like to, it is impossible to name every single one of you. However, I want to acknowledge and say thankyou to all of you who featured in our lives during those powerful couple of years. We would not have managed without your boundless energy and creative humour.

Thankyou to all the members of the groups we belonged to: the Women's Circus, especially the Tech Crew and the Book Crew; the Performing Older Women's Circus; the Lesbian Cancer Support Group; and the Matrix Guild.

Thankyou to everyone who organised, performed, gave money and attended the fundraiser in 1996; to all those who helped shift Maurs into the flat in Gilligan Court in 1998 when she was no longer able to do it herself; to the womyn who painted Maurs' coffin and who were there at the funeral; to everyone who travelled up to Gariwerd in 1999 to scatter Maurs' ashes.

Thankyou to the womyn who organised the rosters and to those who were willing to pick Maurs up and take her into her daily radiotherapy sessions both in 1996 and 1998, and who visited her while she was in hospital. Thankyou to the various members of the households Maurs lived in during 1996 and 1997.

Thankyou to all those who visited Maurs, brought food, stayed to chat, rang, kept in touch, wrote letters, sent flowers and otherwise made sure she was well supported and loved during the last years of her life.

Thankyou to all the members of my biological family and their partners. And a special thankyou to all of you who gave me the support I needed, particularly after Maurs died.

A thankyou, too, to the medical staff at the three institutions Maurs attended: The Royal Women's Hospital, The Peter MacCallum Cancer Institute, and the Melbourne City-mission Hospice Service, as well as to her general practitioner.

Please note: I have chosen not to use the real names of any of the medical staff and have deliberately amalgamated some of their roles so that they cannot be identified.

Thankyou to Susan Hawthorne and Renate Klein for not only agreeing to read the manuscript in the first place but for publishing it. Indeed, thankyou to all the staff and associates at Spinifex Press and in particular, thankyou to Maralann who was the first person, apart from Maurs, to read this book.

East Brunswick,
July 2000.

Dedicated to the memory of
Maureen Catherine O'Connor
14.9.45 – 24.9.98

A woman of remarkable courage.
Generous, open hearted and loving.
She gave the best hugs!

Preface

Jean has been asking me to write down some of my feelings and experiences as I go through this journey of mine. I find it very hard to put anything on paper. All my life (younger) I have been told that I cannot spell and so I cannot write. At fifty-two years I now know that this is a load of bullshit. It is very hard to break a habit of so many years, but I have decided to try.

People I talk to about my Cancer and its prognosis often say, I suppose that I, or you for that matter, could get hit with a bus and we don't know when our number will be called. What they fail to grasp is that I live with the knowledge that I am going to die from this Cancer and I have to face this every day of my life. I wonder if thinking this way allows them to feel okay about my dying. I don't mean to sound smart about this, but if I allow myself to think this way then I may lose my edge on fighting this disease.

Another thing that I realised the other day, is that I am acknowledging my need for Jean. I had been trying to think when this changed, and I realised that it was the night over at her place when I had to call out to her to finish injecting the breakthrough pain injection. Before this I had been holding back.

Maureen O'Connor, mid-1998.

Contents

Introduction

Maureen O'Connor and I met towards the end of 1989 when we were both helping to organise the Lesbian Festival and Conference here in Melbourne.

During the festival I was attracted to this dyke with the friendly grin and her all-encompassing hugs, but was too busy and too caught up in my own emotional turmoil to do anything about it. So I was impressed when Maurs rang me to ask me out for dinner one Saturday in February. Unfortunately, as I told her, I had a fortieth birthday party to go to that night, and with my heart in my mouth asked could we make it Friday instead. We could!

We went to Fitzie's in Brunswick Street, Fitzroy, in Maurs' van. Had a bottle of red with dinner, and talked and talked; I laughed more than I had in months. Maurs drove me home and we sat chatting in the backyard before Maurs went back to her place with just a brief kiss in parting. I lay awake that night thinking it was the best night out I'd had in a long time.

The following Sunday, after I'd been to the Lesbian Co-counselling meeting in Fairfield (my life had reached crisis point), I was passing near Hammond Street, Thornbury, so I called in to see Maurs. She opened the door and immediately invited me in for a cup of coffee.

I stayed drinking coffee till Maurs asked would I like to stay for a pasta dinner, and then it was the video *Malcolm*. Finally, as I was standing up to go at about midnight, I thought, well I've tried. We were hugging goodbye on the nature strip when Maurs said, "You don't really want to go home, do you?" I was so relieved I didn't answer for a moment and she had to ask again, "Do you?"

Of course not. We made love all that night, and Maurs had to go to work at the Ministry of Housing the next day without any sleep. Maurs told me she had a lover and I said I had been involved with someone on and off over the previous two years, but neither of us felt committed to anyone.

I spent the next night with Maurs. By the end of that week Maurs had broken it off with the womyn she was with, and I had decided to make a commitment to a relationship with the other womyn in a do-or-die attempt to resolve the emotional ups and downs of our traumatic affair.

It took another four months for me to realise that it wasn't going to work and to make the final break. In the meantime, Maurs had started a non-monogamous relationship with someone else. That didn't bother me and, after we'd been to see *Peach Melba* at the Malthouse Theatre with a couple of other womyn on 18 June 1990, Maurs and I became lovers again.

So we continued in this way, Maurs sometimes spending time with me and sometimes with her other lover, till the night of the Winter Ball at the St Kilda Town Hall in July. As one of the organisers, I got there early to help set up. Maurs arrived to announce that she'd just been dumped. We spent most of the rest of that night dancing with each other and delighting in it because Maurs and I danced extremely well together, we discovered.

Apart from one disastrous attempt on my part a couple of years later to approach someone I'd loved some years before, Maurs and I were in a committed monogamous relationship from that night on.

We decided from the beginning that we didn't want to live together and we never did. Although it almost seemed that way, as we slept together most nights either at Maurs' place or mine. There were definite advantages in each of us having our own places, and we enjoyed having two houses to share. We could both be financially and personally independent and not have to negotiate about bills and furniture and cleaning rosters. When we were at my house I cooked and Maurs washed the dishes, and Maurs did the meals and I washed up when we were at her place.

We never presumed we'd be together on any permanent long-term basis. We took the relationship a day at a time, as Maurs used to say.

Maureen Catherine O'Connor was born on 14 September 1945. Her brothers Don and Brian were respectively sixteen and twelve years older. Her father was killed in an industrial accident when Maurs was four, and her mother died of cancer when Maurs was seventeen. Don was already married by that time, and when Brian went overseas on an extended trip, Maurs was on her own. About this time Maurs decided she was a lesbian and began a long-term relationship.

Maurs had left school and started work when she was fourteen. She had a series of jobs, as storeman and packer and owner-driver of a delivery van among others, and finally administrative duties in the public service. After a state Liberal government was elected, she took a redundancy package and left the workforce after thirty-plus years of almost full-time work. She was an active member of various unions and a staunch supporter of working-class politics.

The 1990s here in Melbourne were a dynamic time for lesbian events. During the eight years we were partners, Maurs and I were involved in so many of these it would be impossible to describe them all. Having met because of the Lesbian Festival and Conference 1990, we went on to help organise the LezFest 1991 in Melbourne during January. Later that same year we also travelled up to the Sydney Lesbian Festival, one of the very few times we went away together. As I was to discover, Maurs was not into travelling nor keen on conferences and such the way I was. Although I went on to attend all subsequent Lesbian Festivals in various states over the years, it wasn't till the National Lesbian Celebration and Conference in Daylesford in January 1998 that Maurs went to another one.

Also during 1991, both of us joined the Women's Circus. I attended physical training workshops during the year to learn circus skills. I was rapt when Maurs decided to be one of the techies on the end-of-year show, because we could both be on site over those weeks of getting the performance space ready and the show up and running, and during the performance itself. As I did my warm-ups I could look across to where Maurs would be adjusting lights or trailing leads. And she always made sure she gave everyone a hug before each performance. Afterwards, we talked non-stop discussing various aspects of that evening's performance.

Maurs and I worked in our different capacities on the first six Women's Circus shows from 1991 to 1997. They were among the best times we had together. Over several weeks it provided a womyn's communal space that we were not only part of but helped to create.

Maurs became a legend the time we were doing overnight security and she sat up in bed in the warehouse and demanded of an intruder, "What the fuck do you think you're doing?" He scampered back the way he'd come, to be picked up some time later by the cops who Maurs rang to report the break-in.

We did a number of smaller Women's Circus gigs together. In 1994, I was one of the Bitches from Hell—dogs on stilts—on the *Nightmare Barge* being towed down the Yarra River, with Maurs all in black as one of the techies in case we looked like falling overboard.

At the beginning of 1995, when I initiated circus skills workshops for womyn over forty, Maurs agreed to attend and learn how to do balances and be a clown. She was a performer as well as the head techie for the show we put on for International Women's Day that year.

The Performing Older Women's Circus, or POW, as it came to be called, went on to do four shows with me as the director. Maurs provided the technical know-how, as well as being a strong base for double and group balances, where performers balance one on top of the other, using their bodies to create a visual extravaganza that uses torsos, arms and legs as props, or to make a point, or just to thrill the audience. And Maurs was a consummate clown for each performance. I have to say that Maurs was the best clown I ever saw. It's a pity, as with the technical skills she picked up in her late forties, that she hadn't had the opportunity earlier in life to learn these particular skills.

POW gave us the opportunity to learn and develop new skills, and we enjoyed it all immensely. Not least because we were doing it together.

I was already a performer with Amazon Theatre by the

time I met Maurs. When Maurs became involved in the
lighting and sound for some of our performances (as
Dykelighting with one of her dearest friends, Fran Ryan), we
could enjoy and share these times together. Dykelighting
was also involved in the technical production of my one-
womyn play, *Matri-Spiral Descent*, as well as other plays
including Susan Paxton's *We Who Were the Beautiful* in
1993.

I had been a feminist activist since the early 1970s, and
by the time I met Maurs I was involved with numerous
collectives—the Women's Liberation and Lesbian Archives,
the Women's Building Council, Women's Liberation
Switchboard and the Lesbian Writers' Group. While Maurs
and I maintained separate political interests, we were
sometimes both involved in the same activist collectives.

We were both members of Lesbians Unlimited, the
umbrella group set up to cover the Lesbian Festival and
Conference 1990, which then went on to lend money for
various lesbian events. It stopped meeting soon after the
decision not to continue fundraising for a Lesbian Centre
in Melbourne.

Maurs and I were both members of the Lesbian Feminist
Organising Collective for the sixth National 10/40 Conference held in Healesville in 1992. While I attended all but
one of the 10/40s in various states over the years 1987 to
1997, this was the only 10/40 Maurs went to. These 10/40s
were for feminists over forty who'd been in the Women's
Liberation Movement for ten or more years. They were
held at Easter-time, were live-in, had a resident cook; with
workshops, a concert, a dance, fun and games. Challenging
ageism was the main purpose of these conferences.

The following month I helped initiate the Matrix Guild
Victoria Inc. to provide appropriate accommodation and

support for older lesbians, and Maurs joined as a non-active member. Although she didn't attend meetings she was responsible for typing and photocopying the minutes, and posting them.

When the Queen Victoria Women's Hospital was moved to the outer suburbs, a campaign was started to reclaim one of the old buildings for a women's centre in the city. Maurs joined the Access and Participation group and I became a member of Archives and Documentation to ensure that the Women's Liberation and Lesbian Archives would have a space in the building. I lasted a bit longer than Maurs, but even I dropped out when the state Liberal government took over and it became a corporate venture.

During 1992, Maurs and I both went along to a course called Women, HIV and AIDS Awareness, run by Jenny Dodd. We both worked as volunteers for the International Feminist Book Fair in 1994 and attended all five days of events. At a summer solstice full moon party at my place in 1991, Maurs, who'd never launched a book in her life, launched two of my books I'd photocopied to sell, *The Journey* and *Profile of a Co-Addict*.

After years of me being a confirmed Luddite it was Maurs who finally managed to encourage me to buy an Apple Mac computer early in 1994, and provided the venue at her house in Donald Street for my fiftieth birthday party. Maurs also gave me the oil and watercolour paints that started me back painting again after a lapse of over thirty years.

Also in 1994, we did a weekend Reiki course, and started a Lesbian Reconciliation Study Circle as part of the Reconciliation process between Aborigines and Torres Strait Islanders and the non-indigenous people, which ran for eight months. In the lead-up to the World Women's Conference and NGO Forum in Beijing in September 1995, the largest gathering of womyn the world has ever seen, with 30,000 participants, we initiated Lesbians Towards Beijing which eventually became the Melbourne group of the national organisation Coalition Of Activist Lesbians (COAL).

We went on dozens of womyn's marches, attended umpteen lesbian fundraisers, danced our feet off at numerous Women's Balls, listened to heaps of womyn's bands and music and enjoyed ourselves no end at lesbian and womyn's functions during the time we were lovers.

Maurs met my son, Geoff, before he left for an indefinite trip overseas, as well as my father and brother Victor at a family dinner in July 1990. They all took it in their stride, as they'd been doing for years, that I had another lesbian lover. My sister and Maurs met when Marg visited from Munich for a couple of weeks in August 1991. A week later, I met Brian, Maurs' brother, one evening over dinner. It wasn't till the following year, September 1992, that Maurs first met my daughter, Kristi, when she returned from an extended overseas trip. Two years later, Maurs came with me as my partner to Kristi's wedding to Dan, who was from Sweden.

It pleased me no end that my family were friendly towards Maurs and that they all liked each other, and that I got on well with Brian.

In 1996, when Kristi had a son, Sean Daniel, Maurs and I became grandmothers. It was one of the highlights of our relationship to share this most amazing role, and we entered into it with great enthusiasm.

Because Maurs was renting, she inevitably had to move a number of times as houses were sold out from under her. During the time we were lovers Maurs lived in no less that five houses before moving to a Housing Commission flat in

Gilligan Court, West Brunswick, just seven months before she died.

Since my van had been stolen back in 1993 and I couldn't afford to replace it, I was always appreciative that Maurs tried to rent places that were accessible by public transport from my place in East Brunswick. And in the same way Maurs treated my house as home, so I regarded these households as my home for the duration.

As Maurs used to say, we were meant to be together.

1996

1
Surgery

The phone rings. I bound out of bed as I'm half expecting a phone call from Maurs. Sure enough.

"The test shows I've got uterine cancer and the doctor said that I have to have a hysterectomy as soon as possible."

A cold dread takes over. Maurs has cancer. It's unbelievable. She's been spotting blood for some weeks, and we'd assumed it was the onset of menopause. She's fifty, after all. Just to make sure, she'd gone along for a Pap smear test. And this was the result.

"I'll be home in a few minutes. I hope you don't mind me telling you over the phone but I needed to talk to you straight away."

After we hang up I stand riveted, my mind a tangle of jumbled thoughts and feelings, as if all the organs of my body are closing down one by one. I'm encased in terror, unable to function properly.

Only last month a friend of ours, Diana Sands, had died of stomach cancer after it had been diagnosed only three weeks before. I don't want Maurs to die. I don't want Maurs to have cancer either. But she has.

And not only that—my mind leaps ahead—if Maurs has a hysterectomy in a couple of weeks' time, as the doctor has suggested, she won't be able to do the show, *Still Revolting!!!*, with the Performing Older Women's Circus in March. I can't deal with the thought of losing her support. And I don't want to face her disappointment if she has to miss out.

Maurs arrives home, finally. We cling to each other. I seem much more devastated and shocked by the news than Maurs, and cry in her arms.

Later that afternoon, at the POW workshop, I can hardly get through the afternoon, I'm so out of it. It's by far the worst time I've ever had with this particular group of womyn. In the circle afterwards Maurs tells everyone that she has cancer and that it's unlikely she'll be able to do the show after all.

I hear the words and get into even more of a panic. I'm convinced I'm no longer capable of directing this performance and feel paralysed with fear.

Tuesday 6 February
Maurs has an appointment with her doctor to get a referral to the Royal Women's Hospital. When Maurs tells me that the doctor has confirmed she definitely has cancer and that a hysterectomy is inevitable, I realise that I had been hoping that the original diagnosis was some kind of a mistake.

I'm reminded, of course, that this time last year, in the middle of training for POW's first performance, *Act Your Age*, Barb Anthony had dropped out to have a mastectomy after a lump in her right breast had been diagnosed as malignant. It hadn't made sense at the time, and it still didn't—how could someone so full of life and passion get a disease like cancer?

I don't mention to anyone, and especially not to Maurs who has more than enough on her plate, that this right arm and shoulder of mine, which have been quite painful for some time now, seem to be getting worse. On Sunday, for example, as I grabbed hold of a strap as I was getting off the tram for the Gay and Lesbian Pride March in St Kilda, the pain in my upper arm was excruciating. I have no idea what's causing it and it scares the hell out of me. It's impossible for me to mention anything as mundane as a sore arm to my lover who has cancer.

I mustn't forget to post Kristi's birthday present. Even though my daughter's pregnancy is now confirmed, I'm having difficulty getting my head around the fact that, all being well, we'll both be grandmothers in August.

Thursday 8 February

I have lost all confidence in myself and my ability to create a script that will do justice to POW's expertise as circus womyn. Then again, I can't afford to give in to any of these fears. I always worry far too much anyway. While I have this overwhelming and continual sense of dread and feel as if everything I'm doing is an uphill battle, Maurs seems to be coping okay.

I offered to go with Maurs to the Royal Women's today. At first she said she'd rather go on her own but has now changed her mind. Even though I'm not sure how I'll function as a support person, I'm glad I'm going.

The doctor is calm and practical. He books Maurs into the oncology clinic for an appointment on Monday, to be followed by a curette on Wednesday. If the results of the curette show conclusively that Maurs has uterine cancer, they will recommend a hysterectomy.

Surprisingly, this measured approach leaves me feeling a whole lot better. I feel as if Maurs has had a reprieve of sorts. After leaving the hospital, we walk arm-in-arm round the corner to Lygon Street where the café culture reigns supreme. Even though this Italian precinct has changed over the years, it's still one of my favourite places to eat and browse, with its bookshops, outdoor cafés and theatres. It's warm enough to sit outside and have a cappuccino and a cake while we mull over what the doctor has just said. Maurs is so positive she'll survive this cancer that I feel somewhat reassured.

By the time the results are back from the curette and Maurs then has a hysterectomy (supposing she definitely needs one), it's likely she'll be able to do the show after all.

This is such a relief. Not only for Maurs, who has put a a lot of effort into and gets a great deal of fun out of learning these circus skills. With the trauma and terrifying prospect of cancer in someone I love dearly, the whole process of getting this production together has suddenly become almost untenable.

Whatever happens, we have each other. That's the main thing.

Friday 9 February
I wake at 3.00 a.m. worrying about Maurs and POW and the whole damned thing. I'm feeling worse, if anything.

Later in the day Adrienne Liebmann rings to tell me that Jen Jordon, a member of the Women's Circus from its inception, died suddenly yesterday. It's all too much.

Over these past eighteen months or so Jen, Adrienne and I, along with three others, have been part of the Book Crew to edit the forthcoming Women's Circus book. I'm going to miss Jen's fierce insistence that no-one has any right to edit her writing. I only wish I had the guts to stick up for my work in a similar way.

It's raining and cold, matching my mood; snow on the hills for sure. As I don't have the energy or the inclination for doing anything else, I catch up on the backlog of archival material. Something mindless to keep me occupied. Otherwise I'll go mad.

Monday 12 February

Kristi, my three-months-pregnant daughter, is thirty-two today.

Maurs goes into the Royal Women's for her appointment at the clinic on her own. As it's just to let her know what's going to happen on Wednesday, she says there's no need for me to go with her.

I'm utterly exhausted trying to get POW's show together.

Wednesday 14 February

Maurs has to be at the Royal Women's by 7.00 a.m.

Even though a curette is fairly straightforward, it's the first time Maurs has ever had an operation. She's never even been a patient in a hospital before, so she's apprehensive. And cracking brave despite it all. And yet, knowing how tired I am, Maurs kindly lets me stay in bed while she heads off on her own.

Later that morning when I visit, I'm relieved to see Maurs sitting up in bed, still groggy but otherwise okay. Apart from the after-effects of the anaesthetic she feels as if she hasn't had anything done to her.

Maurs has to stay under observation for a few hours and can't leave until she's seen the doctor. As she's already arranged for Ruth Harper, one of the members of POW, to pick her up and take her home at around 5.00 p.m., I stay for an hour or so before heading across to Footscray for Jen's funeral. In her capacity as a solicitor, Ruth has drawn up two documents giving me both Enduring Power of Attorney and Medical Power of Attorney at Maurs' request, so that Maurs is covered in the event of incapacity due to her illness. Because lesbians are not protected by law, these are important documents to have just in case. I find though, that I cannot, because of their implications, even bring myself to read them and put them safely away.

I take part in the memorial gathering at the Women's Circus warehouse space after the service to do justice to Jen's courageous and talented, albeit tortured life, culminating in a bit of flag-waving and ritualistic burning down by the Maribyrnong River. By the end of the afternoon, I feel I've been able to work through my grief.

So much so that, even though it's been a long day, I feel more than capable of getting on with the business of directing POW's three-hour rehearsal that evening. Then I go back to Maurs' place to snuggle against her in bed.

Friday 16 February
While I'm trying to get this production off the ground, Maurs rings to say she has the results of the curette already!

According to the doctor, the pathology report indicates it's definitely a non-aggressive (whatever that means) cancer of the uterus. He's recommending that the hysterectomy be performed on 6 March.

"I told him," Maurs goes on to say, "that as we'll still be in the middle of the show on that day it wasn't convenient for me to have it done then."

"What did he say to that?" I hold my breath.

"He just asked if 13 March would suit me better. How about that now!" She's jubilant. "I said yes, of course."

I'm not absoutely convinced. With beds supposedly at a premium, I'm surprised the hospital staff are willing to do this for a public patient. How come there doesn't seem to be any extreme urgency to cut it out straightaway either, as so often seems to be the case with cancer?

"Maurs," I have to say, "are you sure about this? I don't want you jeopardising your health in any way. The show could manage without you if it has to, you know."

"Jean," she answers, "I'm sure. A week's not going to make a great deal of difference. And he wouldn't have agreed unless he was convinced it was going to be all right, would he? Don't worry," she reiterates as she has all along, "I'm going to beat this, I'm convinced of it."

I'm rapt. More for Maurs' sake than anything else.

"I couldn't bear not to finish the show, you know that," she adds now. "This way I can go into the operating theatre with a clear mind."

Can't argue with that.

Saturday 17 February

It's fantastic. The workshop/rehearsal this afternoon lasts almost seven hours and is very successful. All in all, we (almost) have a show that is more challenging in every way than last year's.

Later, at the AIDS candlelight vigil in the City Square, I'm reminded of that scene I wrote for Amazon Theatre's production of *Della* about a lesbian attending an AIDS vigil. It ended with the words: *I suppose I went because Della is dying and there's no memorial vigil for womyn who die of cancer.*

Not that Maurs is anywhere near dying, I tell myself hurriedly. But I think about all the lesbians I know who have died of cancer.

Tuesday 20 February

I've decided I won't give up my day job. Even supposing I had a day job to give up. I am just not cut out to be a director. The job's too nerve-wracking altogether. And far too much of a strain on top of worrying about Maurs.

A pity really, because I do seem to have the creative drive and the organising skills to be a director. The script I wrote from the scenes devised by the performers during workshops is just about completed. And we've blocked and rehearsed almost all of the scenes of this show within five weeks.

Maurs is still on board and gearing up to organise the Tech Crew. We start bumping in, that is, preparing the performance space for the show, on Thursday. As Maurs is being much more ambitious with the lights this year, I expect it will take us several days to do it all. I'm glad Maurs is here. She's confident and knows what she's doing.

I try not to even begin to imagine what life would be like without her if this cancer is not operable or curable or manifests again. All the fears I have in the middle of the night, I have to put them aside.

Saturday 24 February
Most of the lights are up, with the jigsaw mats covering the floor wall-to-wall. It's looking more like a theatre space, I think, as I look around the warehouse space during the Women's Circus information day.

What I'm doing here, apart from catching up with womyn I haven't seen in weeks, I'm not sure. Maybe to feel part of it again. Since the tour to Sydney to perform for the Sydney Festival in January, I haven't signed up to do any physical training workshops nor any of the gigs for International Women's Day.

Is this an indication that my involvement with the Women's Circus has run its course, perhaps? It is my sixth year, after all. And POW takes up so much of my spare time and energy.

I have an altercation with Donna Jackson, the artistic director of the Women's Circus, about which of us is going to use the warehouse that afternoon—Women's Circus or POW? Maurs has pains in her stomach and lies on the floor with her hands across her pelvis to give herself reiki. During rehearsal,

Rosemary Mann slips and falls off the stilts breaking her elbow.

I have to carry on, taking the performers through the entire script, from the fire at the beginning to the three-high group balances at the end, as we slowly rehearse one scene at a time. It all takes six hours, but we make it.

As the trainer/director I feel responsible for Rosemary's fall, although I'm far too exhausted to let it get to me too much.

Tuesday 27 February

Maurs is very confident about the outcome of the operation. She's certain that as it's uterine cancer it's contained, and the surgery will clear it up completely, as it did for Margaret Taylor, one of the members of POW's music group a couple of years ago. Reminding myself about this relatively successful story relieves some of my fears.

This painful right arm of mine seems to be getting worse. I now have a sore elbow, intermittent pains in my forearm, and excruciating agony in the upper arm if I move it a particular way. Lying on the shoulder at night is almost impossible. I still don't say anything to Maurs about it. The pain is perhaps indicative that some changes in my life are long overdue. Where to start though?

Maurs gets her letter from the Royal Women's, confirming that she's to be admitted at 9.00 a.m. on 12 March. The reality of the hysterectomy hits us so badly we both feel ratshit. But we have to keep going. It's our last run-through for POW's performance this evening. Crazy-making, but there it is.

Wednesday 28 February

I'm awake before 5.00 a.m. full of dread.

By the end of the day, my mood has changed considerably. After last night's ragged run-through, I was doubtful we even had a show. However, halfway through the dress rehearsal all my doubts and fears were swept away as the womyn picked up the performance and ran with it. For the entire one hour, fifteen minutes.

To say that I am on a high would be an understatement.

Thursday 29 February
Opening night, and I take a couple of aspirins for a tension headache. I really must find a way of not worrying so much about every little thing.

I get into outfit and make-up the same as everyone else because I prefer to be on stage, even though I leave most of the performing to the others. It seems to work okay.

I love watching Maurs and Mary Daicos do their very funny clowning routine on the ladder. The show would not have been the same without Maurs. She's not only an inimitable clown, and a strong base for the group and double balances, where the womyn climb on each other and create new forms to impress or intrigue an audience, or to make them laugh. She's a consummate and reliable performer all round, really. Not that I'm prejudiced.

Given how easily and competently Maurs has taken to the physical training and developed her clowning potential over these past twelve months with POW, it's strange that she's stayed with the Tech Crew in the Women's Circus and not diversified into the performance side of it with them.

Sunday 3 March
Three performances down (and last night's was the best yet!) and two to go. The creative process is what life's about, I decide.

Whenever I'm round the Koori community, as we are today at this Brunswick Music Festival street party, I can't help thinking how much we non-Aboriginals have missed out on learning from these resilient and talented people.

Later on, I stand in front of Megaera's drawing of Maurs during the opening of Megaera's big womyn exhibition "Abundant Beauty" at the YWCA. I'm glad I bought this for Maurs for her fiftieth birthday last year. With so little time now before the operation, this nude portrait will also serve as an indelible reminder of how Maurs is now, her belly rounded and without scars.

Tuesday 5 March
I'm in the backyard, happily pottering between the computer in the front room, trying to finish off the story I wrote about the Women's Circus in Beijing, and basking in the sunshine. Then Maurs appears, to tell me she has to be out of her house by tomorrow afternoon. As a temporary measure she's arranged to move into Ellen Kessler's place. Ellen, one of the Tech Crew members of the Women's Circus, has been really supportive since Maurs found out she had cancer.

What a bombshell!

Instead of having a nervous breakdown, as I'm tempted to do, I ring up and book a bus ticket to Adelaide for the National 10/40 Conference next month.

Wednesday 6 March
I wake in Maurs' bed at Tinning Street with my heart heavy as a stone. This is my last time in this little house.

As if Maurs doesn't already have more than enough to contend with: uterine cancer, the hysterectomy in a week's time, and now she's more or less homeless. A crisis point. And not much I or anyone else can do about it, except be supportive and hope Maurs works it out for herself.

Maurs is not the only one who has work to do. It's about

time I took my own problems seriously enough to do something about them. Like moving the Women's Liberation and
Lesbian Archives, for example, which have been stored at my
place now since mid-1992. And this is only one aspect of my
overly committed lesbian feminist activist life that I need to
look at in order to begin instigating the changes necessary to
restore some personal balance.

Tuesday 12 March
By 9.00 a.m., we're both at the Royal Women's Hospital,
where Maurs is checked into Ward 53.

Maurs sits propped against the pillows, still fully clothed,
at one end of the bed. I'm sitting with my feet on the bed
cover at the other end. The rigidly imposed regulations
about visiting hours and other equally ridiculous rules that
applied when I was training to be a nurse in the early 1960s
no longer seem to apply. I'm allowed to be here like this for
as long as I like.

It's not only a comfort to be with Maurs but it's the first
chance I've had to properly focus on this whole cancer
business. I've been totally distracted and preoccupied by
the show, and I know I've got some catching up to do.
Especially if I'm serious about being fully supportive of
Maurs while she goes through all of this.

Dr Jarvis, with several students in tow, arrives to hover at
the end of the bed. When Maurs suggests that she doesn't
want her ovaries taken out if at all possible, he is not
persuaded. In fact, he strongly advises that Maurs have both
ovaries out as a precautionary measure. And has anyone told
her that she'll have to have her lymph glands out as well?

"No, they haven't," she says, her face reflecting the
devastation she is feeling at the thought of it. We've read
enough to know that removing the lymph glands means that

Maurs could have ongoing problems with fluid retention in her legs.

Perhaps noting her distress at the way he's presented this totally unexpected piece of information, he sits on the bed to explain why it's necessary that everything—uterus, ovaries and lymph nodes—be removed in the one operation. He flatly refuses the suggestion that a frozen section be done, and the ovaries removed only after they're tested and found to be malignant, without explaining why. And we're too stunned to ask.

After a bit more palaver, as Dr Jarvis passes his vast knowledge about cancer on to the students (it is a public hospital, after all), he reiterates his earlier advice to Maurs to have everything out, including the ovaries and the lymph glands.

"Have a think about it," he says as he rises to go on with his rounds. "I'll be back in an hour or so." His joking manner grates on my nerves.

As soon as they've gone, Maurs and I hold each other and cry. It's all too much. It's not fair to expect Maurs to make a clear and informed decision in her own best interests when she's just now been told the facts. It's times like this when all my prejudices against the brutality of the Western medical system come to the fore. No wonder I'd given nursing up completely by the time I was twenty-one.

Unfortunately, I have to go because I've arranged to meet my friend Moss in Lygon Street for lunch. Moss and I met twenty years ago because of our mutual interest in writing. "Moss reminded me to tell you," I say when I get back, "that after her ex-lover's hysterectomy for uterine cancer, which was ten years ago now, she recovered completely and hasn't had any problems since. So that's something to look forward to, eh?"

In the meantime, Maurs has decided to go with the surgeon's recommendations and after talking it over with me she signs the agreement form for a radical hysterectomy. It's an impossible decision to make, with no way of knowing if it's the right one. Only the pathology results available a week after the operation will tell for sure.

I stay with Maurs for a while then go for another wander along Lygon Street while she has her dinner. I am full of dread but it's good to be out in the fresh air even if the sights and smells of this colourful street don't move me as much as they usually do. In a somewhat better frame of mind, I return to sit with Maurs on the bed and chat. About the implications of the operation, life generally, the likelihood or otherwise of post-operative treatment, familiarising ourselves with this new environment; confirming our love.

Wednesday 13 March
Maurs is first cab off the rank, as the nurse put it so graphically, and due to have her op at 8.00 a.m. The doctors and nursing staff at the hospital seem not at all fazed by our lesbian relationship and are quite prepared to recognise me as Maurs' partner. As such, I will get a phone-call from one of the surgeons later this morning letting me know how Maurs is and the results of the operation.

I spend a very restless and anxious morning.

Just when I'm beginning to think they've forgotten, Dr Kirk finally rings me to let me know that Maurs has made it through the operation and is in recovery. What a relief.

He goes on to say that the cancer was a lot worse than anyone had predicted. Apart from the uterine cancer there was also a definite cyst on at least one of the ovaries, so taking everything out was the only thing to do under such precarious circumstances. It will depend on the pathology results, of course, he continues, but it certainly looks as if they'll be strongly recommending follow-up treatment in the way of either radiotherapy or chemotherapy to make sure it's all gone.

This is too much for me to take in all at once. I don't want to know that it's more serious. All I care about is that Maurs has survived the operation.

"When can I go in and visit?" I ask.

I take my fortnightly dole form into the Social Security office and am at the hospital by early afternoon. Maurs is propped upright in a bed on the other side of the ward; an intravenous drip with a monitor attached is running saline into her left arm. There's a tube draining the bloody fluids from the wound into a plastic container on one side of the bed and a catheter emptying her bladder on the other. And to complete the hook-up she's got an epidural needle in situ in her lower back.

She's still so groggy she can't speak without slurring her words, and drops off to sleep in between times. She wakes to tell me that the womyn in the next bed has just been told that her ovarian cancer has spread too far for them to do anything about it, and she only has a few more months to live. On the other side an old Chinese womyn is snoring with her teeth out. All three womyn were operated on this morning and are being monitored by a sympathetic nurse.

Maurs is wearing thick elastic stockings on her lower legs to help with fluid retention now that her lymph glands are gone. She's not allowed to eat anything until she's farted because her bowels, which were handled during the op, aren't up to processing food till then.

I imagine all of this is going to take up quite a bit of my time from now on. If anything, I feel closer to Maurs because of what she's going through. And really, when I think about it, where else would I rather be?

Thursday 14 March

I visit Maurs first thing. She's much improved, not so sleepy, talking normally and concerned about the womyn with terminal cancer in the next bed more than for herself.

I glance through one of the books from the Absolutely Women's Health Centre downstairs. My eyes are riveted by the words about putting your finger into your vagina as a follow-up treatment to some kind of internal radiotherapy treatment that I've never heard of before. In fact, there's such a horrifying graphic depicting what looks to me like some kind of mediaeval torture instrument inserted into the vagina that I shut the book in horror.

A whole new world is suddenly opening up. Although I'm entering into it willingly enough, I'm not sure that I'm going to like everything that's involved.

At lunchtime I leave to take the tram down to the fore-court of the Victorian Arts Centre, where the Women's Circus is doing their lunchtime show to highlight the Amnesty International campaign to free womyn political prisoners. It's similar to the show we did at the NGO Women's Forum in Beijing last year. One of the Tech Crew, Ursula, is busy constructing the altars dotted about the forecourt in honour of each womyn being commemorated in the show. She gets on with the job quietly and efficiently, with the same gentle determination she does most things.

When I get back to the hospital, Maurs is sitting out of bed. Already. And I tell her all about what I've just seen. "Ursula's having a dickens of a job getting the altars bricked together in time but they look pretty fantastic even so."

At about 5.00 p.m. I head off to the State Film Centre for the launch of *Apron Strings and Atom Bombs*, a video on the herstory of the Union of Australian Women since its inception in 1950. I get back to the hospital to spend a bit more time with Maurs before I have to leave.

Saturday 16 March

I do the POW rehearsal but my heart's not in it.

Maurs is looking better each day. She had a shower yesterday, incredible though that seems only two days after the hysterectomy. In between times, I went off to visit Dad at the Alfred Hospital, where he's recovering from an exploratory operation. He'd found blood on the toilet paper after wiping himself. It never rains but it pours.

Fortunately, they didn't find anything wrong, but as he's eighty-eight it's taking him a while to recover enough to go home.

Sunday 17 March

This sore arm of mine is likely a result of carrying the world on my shoulders all these years. Or at least the Women's Liberation Movement section of it. Shoulder to the wheel, shouldering problems, all of that.

I'm finding it difficult to get started on this short story I want to write for the Royal Women's Hospital short story competition, combining the two subjects uppermost in my mind, Maurs' cancer and my daughter's pregnancy.

I leave it and go to be with Maurs. She has improved to the stage of complaining about the meals, the uncomfortable bed, the way the other patient talks incessantly about her condition, the continual noise, not being able to sleep at night, the unsympathetic doctors, and how bored she is with being there.

It's good to see she's well on the mend.

I mention a few of my own concerns. I'm not sure I ought to go away to Adelaide for the National 10/40 conference.

Maurs is adamant. "Jean," she reiterates firmly (we've had this conversation before) "it's absolutely essential for you to go away, especially as you're so exhausted and need a break. Besides," she continues steadily, "I'm going to need your support more than ever once I start treatment, and you'll be no use to me or yourself if you continue on the way you are."

I need to be reassured Maurs doesn't think that I'm deserting her in her hour of need.

"I've decided what we need here in Melbourne is a lesbian cancer support group," I say out of my long-time activist commitment to rectify a need by organising a group. "You know, like the one that was started in Sydney." However, I'm reluctant to be the one to start it, partly because I'm doing too much already and partly because as I don't have cancer myself it might seem a bit pushy. The fact of the matter is that I need a lesbian support group myself.

Maurs says, "Just take it easy. You don't have to do everything, you know."

But if I don't who will? And I need to be supported now.

I head off to meet Morgana Oliver for coffee. For many years, Morgana was Kate Lewis' partner, while Kate was fighting the cancer which ended with her death in 1992. So she knows what it's like to be where I am now. However, I note in myself that there's a hard core of resistance to Morgana's gentle and sympathetic probing. I can't or don't want to respond in the way she seems to expect. I'm nowhere near ready to deal with my deep-seated fears.

It's almost a relief to go back and sit beside Maurs, whose demands on my love and energy are quite manageable.

Monday 18 March
Such is my ignorance of these matters that I've had to memorise the words "oncology and dysplasia" featured on the noticeboard at the entrance to Ward 53, in order to

look them up in my Boston Women's Health Book, *Our Bodies, Ourselves*, to see what they mean exactly.

Each day as I pass the open doorway of the chemo-therapy room I can't help shuddering at the thought of those deadly poisons womyn are allowing to drip into their veins. I quickly glance in and away again, trying not to stare at these womyn sitting in armchairs, attached to the intravenous drips and wearing their various hats which only partly hide their bald heads.

I only hope Maurs doesn't have to have chemo. This dreaded and debilitating possibility hasn't been ruled out entirely, as yet.

By the time I get there, Maurs tells me she has had half her staples out already. "Want to see?" She discreetly lifts the bedclothes to enable me to peer closely at the angry red scar running in a crooked line (Maurs has jokingly complained to Dr Kirk that he can't cut straight) from the shaved line of her pubic bone, over her plump stomach, to wind around the left side of her navel.

Sure enough, only every second staple is still in situ and the incision appears to be healing well in between.

I ask Maurs what all those people are doing standing so still and silent at the far end of the corridor. She informs me that a womyn from the Cook Islands was brought in last night to die. Later we hear a child sobbing and screaming. "I think she just died," I say.

The child, a girl of about twelve, is being comforted as she is led away down the corridor. "But my mother is dead," she calls out in great distress as she passes the open doorway.

The nursing staff continue on as if it's business as usual and someone hasn't just died a few rooms away. No-one comes to tell us what's happening, let alone see if we might be upset by any of it. All the while the womyn with the ovarian cancer continues to explain to her mother that she's going to die within a few months. I start crying and Maurs holds me.

Tuesday 19 March
We get the pathology results today.

Straight after a POW gig at Moonee Ponds, I'm back at the hospital. Maurs, dressed and packed, is sitting on the bed waiting for Dr Kirk to arrive, which he does eventually. Sitting next to Maurs, he carefully takes her through the results before explaining the kind of treatment they're recommending. I stand helplessly trying to take in as much as possible.

It is much worse than we feared.

Maurs had ovarian cancer in her right ovary, as well as uterine cancer that had spread to her left ovary, to at least a couple of lymph nodes, and into one of the ligaments. They are recommending that Maurs has radium treatment starting in two weeks' time, five days a week for five weeks, and then chemotherapy once every three weeks for six treatments.

The side-effects will be possible damage to her bladder and bowel (radium), and nausea and hair loss (chemo). All this will be part of our lives for the next six months, at least. Till after Maurs' fifty-first birthday in September.

Just as I'm thinking I ought to be jotting this down so we'll remember it, Dr Kirk says he'll give Maurs a photocopy of the report right away and put all this information onto an audio cassette, so we can listen to it when we're not in a state of shock. We just want to leave, get home, shut the door on the world, light the fire and comfort each other.

When we get home, Maurs rings a few womyn to let them know the results, so they'll pass the news on to others. I admire her willingness to be open about the cancer and the proposed treatment. Especially when I know she's more upset by this than I am. And that's saying something.

There's a knock on the door and my heart sinks. We're in no mood to talk with anyone right at this moment. We need this time to lick the raw wounds of our grief and anguish. However, when I reluctantly open the door it's a courier with a bunch of flowers and a note from Sabin Fernbacher, an Austrian friend I met through Amazon Theatre. Which makes us both cry.

Sometime later, there's another knock. Same thing. We don't want to be disturbed. But it's another bunch of flowers plus a box of chocolates.

As these flowers sit on the table, glowing in their vibrant colours, we're reminded of how loved and supported we are by these friends of ours. The lesbian community has rallied with visits to the hospital, sometimes two or three times a day, and good wishes all along the way. And now, in this desperate hour of need.

Wednesday 20 March

We spend the day together at home, crying, going over the pathology results yet again, crying, comforting each other, crying. By the end of the day we're getting used to the idea of this long tedious business of treatment. We're going to survive all this.

"I know I had to cheat to do it," says Maurs, "but do you realise that I've actually reached menopause before you." This is a standing joke between us. I figure that as I'm eighteen months older I get to experience everything, including menopause, first.

Not so, it seems.

Thursday 21 March

Maurs has the remainder of her staples out. While the wound looks fairly well healed, there's a great gaping hole just below her navel which is nasty-looking. Maurs needs such a drastic bombardment of radium and chemo (with no guarantees at the end of it) because of the life-threatening nature of this disease. She had two different kinds of cancer plus secondaries, so the cancer had spread already.

At least her legs aren't swelling up much, although she'll continue to wear the stockings for a while yet. Indeed, Maurs is recovering well for such major surgery and hardly complains about anything at all. I'm glad she's staying here with me and I'm pleased I can cook and do other things for her while she needs this.

Friday 22 March

I finish writing the short story for the Royal Women's competition, "In Full Bloom". It is more about cancer than it is about motherhood since, let's face it, the cancer is uppermost in my mind.

We're not going anywhere or doing anything much. In a way, I'm enjoying this enforced inactivity and taking advantage of it to instigate a long overdue look at some of my own insecurities.

Saturday 23 March

Maurs attends the POW workshop today to say hullo and to reassure everyone that she is even better than could be expected under these circumstances. Her constitution might be as strong as an ox (which Maurs puts down to her weeks of physical training before the show) but she is exhausted by this, her first big outing since the op, so she has a sleep in the front room at my house afterwards, till Maralann, one of the POW members arrives to chat and give us both huge hugs. Maralann and I met at the physical training workshops at the Women's Circus initially and she has continued on to be one of the trainers and performers of POW, as well as a techie for the Women's Circus. She's always ready to listen, or help where she can. Both Maurs and I appreciate her concern.

Monday 25 March
On this sunny Monday morning, with Maurs sleeping here beside me, I'm reading the relevant chapter in Dr Trish Reynolds' book, *Your Cancer Your Life*, in preparation for the appointment at the Peter MacCallum Cancer Institute tomorrow morning to discuss the radiotherapy treatment Maurs will need to have over this next couple of months. I jot down some questions we will need to ask as I go along.

It's comforting to read a book by someone I know. I'm impressed by the wealth of detail and the inside information about what to look out for from a medical profession that I know, since my nurse's training days, does not always have the best interests of their patients at heart.

2

Radiotherapy

Tuesday 26 March

The Peter MacCallum Cancer Institute is now in a newly renovated building in St Andrew's Place, East Melbourne. The modern surroundings make this next part of the process seem less fearful. It reminds me, though, of the time my mother was having chemo at the Peter Mac when it was still in the old building in Lonsdale Street in the centre of the city, back in 1970. Not that I ever went there. Even though the doctors had told us, just before Christmas 1969, that Mum had only six more months to live, they recommended she have chemo anyway. It made her so ill that my mother, who accepted most things without complaint, asked me if she should continue with the treatment. When I said it didn't seem like a good idea under the circumstances, she stopped having it. I was impressed with her unexpected readiness to buck the system. She died on Thursday, 28 May 1970, three months before her sixtieth birthday.

I know Maurs has been told she ought to have chemo, but I'm trying not to think about it. The radiologist finally arrives. After Maurs has explained her concerns, he says that in Maurs' case they are recommending five weeks of daily radium treatment, as we'd been led to expect, and that without it her chances of recovery are going to be a lot lower.

He then says (and this rivets me to my chair with horror, recalling the diagrams I'd seen in the book Maurs had borrowed) that they think it would be in Maurs' best interests to have several hours of internal radium treatment. What this involves, is two rods packed with gauze, inserted into Maurs' vagina while she is under anaesthetic and then left there. While she stays flat on her back without moving, they burn the area to avoid any further possibility of cancer.

We leave the hospital stunned by the implications of this massive bombardment of potentially damaging rays. Without it, the doctor has said, there is every indication the cancer will manifest again. What choice does Maurs really have in the face of such an implacably presented potential for disaster?

Thursday 28 March
Maurs rings at about 4.30 a.m. to say she's been vomiting and has ordered a taxi to take her into the Royal Women's.

"Pick me up on the way through and I'll go with you," I offer. Just when Maurs was beginning to feel well enough to stay at her new room at Ellen's place for a change, too.

"You don't have to," Maurs says.

"I know I don't have to," I say, "I want to. Otherwise I'll just lie here and worry." When the taxi arrives, I notice Maurs' face is drawn with pain, but she's quietly holding on.

When we get to the hospital, the night sister on duty in casualty tries to fob us off. "What makes you think you have a pain in your stomach?" she queries. "Are you pregnant?"

"No way," said Maurs, grimacing through the pain. And explains why.

"You were a patient on Ward 53? Why didn't you say so in the first place?" Her whole attitude changes. "We take special care of the womyn on Ward 53. Anything you want, you just have to ask."

Maurs is quiet, too quiet, from fear of what these symptoms might entail as well as the pain, I suspect. The intern doctor on duty figures it might be a post-operative blocked bowel and sends Maurs upstairs to be admitted for observation and to get something for the pain—an immediate necessity as it's getting worse.

I accompany Maurs to see her settled into bed before I trail off home again for a shower and to finish off the POW script for an Amazon Games gig on Saturday. Doing the script helps keep my mind off frightening tangents. Then I tram back in again to hear that the diagnosis has changed. It's likely to be her gall bladder that's causing the pain.

Sure enough, an X-ray confirms that a stone has shifted to block the duct. "It's been so long since I've had an attack, about four or five years now, that I'd completely forgotten all about it," Maurs says, quite cheerful, now that she knows it's nothing more serious.

But it does mean that she has to have another operation. The surgeon from the Royal Melbourne Hospital calls in to discuss booking her into theatre within the next week or so. "Oh dear," I suggest. "I think I ought to cancel going to Adelaide."

"No way," Maurs is firm. "You're going to the 10/40 and that's final."

"But—"

"No buts."

I feel like a deserting rat. But, as Maurs points out, several of the Women's Circus Tech Crew, members of POW and other friends have been in to visit, so she'll be well looked after. It's a difficult decision, but I decide to go. I am absolutely exhausted. If I don't have this time away I'm going to collapse in a mangled heap and be no good to anyone.

I need to let go of that fear, get my own shit together, and let Maurs deal with her own stuff as she wants to, because basically it's not really any of my business how she deals with all of this.

Friday 29 March
I really will have to see a doctor about this arm of mine when I return from Adelaide. I don't think I've had an uninterrupted night's sleep for weeks now. And it's getting worse. Maurs is still insisting I go to Adelaide and has already arranged that someone take her in for her first radiotherapy session on 10 April.

This gall bladder operation is straightforward. They'll take it out through one of about four nicks they'll cut in Maurs' abdomen. It won't be nearly as traumatic as the radical hysterectomy. Thank heavens for small mercies.

Nor is a gallstone as frightening as the threat of cancer.

Saturday 30 March
We go to the Amazon Games, which is an annual event for womyn and girls to have fun trying out various sports and physical activities. Instead of getting involved myself in any of the games, like archery and tunnel ball, I spend quite some time, along with everyone else, being amused by the arm-wrestling competition. The lesbian community is demonstrating a remarkable degree of interest in and sympathy about Maurs and her condition. If I'm asked once how Maurs is, I am asked a thousand times. I can appreciate that this degree of concern is because of the high profile Maurs

has in the community, and it's gratifying to know that dykes do care and look after their own when the chips are down. But having to repeat the same story over and over gets to me.

Maurs spends most of the day sitting quietly out of the way in the stands. Even though I recognise that it's easier for everyone to ask me these difficult questions than bother Maurs, when the enquiries get too much I point out where Maurs is sitting so they can see her for themselves.

Maurs is so supportive. Just before POW is due to go on, she gets a chair and sets it up immediately in front of where we're going to perform. And then laughs, claps and cheers all the way through the performance.

Sunday 31 March
It's our last day together for awhile. We stay in bed and make love. And for the first time since the operation Maurs comes. In my mouth. Such a relief, especially for Maurs, as it was beginning to seem as if the surgery had done some permanent damage.

I rest my face against Maurs' inner thigh, my mouth still wet, my hand firmly covering the labia as the throbbing slows to a halt finally. Such bliss on this Sunday morning in autumn.

Tuesday 2 April
I'm in Adelaide and realise we were so intent on getting to the bus yesterday morning that I forgot to listen to the five-minute segment "Left Opinion" I'd taped for 3CR last week. All about Maurs and the cancer.

"Well . . ." I say, when Maurs eventually comes to the phone, "it's taken me a while to track you down."

"I had another severe gall bladder attack yesterday,"

Maurs explains, "so they decided I'd be better off in here," in Ward 53 at the Royal Women's.

Friendlier at least, where she knows the staff and is known. "What time do you go to theatre?" I ask.

"At ten. I've put Brian down as next-of-kin. Temporarily," she hastens to add.

I feel a stab of . . . what? Annoyance, disappointment, hurt? But what can I expect, being some hundreds of miles away? I give her the phone number of my billet. "If anything does go wrong I want to know about it straightaway," I tell her.

"Of course. How was the bus trip?"

We talk of this and that. I wish her luck with the op, tell her I'll ring again tonight to make sure she's okay. After I hang up, I decide to write down all of these experiences we're having because of the cancer into some kind of story.

At 1.00 p.m. I ring again to make sure Maurs is okay and unexpectedly find that I'm allowed to speak to her.

"I'm not with it yet," Maurs says around the ice they've given her to wet her mouth. "I'm just doing whatever I'm told."

"How many cuts?" I ask.

"Three, I think. I haven't looked yet. One's on the other one near the belly button, they tell me. Or four."

Relieved, and with a sudden burst of contentment, I head off out for the day to explore Adelaide. Away from the phone and all my commitments for a few hours of blessed solitude.

Wednesday 3 April
Because I don't want to get into any discussions about cancer at all for the moment I haven't mentioned anything about it to the womyn I'm billeted with. Then Maurs leaves a message on the answering machine about leaving hospital.

"Why is Maurs in hospital?" she asks.

"She had her gall bladder removed," I answer.

"Isn't that rather a big operation?" I can see she's puzzled.

"Not really," and in the overall scheme of things it's not, but I don't go into any more details. I'm only glad she doesn't push the issue. I'll be talking about the cancer at the 10/40, and that will be soon enough.

Friday 5 April

I'm at the 10/40 and because it's raining right on dusk we sit in the chapel with our candles, and gaze through the huge windows as the bush gradually fades from view and the candle flames are reflected back to us. As we mention the names of our many lesbian friends who've died over the years, including Kate Lewis, Morgana's lover, whose death started these candle ceremonies at the 10/40s, I'm struck by the number of us who've died of cancer.

I can't help wondering if Maurs will be next. Will I be saying her name too at some future conference? I can't help crying at the thought of what might happen in spite all the treatment.

Tomorrow I'm facilitating a workshop to get some feed-back about what I need to know about being a grandmother. I'll be taking notes for Maurs as well as myself.

I need to be prepared, as Kristi is due to arrive at the beginning of July and the baby is due about mid-August. I can see it now, Maurs in the middle of chemotherapy and our grandchild demanding attention.

Thursday 11 April

Sabin Fernbacher is organising a bank account for lesbians in the community to make donations so Maurs can use the money for whatever she wants. It's an excellent idea because without it Maurs hasn't a hope of being able to afford any kind of alternative care, which she's going to need—a naturopath and counselling, at least. Ellen Kessler has rallied a whole range of entertainers for a fundraising benefit at Rascal's Hotel in Richmond on 21 April. Maurs was very embarrassed about this at first, but has come to terms with the necessity of having some extra money.

Maurs told me on the phone last night that her first radiotherapy session has had to be postponed till today because the machine had broken down.

Sunday 14 April
Maurs has small blue tattoo markings on both hips and on her back so the radium treatment can be pinpointed to the exact spots with precise accuracy each time. As well as blue marker lines.

"It's a treasure map," I tell Maurs. "I have to read it so I can find the treasure."

And I do. Find the treasure, that is. Nestled between the labia folds of her cunt, tufted like a beard below the shorn mound of her pubis.

"The treasure map has led me directly to here," I say, as my fingers part the hair and begin stroking the smooth hardening softness in between. Maurs isn't answering my nonsense. She's too busy concentrating.

It doesn't seem to matter that we make love these days when it's more convenient.

"You don't mind," I check with Maurs, "that we're not in any hurry to go to bed these days?" Although we do still seem to manage to make love a couple of times a week.

"Why, does it bother you?" she asks.

Not at all. There's a peaceful rhythm to our less passionate lovemaking that seems to suit our middle-aged sexuality. The obsessions and angst of more youthful days are left behind without regret.

Wednesday 17 April
"Did I tell you what happened?" We are sitting in the basement waiting-room of the Peter Mac.

"No, what happened?" Maurs asks.

"I got my first acceptance letter in the mail this morning." I'm holding the blue gown and the green card as if I'm the one going in to have radiation treatment. "Not that it's any indication that the short story will be published." This many rejection slips down the publishing track I'm less than optimistic. "And a pity it's a United States anthology, in a way." It's not as if I haven't tried to get published in Australia.

Maurs knows about this, of course. I'm just making conversation while we wait. "Well, I think it's fantastic." Maurs is always supportive of my writing.

"Mrs O'Connor," a womyn in uniform calls out.

"It's not Mrs," Maurs says, somewhat impatiently, as we stand up. "It's Ms, and I'd prefer Maureen."

I stand outside the small changing-room while Maurs gets into the blue gown. "This is what the men wear," Maurs explains, as we go round to a curtained cubicle to wait some more. "Those flowery gowns were far too skimpy, so I asked for a bigger one and got this." She sits and smooths the blue fabric over her knees.

Another staff member appears. "This is my lover, Jean," Maurs introduces me. "I've arranged for her to come in with me today so she knows what's going on and understands this whole process I'm going through."

"A good idea," she smiles and gets me a chair. Support people are encouraged, it seems, judging by the numbers of us in the waiting-room.

"Okay, Maureen, it's your turn."

We stop halfway down the corridor for Maurs to wait in a chair till the previous womyn—in a pale flowery print gown —comes past and we can proceed into the radiotherapy room itself.

A large machine dominates the space. So she'll be more comfortable, Maurs insists that bubble wrap be placed in the incline where her stomach will go before she gets settled on the treatment table face down. As two young womyn arrange the wedges under Maurs' arms, place a pillow under her legs and align her whole body just so, an older womyn explains what's going on and what will happen.

The table moves up and into position. The blue tattoo marks on Maurs' body show clearly where the rays have to be directed for the minimum amount of damage. As the narrow bands of red light fall the length of Maurs' spine and across her hips, one of the womyn touches up the lines and crosses already there with a blue marker pen to confirm the positioning.

"Tear along serrated edge," I joke, as a broken series of lines crosses Maurs' back. Everyone's too busy concentrating to respond.

The tattooed dot, precisely placed so many centimetres from the base of Maurs' spine, is circled as one of the key markers, with a lined arrow pointing upwards. Maurs' head is turned to one side so we can see each other, and I'm glad to be there chatting, listening and taking it all in.

The two young womyn check and double-check with each other to make sure the measurements are precise and everything is correct, I'm pleased to see. Then they key the written instructions into the electronic overhead gadget, which is like a large remote control unit with lots of red lights and buttons hanging by a cord from the ceiling. The huge machine rotates around Maurs' body and locks into position underneath the table for the first dose. It's time to leave.

I stand outside where I can see the screen showing Maurs lying on the table inside. Again, all the details are checked and double-checked on the two computer terminals before the dose is administered for five seconds.

"Lots of small doses like this over a longer period of time means less tissue damage," the staff explain to me, as we all troop back to where Maurs hasn't moved.

The machine moves round to aim at Maurs from the top this time. Once everything is in position we go back outside again—a gate is shut behind us each time—to watch as Maurs is zapped yet again for the obligatory five seconds.

This whole procedure happens twice more to each of her sides in turn. After the last one, the table pulls back and lowers. Maurs slowly unfolds herself from the table, moving her neck where it has stiffened from being held to the side. As we walk back to the dressing room, we pass the next couple of patients, one sitting on the chair in the corridor, the other reading a magazine in the curtained cubicle. Maurs picks up her green card.

"Six down, nineteen to go," Maurs comments as she hands the card back to the receptionist at the front desk.

"You have your weekly appointment to see the doctor tomorrow," the receptionist reminds her. "So come here first before you go back upstairs. That way you'll already be in the queue and won't have to wait."

As we step outside I am thankful for the fresh air and the windswept streets after the hothouse atmosphere inside. Maurs immediately lights up a cigarette. I don't say anything.

While Maurs goes to the Royal Women's, I head off to my doctor's appointment at the Community Health Centre about this pain in my arm. When I did tell Maurs about my sore shoulder she was annoyed that I hadn't told her sooner and made me promise that I'll always tell her about such things in future. Fair enough.

Dr Patricia, who is Maurs' GP as well, talks for so long about Maurs and her condition that I have to interrupt to explain that the real reason I'm here is that I have a sore arm. After an examination, Dr Patricia gives me a referral for an X-ray, writes out a prescription for anti-inflammatory tablets and suggests I might need to have a cortisone injection into the shoulder.

"I'd prefer not if it can be managed some other way," I say, having heard that such an injection is excruciatingly painful.

"I see here in your file that you're nearly due for another Pap smear." She looks up as I make a noncommittal grunt. This is the doctor who did the Pap smear on Maurs and look what's happening to her. "I'll just mark down to give you one when you come to see me next week to get the results of the X-rays, shall I?"

I've read somewhere that because of early detection, the number of deaths from cervical cancer has fallen significantly, and this is one of the very few types of cancer where this has occurred.

I decide to have the X-ray straight away. For the second time that day I am in a room with an X-ray machine. Only this time, I'm in the blue gown, the room is dark and dingy, and the equipment has obviously seen better days. In fact, it looks positively antique compared to the machine at the Peter Mac.

Thursday 18 April
After hearing the Australian writer Robyn Davidson, who wrote one of my favourite books, *Tracks*, read from her latest book at the Comedy Club, I spend a restless night.

"Maybe I need an adventure," I say to Maurs. After all, compared to what RD's been up to over the years, my life seems dull and constrained.

"Life is an adventure," Maurs answers.

"You're right," I agree. It's one of the reasons I feel almost content about being included in this whole process that Maurs is going through: it feels like a journey we're both on together.

The phone rings. It's my sister Marg in Munich ringing to wish me a happy birthday. She compliments me about my article in the copy of *Journal of Australian Lesbian Feminist Studies*,[1] which I sent her for her recent birthday, and we compare differences in our quite disparate lifestyles: she's just back from celebrating her fiftieth birthday raging on a houseboat on the Thames in London, while I was at the 10/40 in Adelaide. Suddenly I realise I haven't yet written to tell her about Maurs having cancer.

It's not easy explaining all this over the phone and across thousands of miles, and I hang up feeling wretched. Not least because, twenty-six years ago, I had to write and tell my sister, in London at the time, that our mother had cancer, a couple of weeks before she died.

It was one of the hardest letters I'd ever had to write because it had taken me several months to come to terms with the prognosis myself. At the age of twenty-five, when I was told my mother had six months to live, I went into total denial, not ready to believe the terrifying reality that my beloved mother had terminal cancer.

Later in the morning, as Maurs and I sit in the waiting-room at the Peter Mac, I say, "No wonder I love you, you take

---

[1] *Journal of Australian Lesbian Feminist Studies*, No. 5, December 1995, editors Alice Petherbridge, Jean Taylor, Louise Enders, Sarah Yeomans, Tania Lienart.

me to all the nicest places." Maurs laughs.

Afterwards as we stroll up to the tram stop we kick our way, like kids, through the heaps of autumn leaves that have accumulated in the gutter and in huge piles on the lawn under the trees, laughing for the joy of doing this satisfying thing neither of us has done in years.

Monday 22 April
The fundraiser at Rascal's for Maurs yesterday was an overwhelming success in every way. Dozens of lesbians donated their time and energy and talents as singers and musicians, sound techs, performers, and what-have-you.

Ursula and Sabin Fernbacher had a great time introducing the acts, including Tiddas, the dynamic singing trio of Lou Bennett, Amy Saunders and Sally Dastey, which was an absolute bonus, as far as Maurs was concerned. We've been going to their gigs for years and love their music. The harmonious blending of their voices is a joy to listen to. Maurs cried when they dedicated "Come into My Kitchen" to her. POW did the same performance we'd put on for the launch of the Spinifex Press book *Radically Speaking* the day before. We both agreed that Ellen, who was responsible for most of the organising, did an amazing job.

The atmosphere was fantastic, and despite her exhaustion after her first week of radiotherapy Maurs stayed for the entire time and thoroughly enjoyed herself.

Tuesday 23 April
Reading Ian Gawler's *You Can Conquer Cancer*, I realise that I need to build up my own immune system in order to actively reduce the risk of cancer. Will definitely start bringing a lot of the healing practices that Gawler (and others) recommend into my everyday life. Like meditation.

A healthy diet. Reduced stress. Writing my personal herstory. And exercise.

Wednesday 24 April
Clutching the X-rays of my right shoulder I front up to Dr Patricia's office.

"Are you having a Pap smear done today?" she asks.

Having prepared myself, I nod. "If you have a mirror handy I also want to have a look at my cervix, if that's okay with you."

I haven't seen my cervix in years. Probably not since the late 1980s. Looking at it was something I started doing in the 1970s, using the plastic speculum I'd been given when the Women's Health Clinic in Johnston Street, Collingwood, closed down in 1975.

Dr Patricia is using the smallest speculum I've ever seen. I didn't even know speculums came in different sizes till Maurs told me that Dr Patricia had used a small one on her to make the procedure a lot less painful than it usually was. The speculum inserted, Dr Patricia takes the smears first, then hands me the mirror to hold at the correct angle between my outstretched thighs. I can see the cervix immediately. A glistening, pinkish-red knob with the characteristic side-to-side slit opening in the centre indicating I've given birth. It looks healthy. Dr Patricia tells me there's still no sign that menopause is imminent.

My sudden interest in my cervix is in response to Maurs' hysterectomy. It's as if I need to check on mine just to make sure it's still there and okay, while I can.

Dr Patricia tells me the X-rays show that I have some arthritis in the shoulder joint. I'm to keep on with the anti-inflammatories and make an appointment with the physiotherapist. Which I do.

Sunday 28 April

"You're crying for joy, aren't you?" Maurs asks, as we lie together in the aftermath of our lovemaking on this sunny Sunday morning.

"I am now," I say, as an irrepressible burst of laughter passes my lips, which is one of the reasons I love her to pieces.

Later on, my son Geoff visits and, because the sun is shining, we sit outside in the backyard. I get the wool I bought yesterday while I was in town with Maurs for her thirteenth dose of radiotherapy (fifteen to go) and start the rug I want to make for our first grandchild in purple, green, yellow and red. The bright colours merge and form shape quickly as my impatient fingers flash the crotchet hook in and out. I don't stop until one square is completed.

"What do you think?" I pass it across to Maurs, not really expecting her not to like it. "Will she approve?"

"Bright colours are good for young babies," Maurs says on cue.

My son looks sceptical. As much for the proposed rug as for my assumption that the baby will be a girl, I suspect.

But I can't complain. Geoff has been very supportive. He visited Maurs in hospital, he's on the roster to take Maurs in for her radiotherapy and both he and my brother Victor attended the fundraiser. A few years back, when his lover at the time was having treatment for cancer, I remember being impressed with his caring concern for her welfare. So it's perhaps not surprising that he's doing more than his fair share for Maurs, but I'm grateful, nevertheless.

Saturday 4 May

I am reading *Heal Cancer: Choose Your Own Survival Path* by Dr Ruth Cilento and am utterly absorbed. You have a good chance of healing cancer, she says, with a combination of strategies: meditate, be creative, have a positive attitude, give and receive love, strengthen the immune system with fresh fruit and vegetables (mainly taken in juice form in order to absorb more) and eat a strictly balanced diet. And alter such life-threatening habits as stress-related behaviour, a high fat diet, addictions such as smoking and don't do anything, including exercise and sport, to excess.

It all makes sense but requires a level of commitment I'm not sure I'm capable of taking on.

Monday 6 May
We are sitting in the quiet room of Ward 53 next to the boxful of toys and other assorted paraphernalia. Dr Kirk is telling Maurs that she has only a fifty-fifty chance of survival even with the chemotherapy he's recommending.

He doesn't think that a healthy diet would do Maurs any harm when she mentions that she's working in conjunction with her naturopath to build up her immune system in preparation for the onslaught of the chemo. Which, among other things, Dr Kirk tells her, will cause temporary hair loss, maybe some permanent hearing impairment, and make her nauseous in the extreme. And it will also lower her resistance to disease by killing off her white blood cells to life-threatening levels.

"While you're having the chemo, if you do get an infection come and see us straight away," he emphasises, "so that we can deal with it before it gets out of hand."

Given the severe limitations of the standard procedures —surgery, radiotherapy and chemo—the major thing Maurs has going for her at the moment is her positive attitude and her willingness to explore her options with an open mind. We walk round the corner to Lygon Street to try and restore our equilibrium by relaxing over cakes and coffee at one of the tables on the footpath.

When I get home I find a notice in my post office box from Dr Patricia informing me that my recent Pap smear was normal and recommending I have another one in a year's time.

Wednesday 8 May

I'm absolutely furious because I have to put in my dole form unexpectedly this morning. However, on the tram up Sydney Road I realise my anger is a symptom of this overall situation.

Yes, I'm angry at Social Security for fucking me around. But I also identify that this anger has more to do with the cancer and the debilitating treatment Maurs is having to endure. And that feeling of being trapped in a terrifying situation not of my own making and having to deal with it whether I like it or not. Just thinking of this makes me feel better.

I've always been able to express my anger and, as a working-class female, there's a lot for me to be angry about. However, I've had to learn how to express my anger in appropriate ways and channel it positively, rather than just rage at others, as I used to do in the past.

That evening, I ask Maurs to check out the mouth ulcer I've developed. A sure sign of stress. I'm dozing off by the time Maurs gets into bed. I switch out the light, turn over to lie on her shoulder in the curve of her left arm and am instantly asleep.

Thursday 9 May

Because it is now too tiring for Maurs to go into the Peter Mac by public transport every day, Sabin Fernbacher has organised a roster of people to drive her there and back. Which is why we both find ourselves waiting an unprecedentedly long time for today's radiotherapy with someone else for company. The machine's broken down, we're told eventually. Well then, could she see the doctor for her weekly check-up while we're waiting for it to be fixed, Maurs asks? Sure.

Unbelievable. Maurs strikes a doctor who chats about his own problems rather than what's happening with Maurs. Maurs sympathises, but in my head I'm asking who's the patient here? I manage to keep my mouth shut.

Back in the waiting-room I amuse Maurs and myself by enacting outrageous scenarios with the children's hand puppets.

"We'll pretend she's not with us," says the other womyn, who's embarrassed.

As we walk back to the truck I say, "Want to hear a sick joke? When you leave the Peter Mac, how can you tell which people are the ones who are having treatment for cancer?"

"I'm not sure I want to know," the womyn protests.

I tell her anyway, "They're the ones who, as soon as they're out the door, light up a cigarette."

"That's a terrible thing to say," she admonishes me, with a glance at Maurs to see how she's taking it. "It's sick." Not that this stops Maurs from smoking.

That evening we attend our first meditation class for beginners. The meditation program is free because, according to the leaflet I picked up, the group believes that meditation, which involves getting in touch with our true selves, is not something to be bought or sold. We sit on chairs in a loft with high vaulted ceilings, close our eyes and are guided through the initial stages of the technique in a gentle and informative manner.

As all of the healers we've been reading recommend meditation as a way of life for everyone, and even more essential for people with cancer who want to get well again, we leave the class feeling we've at least made a start.

Friday 10 May

I'm sitting up in bed trying, somewhat belatedly, to recap some of the events over these past few hectic days when Maurs walks in with two brimming glasses of murky liquid. Maurs has taken to juicing fruit and vegies according to the recommendations of Dr Ruth Cilento et al.

"What is it today?" I ask, accepting the glassful of raw nourishment.

"You have to guess," says Maurs and before I can answer she tells me. "Carrots, pear and celery."

It's delicious.

Saturday 11 May

With a new trainer, it's a relief to be part of the POW workshop without having to take responsibility for running it. Beforehand, I call in to the Peter Mac and spent my third radiotherapy session for the week with Maurs.

As we are leaving the building, Maurs lights a cigarette. "Have you thought about giving up smoking?" I ask cautiously. I've been thinking a lot about this lately, about how Maurs is still addicted.

"Yes, I have," says Maurs, "but not at the moment. I couldn't handle it."

"Perhaps before you begin chemo might be a good time," I suggest. "Your body will have enough to contend with trying to deal with the chemo without the extra poison of nicotine as well."

"Don't push me, Jean. I said I'm not ready yet. Okay?"

I keep my fears to myself. And we go and kick through the growing piles of autumn leaves at the end of the street instead.

There're a few of us sitting together at the performance space, La Boite, waiting for Lou Bennett from Tiddas and

Ruby Hunter, both Aboriginal singers, to entertain us in
their inimitable ways. Mention is made about me becoming
a grandmother.

"I'll never be a grandmother," Ursula says, meaning she's
never had children therefore it's impossible.

"Well, I'm going to be a grandmother," contradicts
Maurs, in a similar position to Ursula as far as children are
concerned.

I'm very glad that Maurs is so accepting of this new role.
Grandmothers, I'm coming to realise, are not what you'd
call big news in the lesbian community.

Tuesday 14 May
Maurs has been going to yoga classes for physical exercise
till she's well enough to go to the more strenuous POW
workshops again.

We're at the Royal Women's for the first of the eight
weekly Living With Cancer sessions being run by two of the
nurses we know from Ward 53. These sessions are free and
have been devised by the Anti-Cancer Council to provide
much needed support and information to cancer survivors
and their friends.

While I crotchet some more of the squares for the baby's
rug, we watch the introductory video and introduce ourselves. It helps to know that other womyn have experienced
similar fear and trauma. And no-one bothers when Maurs
and I say we're lesbian partners. I find the two hours of
talking about nothing but cancer and related issues is just
what I need.

Friday 17 May
It's definitely going to take me some time to get used to this
meditation business. It's amazing how long a mere five

minutes takes to pass when I'm sitting cross-legged on my bed with my hands on my knees and my eyes closed.

Yesterday, Maurs and I spent the morning at the Peter Mac watching the video and being instructed about the intracavity caesium. It all sounded horrific, although the video concentrated more on the breathing and leg exercises that patients need to do while they're flat on their backs not moving during treatment, than on the insertion of the rods into the vagina. Under anaesthetic, fortunately.

The social worker showed us the plastic cylinder (resembling a plain dildo) that has to be inserted into the vagina for approximately ten minutes every day after the operation to prevent the raw lining of the vagina from fusing together. All three womyn paid $10 for one of their very own. The social worker then explained about the douche of bi-carb of soda to aid the healing process. In Maurs' case the radiology will last for approximately fourteen hours. We were horrified to hear that the quite elderly womyn in a wheelchair will be having two doses of twenty hours each time. Afterwards, Maurs had an electro-cardiagram done to make sure her heart is fit enough to withstand the operation, some more of the inevitable blood tests, and a chest X-ray. Before going downstairs for her second-last radiotherapy zap.

Today, I tram into the Peter Mac to be with Maurs for her twenty-eighth and final radiology session. Five and a half weeks all told, and because they have it down pat now it's all over in a matter of minutes. Then, the two womyn on the transport roster who picked Maurs up this morning, drive us round to Café Rumours, one of the gay-owned cafés in Brunswick Street, where we have milkshakes and mud cake to celebrate the end of yet another one of these barbaric treatments.

3

Intracavity Caesium

Sunday 19 May
I jolted my shoulder so badly yesterday when I was helping Maurs move into a shared household in Bruce Street, Coburg, that I had to sit down the pain was so excruciating.

This week, I managed to do an article for *Lesbiana*, the local monthly lesbian magazine, with the theme of cancer. I'm finding it helps to write about it.

Fairlea Women's Prison is closing and we go to the final protest, Wring Out/Ring Around, where the hundreds of protesters form a ring around the prison and hold hands in solidarity with the prisoners who are protesting about the imminent closure and being moved to a privately run prison. It's another predominantly dyke event, and we spend a pleasant afternoon listening to the music and chatting to our friends who drift up to say hullo and find out how Maurs is.

Tuesday 21 May
Maurs found a naturopath who has been treating her over this last little while with some foul-tasting mixture and now

slippery elm bark, among other things, in preparation for the chemo next month. She also rang the Housing Commission yesterday to enquire about emergency housing, and seems to be taking vitamin tablets by the dozen.

Dr Kirk is the speaker at this evening's session of Living With Cancer. He explains what cancers actually are and answers everyone's questions in an easily understandable fashion. I want to know about his attitude to non-traditional treatment, and he admits it's not encouraged at the Royal Women's.

Even these sessions are being done by two nurses in their spare time entirely without pay. This is a disgrace when you think of the billions of dollars that go into cancer research and treatment every year, so long as it's along well-established lines.

Wednesday 22 May
Every second book I read is a murder mystery. Alternating murder mysteries with the books about cancer makes for a more balanced and palatable reading regime.

I tell Maurs that, because her smoking is making me anxious about her health, and she's taking her time giving it up, from now on my house is smoke-free. She tells me she doesn't have a problem with that.

I think with everything going on in my life I might be cracking up.

Sunday 26 May
After Maurs is booked into Ward 9 at the Peter Mac for her intracavity caesium operation tomorrow morning, we are told about all the procedures.

The main thing is, once Maurs is hooked up to the radiotherapy machine, every time anyone goes into the room the machine has to be switched off. I'll only be allowed to go in to her for no more than fifteen minutes at a time. Otherwise the whole process will take even longer than the eleven or so hours Maurs is down for.

Heaven forbid.

We take down the name tag above Maurs' bed and it's a simple matter to cut out the "r" in the Mrs and put it back together again as Ms.

All this horrific treatment Maurs is going through, plus the cancer, has brought us closer. We no longer take being together for granted and make sure we have fun in each other's company wherever we are.

Before I go to sleep I eat a whole 200-gram block of dark rum and raisin chocolate and draw a picture of myself lying curled up under Maurs' bed at the hospital.

Monday 27 May
It's early morning and I'm meditating. The phone rings. It's Maurs.

She's ready to go but no-one's arrived to take her to theatre yet. She announces, "I'm off to Adelaide for ten days on 1 June," to stay with her good friend Joan Russell, where she can recover from all the radiotherapy she's had before she has to start chemo on 17 June.

What with one thing and another it's about five o'clock by the time I visit Maurs. I discover that, because it's taken about five hours or so to set the computer, Maurs has only just been attached to the machine. So I stand helplessly outside the plastic chain barrier across the door that warns me the machine is on, as Maurs tells me how much it is hurting her and trying not to cry.

This image of Maurs in pain and uncomfortably flat on her back unable to move is not the impression we got from the video. All I want to do is go in and give her a hug, but they tell me it's too soon and will only add to the time if they have to keep turning the machine on and off. As if the five hours they took setting it up in the first place was nothing. How long do they think it takes to hug someone?

"I have to be on this for 11 hours 36 minutes, so they tell me." Mediaeval torture, although slightly less time than we'd been told originally. Maurs holds up her arm. The drip has come out and she's bleeding. She rings the bell so I can get in to see her properly.

"I want you to have a look at it," says Maurs to me, after one nurse has put a dressing on the back of Maurs' hand and gone off with the almost empty saline bag and intravenous paraphernalia, and another nurse is off looking for a container to empty the urine out of the full bag attached to the side of the bed.

I carefully lift the bedclothes. I hardly dare look at the cords from the machine that run straight into the packing spilling out from Maurs' swollen cunt. I can't see them, but the rods inserted into the vagina are packed with a considerable amount of gauze, to help keep them in place and protect the surrounding area. The radium is being aimed at the top end of the vagina where the uterus and cervix were cut away, as that is one of the most likely places for the cancer to manifest again.

I notice the labia is also closed round the tube of the catheter curling into the bag that the nurse is even now emptying into a plastic jug.

"Oh my darling," I murmur as I smooth the hair back off her forehead and try to kiss her better.

I have never seen Maurs looking so distressed. After the hysterectomy she was sleepy, then mainly bored. Five weeks of radiotherapy had made her tired. But this is something else again. It's as if she's impaled to the bed by these rods.

She's in pain, not allowed to move, and entirely at the mercy of the machine in the corner that is designed to send deadly rays into the most intimate part of her body.

With the machine back on I'm on the other side of the barrier when dinner arrives. The ward womyn leaves the tray on the chair I've been sitting on, so I have to stand. When I inform the nurse the meal has arrived, she says she's been told it will be another half-an-hour before the machine can be turned off again in order for Maurs to eat. I can hardly believe anyone can be that uncaring.

Another sister comes along. She not only switches the machine off so she can turn Maurs over onto her side to give her some relief for her back (after all, it is hardly Maurs' fault they took so long to hook her up in the first place) but also gives her something for the pain.

Thus Maurs is able to lie on her side in a more comfortable position while she eats her toasted ham and cheese sandwiches and attempts some of the too-sweet jelly. (We've been told that it's better to eat only a small amount so Maurs isn't tempted to shit before the rods are taken out.) And I'm allowed to stay there and give her little kisses in between bites.

I leave soon after Maurs is given a shot of morphine, before being moved onto her back in anticipation of a few hours of television viewing to take her mind off what she's going through. I'm late for the POW meeting, and because punctuality has always been one of my strong points, I'm now anxious about this as well. But what the hell, I tell myself. It won't hurt for a change.

Tuesday 28 May
I'm meditating when the phone rings.

"I thought we'd agreed you weren't going to ring

between seven and eight in the morning," I remind Maurs, annoyed because it takes all my concentration and effort to learn to meditate, and this is the second morning in a row that I've been interrupted.

"I'm sorry. I thought it was later than that. I've just had the packing and the rods taken out and it hurt." She starts to cry. "I'm sorry, I'll ring back later."

I'm immediately contrite. "That's okay, darling. I'm glad you rang, tell me about it."

We talk. Maurs tells me how much it hurt as the stitches through her labia majora to hold it all in place were cut and removed (they must have been underneath as I hadn't seen them yesterday). Then yards and yards of packing had been unravelled out. "It felt like a whole pillow was stuffed up there." That was the worst of it. Finally the rods themselves, resembling the rods put into the toes of shoes, according to Maurs, were removed. It was all so extremely painful Maurs had had to grip the end of the bed to help her bear it.

As Maurs had kept saying last night, it had to be boys that invented something like this. If they had to have rods shoved down their dicks they wouldn't be so complacent about it. "They gave me another injection and a couple of sleeping pills, so I managed to get a good night's sleep," Maurs goes on to say.

A bloody good thing if you ask me. "What time shall I pick you up?"

"Whenever you're ready. I've had my first douche and the nurse has shown me how to use the apparatus when I get home. I've got my dildo, not that I'm too thrilled about that because they didn't have a small size and I'm not sure I'll be able to use this one. Oh, and by the way, don't forget to buy more wool for the baby's rug on the way through the city, will you?" she reminds me. It's typical of Maurs that she is still considering my needs despite her own suffering.

Maurs is asleep in the chair by the side of the bed when I get there, her feet propped up on a stool. She tells me how painful it is sitting down. We take a taxi back to my place.

Maurs lies back on the bed while I hold the mirror so she can see for herself what her poor bruised and tender cunt looks like after all the messing about it's had. There is one particularly large purple bruise on the left side and another smaller one opposite. Knowing how rough doctors can be with patients under anaesthetic it's awful to think about how she came to get these.

"It almost looks as if you've been sexually assaulted," I say, trying not to look as horrified as I feel about what this whole procedure has done to Maurs both physically and psychologically.

"It feels as if I've been sexually assaulted," Maurs says, with feeling. "I feel violated by this whole damned business. I'm never going through this ever again."

I gently smooth baby oil onto Maurs' swollen genitals, especially round the perineum, that tender place on womyn, trying to restore the balance and soothe away the pain. I love Maurs' plump cunt and tell her so before we curl up together and go to sleep.

Wednesday 29 May
I did over half-an-hour of meditation for the first time this morning. Maybe it means I'm finally getting the hang of it.

Maurs lubricates the nozzle of the hose attached to a plastic bag full of water, and sits down on the toilet to insert it into her vagina. While I hold the bag aloft, Maurs releases the clamp and the warm bi-carbonated water pours into her vagina and out again into the toilet.

The douche is over in less than a minute.

"I still feel funny about it," says Maurs.

As it's cleaning out all the residue from the radiotherapy until the vagina is healed enough to do this for itself, it's an essential part of the healing process. But I can understand Maurs' reluctance about it.

"Now for the other." She undoes the packet containing a cylinder that looks far too big for a long-time lesbian who has never had children. "This is the medium size."

"Bloody hell," I exclaim. "What must the large be like?"

Even with the lubricant, it's far too painful for Maurs to get this cylinder-thing into her red-raw vagina. I leave her lying on the couch with the rug over her and her finger doing the job of preventing her vagina from closing off altogether.

On a closer examination of Maurs' cunt, before we go to sleep, I find a couple of longish scabs where she's been scratched—probably by the careless handling of surgical instruments. Plus two small scabs that could indicate where one of the sutures went in and out on the right labia. This is besides the bruising still much in evidence.

When I part the labia some more, I can quite clearly see the red raw entrance to the vagina. What must it look like inside where the radium's been doing its damage?

Thursday 30 May

After the way her vagina looked last night, it's no wonder Maurs is bleeding this morning. I'm surprised she can put the nozzle of the douche into her poor, beleaguered insides, the way they are at this stage.

"I'm not cancelling the trip to Adelaide for anyone," Maurs mutters, to cover, I suspect, her anxiety about what the bleeding might indicate.

"I'm not all that happy with the way I was treated by the doctors on that operating table either," she goes on, "They need to be made accountable for how they do these barbaric procedures." Maurs stomps off to the Peter Mac in a high dudgeon to have them check out the bleeding and to tackle them about all of this. As Maurs rarely gets angry, this is quite a transformation.

I hark back to the video in my mind. There was no mention of how uncomfortable, awkward and painful the whole procedure was going to be. The reality was so drastic, all Maurs wanted was to be drugged and out of it for the duration.

Friday 31 May
"Success!" says Maurs' triumphant voice from the next room. "I didn't think it would ever stop." Then "Um, um, I can't reach the rug."

I go in. Maurs is lying back on the cushion, knees wide apart, feet touching, in the familiar diamond position, with about two inches of the white cylinder sticking out of her vagina, one hand holding it in place. Now there's a sight I never thought I'd see. I cover her legs with the rug to keep her warm for the next ten minutes. Maurs glances at her watch to time herself.

Maurs had picked up this smaller and more convenient version of the cylinder from the doctor at the Peter Mac yesterday. After she'd expressed her anger at the way she'd been treated, what she thought of his technique, and how violated she felt by the whole procedure.

If nothing else, this cancer is clearing away a lot of our old habits of accepting authority towards a more positive and practical approach to the way we live our lives.

I ring Dad. He says he doesn't have to go back for a

check-up for another six months because the last examination showed that the lung cancer in his right lung hasn't grown at all. I'm just pleased, after all that Maurs has been going through, that his doctors are not suggesting he have any of the debilitating treatments Maurs has been suffering. At his age, almost eighty-nine, the cure would be worse than the complaint.

He also says that he's mentioning Maurs in his twice daily meditations. Between Kristi's prayers, Dad's meditations and the support of the dyke community, Maurs is well covered.

We've also been trying to get out a bit more, to see films, have dinner, and generally spend some fun time together to balance it all out.

Monday 3 June
Issue 47 of *Lesbiana* not only includes my article "The C-Word and Other Lesbian Issues", there's an article by Rosemary Mann, Jenny Teeney and Trish McGuane about the death of Sue Morton in a hospital rather than at home as she and her partner Rosemary had wanted. Even when it became obvious the cancer had run its course and Sue was going to die, the doctors refused to allow her to leave, in direct opposition to Sue and Rosemary's directives. The article ends with the suggestion that a support group for lesbians might be appropriate in these and other similar circumstances. But, with its emphasis on death and dying, it's too close to the bone for me to contemplate at this stage, and not quite what I'm looking for.

Thursday 6 June
Even though Maurs is away, I'm glad I went along to the Living With Cancer session on Tuesday because I'm not getting that kind of support anywhere else at the moment.

I'm taking advantage of this time to myself to hibernate and catch up with my own work and myself, my life. In fact, what I've been doing recently, the meditation, getting back into my writing, cutting back on my activist work (including the Women's Circus), being with Maurs more, being on my own more and relaxing, is just exactly what I need to do.

It's a great pity Maurs won't be here for the Lesbian Art Exhibition opening at the Brunswick Mechanics Institute tomorrow night. Especially as I've put one of my paintings, "A Study in Red", into an exhibition for the first time in my life. It was Maurs' gift of the oil paints that started me painting again for the first time since I was sixteen.

When I visit the shoulder physiotherapist over in Prahran, she tells me that a lot of middle-aged womyn have this kind of injury. It's all part of growing older. She seems so sure about it that I believe her when she tells me that I have to have a hydrodilatation done. This procedure involves injecting fluid into the shoulder joint. She's so convincing that I wonder if I ought to take her advice and be done with it. But only after I've talked to my doctor about it. I don't want to stuff it up even more if she happens to be wrong.

Maurs has been having a wonderful time over in Adelaide, so she's been telling me on the phone whenever she rings. And thanks to Fran and her partner we've got tickets to go and see k d lang at the Palais when she gets back.

Thursday 13 June
Maurs is home again, all is well with the world.

Maurs had her first session with the hypnotherapist yesterday to help her stop smoking. When she got back here she looked so utterly lost and out of it that I was worried. I can't help thinking what an incredible lot she's taking on.

Between seeing her naturopath to build up her immune system in preparation for the chemo sessions starting on Monday, trying to sort out a healthy diet with supplements and giving up cigarettes after thirty-plus years, it's all a bit much.

"When did you start smoking, Maurs?" I asked.

"At about seventeen or eighteen after my mother died," she replied.

She's also confronting her quite understandable fears about the chemotherapy itself. Especially so, as it's only adjuvant treatment anyway. Adjuvant chemotherapy is used when there's no definite sign of cancer but can still get rid of any stray cancer cells that may be lingering about in the system before they can develop to life-threatening proportions.

However, there's no way of knowing for sure. It's all so personal and therefore too difficult for Maurs (or the doctors either, I suspect) to know what to do for the best with any degree of certainty. But, as the doctor advised Maurs, if the chemo causes her undue stress she can consider stopping it after three sessions.

I rang the Anti-Cancer Council to obtain information on ovarian cancer. How, I wondered, do they know when and if there's a recurrence of the ovarian cancer? When it's almost impossible to detect, as in Maurs' case, for example.

Sure enough, they can do what's called a second look operation, either a laparoscopy or major surgery. As no-one has mentioned this before, it makes me wonder what else they're not telling us.

Lately, just the sight of Maurs smoking makes me fearful at the thought of how it's undermining her precarious health. And yet after dinner last night Maurs looked so lost. Like a little kid whose toy has been taken away. She seemed shrunk within herself, a bewildered look on her face.

4

Chemotherapy

Monday 17 June

We step into the chemo room at around 9.30 a.m. And after all these weeks of nervously glancing into this room as I passed by, of dreading the time Maurs would find herself here, of being apprehensive about what it involved, I find it's all quite different to my imaginings.

We're in a room the size of a largish lounge-room, with several big comfortable recliner armchairs lining the walls. There's lots of joking and kidding about because these womyn, both staff and patients, have come to know each other over these past months of surgery and treatment. As I sit next to Maurs, crocheting the yellow and red on the squares for the baby's rug I marvel at how far I've come since I first set foot in Ward 53.

"Wear your gloves next time," Sister advises, as she slaps the back of Maurs' hand to get the vein to come to the surface. Having warm hands makes it easier to find a vein.

I don't really know what to expect as I've never been this close to a chemo session before. That it is happening to

Maurs makes it both easier (I have a personal and immediate reason for being there) and harder (because I'm here with someone I love).

It seems, from what everyone is saying, that nausea and vomiting are almost standard reactions to chemo. Anti-nausea injections and tablets are given as a matter of course, although they don't always work. With any luck, Maurs might be able to handle the chemo as well as she did the surgery and the radiotherapy.

Whenever anyone has to go to the toilet, which they have to do quite frequently owing to the amount of saline they use to flush and dilute the chemo poisons going into their systems, they take their stands, with the intravenous bags swinging from the top, with them.

"My urine's pink," Maurs announces with some pride when she gets back after one of her trips. As she's on pink Rubicin, we expected this to happen. Maurs mentions she can hardly wait to lose her hair so she can shave it all off. In the lesbian community this is more a fashion statement than anything else.

"Are you going to shave yours in sympathy?" one of the nurses wants to know.

"Not likely," I reply. "This is the longest my hair's been in over thirty-five years." Although I'd be tempted if that wasn't the case.

We're the last to leave at 7.00 p.m. A long day. Maurs isn't feeling too badly but when we get home she decides to sleep with a bucket by the side of the bed, just in case. I've given up on getting to the Matrix Guild business meeting this evening, where we're planning to start a business to raise the money for housing and lifestyle options for lesbians in old age, because I don't want to leave Maurs by herself. Especially when we don't know how she'll react to the chemo mixtures she's had.

Tuesday 18 June

It's our sixth anniversary today. As I write this Maurs is, thank goodness, symptom free. Maybe it is, as she says, because of all the naturopathic remedies she's been taking. Also the anti-nausea injection last night and the tablet this morning, too, I expect.

Everyone, all eight of us, is present for the Living With Cancer session this evening. Including Maurs, four womyn have had cancer, two of us support people plus the two nurses who have been doing a great job presenting the information. An eclectic group and yet it works quite well, bonded, as we are, by the cancer and the trauma of the ongoing treatment.

"Today, Maurs and I are celebrating our sixth anniversary together," I say at one point, and they all offer us their congratulations.

Thursday 20 June

Maurs has been constipated—that's all. She finally resorted to buying some glycerine suppositories.

Uncomfortable though constipation undoubtedly is, if that's all she has to worry about it's nothing to what others have had to put up with. No nausea, no vomiting, it's wonderful.

I'm inspired to write a small poem in praise of Maurs' courage to give to her.

I'm obsessed. Each time I think I've had enough of the books on cancer I start another one.

Sunday 23 June

I wake crying about my mother and her too-early death from cancer at fifty-nine. For some reason, the memory of this is making me very sad on this cold, grey, rainy morning, triggered, perhaps, by the fact that Maurs was not well in the middle of the night and went to sleep sitting up on the couch.

Or else it was hearing from Sabin Fernbacher about how upset she is that she hasn't yet had a letter from her mother in Austria to let her know about how her mother's recent mastectomy for breast cancer went.

Or learning from Ursula that Marianne Permezel, who used to be the musical director of the Women's Circus, also had a mastectomy a few days ago for breast cancer and needs follow-up chemo to combat the spread of a particularly aggressive form of this disease. At the age of thirty-three.

I've noticed a slight tension and a feeling of ambiguity about Kristi's forthcoming visit because we'll have to re-establish our relationship all over again, knowing that she'll be leaving after a couple of months.

There's also some apprehension about what I might learn from the doctor next Wednesday when I get the results of the ultrasound on the shoulder. And there's always Dad who is becoming increasingly infirm with all his health problems: blindness and diabetes as well as lung cancer.

Is this the winter of my discontent?

Sunday 30 June
It's a blue moon (as in, once in a . . .)

Every morning now, after my first cup of coffee, I meditate for at least fifty minutes to an hour, which balances me and sets me up for the day. I do another couple of ten-minute sessions through the day whenever I can manage them.

I had a cortisone injection into the shoulder last week, which doesn't seem to have made much difference. So much for the wonders of modern science.

I rang Marianne Permezel yesterday and spoke to her

lover, Jane. There was an instant rapport between us, even though we hardly know each other, because we're in similar positions, having partners who have had radical surgery for cancer with all the worry and hope that entails.

After reading Neti Davidson's article in *Pandora*[1], a Melbourne women's issues journal, it's obvious her cancer has given her a quite different perspective on the disease to the experiences Maurs is having, because she hasn't had to have surgery, and her chemotherapy was in tablet form rather than the intravenous treatment Maurs is going through.

I met Neti through her lover Anne Stafford, who died from cancer in 1988. But not before Anne had taught me by her example that dying can be an extremely courageous and empowering experience for everyone concerned.

There's a lot of cancer about. We do need to talk more, exchange information, support each other, and demystify this whole multibillion-dollar industry that the boys have set up for themselves. Take the healing processes back into our own hands, so we know what's going on and can actively participate in our own diagnosis and treatment.

Tuesday 2 July
Maurs and I go out to the airport with Geoff to meet Kristi off the plane from Papua New Guinea, where she and her husband have been working for the past twelve months. I'm beside myself with excitement. And absolutely intrigued that my daughter is so obviously seven months pregnant.

We're (nearly) grandmothers!

On the way back from the airport, Kristi asks if we'll be too disappointed if it turns out the baby is a boy. Is she trying to tell me something?

---

[1] No. 6, 1996.

Wednesday 3 July

I offer to be Kristi's support person till her husband Dan gets here. I'm now convinced that the baby is a boy.

Maurs, bless her heart, is being her usual supportive and cheery self. Like a little rock, she is, and just what I need.

I'm just glad that, this far into the treatment, I can now afford to give some of my attention to Kristi without neglecting Maurs. That I've just about given up most of my feminist activist work helps.

And the sun is shining, too. What more could I possibly want?

Thursday 4 July

Pat Rooney from POW Circus calls in on some business. She tells me that she's just had a biopsy on a lump in her breast which is "so big" and she holds her thumb and forefinger in a circle the size of a golf ball.

"I keep telling myself it's not as bad as losing Ian." She's biting her lip to keep from crying. Her only son Ian was killed in a motorbike accident.

I remember how I felt after my third child, Michelle, died.

"We're going down like ninepins, aren't we?" As she turns to leave, her Scottish humour reasserts itself. "Oh well, if it has to go I've always got another one." She's holding her left breast where they've packed it with ice to dull the pain of the diagnostic mammograms and the biopsy needle.

As Pat gets into the car I bend down to offer my sympathy to Pat's friend and housemate Jean Gardner, whose face looks like mine must have done back in February. As if she's just been hit by a bus.

Saturday 6 July

It's just occurred to me that I am the same age as Mum

when she became a grandmother for the first time. How about that now?

I lean against Maurs at the dance performance "Tracks", and watch the seven Warlpiri womyn from Lajamanu take it in turns to paint each other's round melon-sized breasts in slow unhurried movements.

They are seated cross-legged on a rug on the polished floorboards, for all the world as if they were at home in their own country in the desert of Central Australia, instead of downtown Carlton in the middle of winter. They shed their coats, oil their breasts and shoulders, and quietly submit their bodies to the designer's stick dipped in paint over and over again. We in the audience sit riveted to our seats in awe of this most ancient of ceremonies being enacted before our yearning eyes.

A friend, sitting behind us, leans forward to ask how Maurs is and whether, because of the chemo, her hair has started to fall out yet. "No, not at all," Maurs answers.

Sunday 7 July
Maurs comes back to bed and we get into our usual kissing, cuddling, back scratching, breast sucking, talking about this and that, which can go for ages before we make any genital contact.

"I could go down on you this morning, if you like," I offer.

Later on, as my fingers stray as far as Maurs' cunt, she grumbles about not having much hair down there any more.

"Nonsense," I say, "there's not much on the top bit, certainly," because it still hasn't grown back since it was shaved for the op, "but in between here," I finger the hairs on the labia, "there's . . . oh, not much there either. Oh," my fingers continue to explore. What only last week was the usual substantial labia hair is now a sparse straggle, "When did that happen?"

As I'm down there anyway, I take the opportunity to look more closely at this new development. Sure enough, there's hardly any hair anywhere at all. Parts of her cunt feel quite smooth to touch.

"I'm bald," Maurs moans.

It's too soon to tell if this is because of menopause and permanent—some womyn do lose their pubic and under-arm hair after menopause—or because of the chemo.

"You always said this would happen." Small comfort for the loss of this outward manifestation of her adult womyn-hood after nearly forty years. "How's your mucus going?" I ask about the post-operative discharge from her vagina.

"There's not as much as there was, but it still comes and goes; thick like concrete when it dries, though, and hard to wash off my knickers."

This reminds me of what Kristi has been saying about how acidic her mucus is at the moment. So much so that it's making holes in the crotch of her knickers and she's had to throw them out and buy new ones.

The lack of pubic hair doesn't seem to have affected Maurs' ability to make love.

Maurs comes back from the bathroom to announce that the hair on her head, which has hitherto been holding on tenaciously and against all predictions, started to fall out while she was in the shower.

"See?" She demonstrates by pulling on a tuft which comes away in her fingers. "It's coming off. I'm not vain about many things but I am about my hair. I'd rather be completely bald than have it straggly and bald in patches."

Not a problem. This has been on the drawing board for a while just waiting for the right moment. "Can it wait till after tomorrow's chemo session?" I ask.

Mind you, it still looks like a full head of hair for the moment. Time and this next chemo session will tell. Maurs has already been given beanies which will come in handy any day now.

Monday 8 July
It's all so much easier the second time around because we know what to expect. We know that Maurs' response to the chemo is nowhere near as drastic as we'd been led to expect, probably because she's been looking after herself so well.

Maurs settles in, with the saline dripping into her veins to start with, while I sit knitting another pair of socks. Maurs has brought in some k d lang tapes.

Both Dr Jarvis and Dr Kirk visit. They set Maurs to rights about even suggesting that she might stop the chemo after the third session.

If the chemo was upsetting Maurs' system, they would consider stopping it after three. As it's not, they feel it's best to keep going for at least five, if not all six, even though it's adjuvant treatment. So that's the end of that good idea.

I head off to have lunch and go on the guided tour of the proposed Queen Victoria Women's Centre. In the beginning stages of a complete renovation there's not much to admire.

Since the Liberal Premier, Jeff Kennett appointed the Queen Victoria Women's Centre Trust to oversee the process, the building now has to be financially viable. This rules out any possibility of the archives moving into the building, as was originally intended. Not to mention it won't be womyn-only except for one small lounge area on the second floor.

Maurs announces to all and sundry that the next time they see her she'll be bald because I'm going to be shaving her head the following day. Each time I feel a slight twinge of apprehension. Obviously I'm not as prepared as Maurs is about shaving it off.

Tuesday 9 July

Pat Rooney calls in. The lump is very likely benign, she tells me. What a relief. Because pre-cancerous cells are in evidence she'll have the lump removed in a couple of weeks.

Having recalled that when we were together I used to keep one of my ex-lover's hair clipped so short as to be almost bald, I feel better about doing the same for Maurs. I fine-scissor her hair right back to the scalp. It's already patchy in parts anyway and even more so by the time I've finished with it.

The result is not all that brilliant, really. It's more a sign of courage and a validation of what Maurs is going through.

Wednesday 10 July

It takes a lot to reduce her to tears but Maurs is unexpectedly crying on my shoulder this morning. She is mourning the removal of her uterus and ovaries, which precipitated her into menopause before she'd had a chance to prepare for it or realise the significance of this crucial rite of passage. And for the loss of all her hair. On her head, her cunt and under her arms (chemically induced though it is). So many, too many changes all of a sudden.

I run the electric clippers over her head to finish off the cut I gave it yesterday. It makes a heck of a difference because it's now all smoothly short and the same minute length all over. Just barely past a shave. Almost trendy even.

As for me, between POW's forthcoming gig, Maurs' chemo, Kristi's pregnancy, and the difficulty of getting rid of the archives, it's just as well I'm taking it easy these days and I'm not too preoccupied with other things.

Friday 12 July

"This is my one gesture for NAIDOC Week," I tell Kristi, as we head off on the National Aboriginal and Islander Day Observance Committee march down Gertrude Street towards the city. Kristi leaves the march at Elizabeth Street to go off to her ante-natal appointment. It's raining so lightly I don't even bother to put up my umbrella, as we wind our way up the hill to admire the Koori art exhibition and have a barbecue lunch to celebrate.

Kristi arrives home. "Do you want the good news or the bad news first?"

I can't bear the suspense, "The bad news."

"The doctor found abnormal cells on my cervix, little white lumps, the worst possible. I could actually see them myself on the screen."

"What did he have up there, a closed-circuit TV camera?" My mind refuses to take this in.

"He did a biopsy right there and then. I could see it all happening. He just pulled off a bit of my flesh. I'm all sore now. It hurt." Her face is drawn with pain, anguish and exhaustion.

"Oh darling." I gather this precious daughter of mine into my arms, to comfort and hold, not wanting this to be happening, to soothe away the hurt. Kristi starts to cry, which almost penetrates my defences. However, I don't want to give into this myself just yet.

"When will you get the results?" I ask.

"In two weeks." Her eyes are bright with tears. "He said if it's serious and I have to have treatment it would have to be after the baby's born in four months' time."

We're still standing wedged in the kitchen doorway. With shock, probably. Kristi is concerned about getting back from Papua New Guinea if it's necessary. The doctor has advised her not to worry and to take it one step at a time. I agree.

We can't afford to dwell on this now. Kristi needs all her strength for the baby. "What's the good news?" I ask.

"I had the ultrasound and it looks as if it's a boy." Kristi smiles. She's been hoping for a boy.

As this confirms my own intuitive sense, I'm prepared to believe the doctor's interpretation of what seem like incomprehensible blobs and blurry outlines on the ultrasound photo Kristi shows me.

"Say what you like," Kristi mimics the doctor's words, "but that's a scrotum, if ever I've seen one."

It's true, once it's pointed out, the small double rounded image does look more like a fused scrotum sac than two distinct labia, even to my inexperienced eye. As I've already got used to the idea of a grandson, all I really care about at this stage is that mother and child are both healthy. Sean Daniel, it's a great name too.

I have to remember: cancer is not a death sentence. Whatever happens, in whatever way, whatever the biopsy results are or the diagnosis, Kristi is still my most treasured and lovable daughter. I'm not going to lose her.

Besides, she's survived so much already and has a will of iron.

As I do the dishes before I leave for the POW rehearsal, I find myself crying out of control. I don't think I could stand one more diagnosis of cancer in someone I love. Coping with what's happening with Maurs is as much as I can handle right now. I dry my eyes and pull myself together to say goodbye to Kristi, glad she's planning to go to her brother's for tea tonight and won't be on her own.

Not wanting to ring from home while Kristi's there, on the way to POW's workshop by train, I ring Maurs from the Footscray railway station to share some of this devastating load. She's sympathetic and understanding, while I sob down the phone.

As soon as she arrives at the warehouse for POW's rehearsal, Pat Rooney tells me the results of the biopsy are not back yet, although it does appear very likely that it's not cancer. Thank goodness for small mercies.

Saturday 13 July
It's better that we just take it easy for the time being rather than worry ourselves unnecessarily. As the doctor said, time enough if and when it's appropriate. I've been surprised that I've been able to put my fears about all this on hold. A necessary way of coping, I suppose.

Maurs says she's still a bit nauseous although not vomiting at all and that the diarrhoea (yes, diarrhoea this time) has stopped. It's probably best that she doesn't go to Geelong with POW tomorrow, unfortunately. But she will be well enough to go to Wonthaggi with me for the gig next Friday, she says. As both towns are some distance from Melbourne, it will take an effort to get there.

"Would you do me a favour please, Mum?" Kristi asks, after I've finished covering the noticeably ropey varicose veins on Kristi's right leg with the elasticised bandage.

Kristi is concerned that the baby hasn't moved this morning. "It's probably just that he's tired because I had a late night last night. But would you mind putting your ear on my stomach and listening for the heart-beat?"

Kristi's swollen stomach feels very hot against my ear, I am startled to notice, and it takes me a moment or two to adjust to a convenient position. Then I hear a distant sound like the pounding of tiny horses' hooves, poom-poom, poom-poom (very quickly, loud-soft), poom-poom, poom-poom. I realise I can actually hear his little heart beating. And am moved to tears.

What an extraordinary sensation. I'm amazed at how clear it sounds and the awesome potential it conveys in all its vigorous tenderness.

Wednesday 17 July
Another day, another dole form.

My heart is frozen. I'm waiting, suspended, I can feel it. For the results of Kristi's biopsy. For the baby to be born well and healthy. For Maurs to be finished her treatment.

I've been wanting to write something to include in the Daffodil Day competition that raises funds for cancer research. Inspired by the dark-blue woollen beanie that Maurs is now wearing most of the time on her bald head because of the cold, I find that when I do put pen to paper it comes out as a poem rather than a short story: "My Darling is Wearing a New Blue Hat".

Thursday 18 July
The juice extractor is still on the bench in the kitchen. It hasn't been used since before Maurs went to Adelaide. What does this mean? I ask myself. It seems the only discipline gleaned from the cancer books that I practise these days is the meditation.

Kristi arrives back from her ante-natal appointment. "Do you want to hear the good news or the bad news first?"

Not again. I bury my head under the bedclothes. I don't want to know anything any more.

"The good news is that the results of the biopsy indicate medium level abnormal cells."

I sit up. It's not cancer! Thank goodness for that.

"The bad news is that I might have to stay on in Melbourne for about six weeks after the baby is born for treatment."

Better here than stranded in the wilds of Papua New Guinea with a young baby. "What kind of treatment?" Kristi has already had one cone biopsy on her cervix, several years ago now.

"Laser. They'll just burn off the abnormal cells, apparently."

"After Dan goes back, you can stay here," I offer, ignoring the probability of being woken in the middle of the night for those weeks. I can cope. I'll be a grandmother.

At the meditation session that evening, Maurs says that the reason she's learning to meditate is because she has cancer and believes meditation will help her to get rid of it. Afterwards a young womyn comes up to Maurs to say her mother had cancer and is now well again and to keep hanging in there. "Don't let anyone pity you," she adds.

Tuesday 23 July

Feel teary this morning. Need some comforting. All this giving out is getting to me, and I haven't had any time to myself lately.

It has a lot to do with having the hydrodilitation on my shoulder yesterday, I expect. The after-effects of the local anaesthetic made my whole arm uncoordinated for several hours afterwards. The long needle hurt as it was being put into my shoulder, and again as it was being manipulated into the correct place. Then the first large syringeful of fluid built up the pressure in my shoulder joint to such a painful level that I muttered out loud. When the doctor put the second syringeful in I actually felt the adhesions break apart. It felt all right after that. Just a bit strange and uncomfortable.

Maurs, bless her, drove me there and waited to bring me home again. With any luck, it will take just a couple of weeks for it to be fully recovered.

Kristi is beginning to look like the side of a house. Any

day now. She has a bad cold, which came on as soon as she knew the results of the biopsy.

Maurs is staying away because her resistance to disease is lowered by the chemo and it would be too harmful for her, especially with her third chemo coming up in a week's time. This gives her a chance to watch as much of the Atlanta Olympics on television as she likes, over at her house in Bruce Street, till all hours of the day and night.

My ear blocked up with wax yesterday, as it sometimes does. I feel quite disoriented because of it and am not functioning properly.

Friday 26 July
I'm constipated, what's going on? My shoulder's still not 100 per cent, but not quite as bad as it was. Or am I just getting used to its limited mobility? By the amount of wax that is finally syringed from my ear, it's no wonder I was having difficulty hearing.

Dan arrives from Papua New Guinea and we pick him up at the airport. Geoff drops me off before driving his sister and brother-in-law over to the house they've arranged for themselves.

Blessed solitude.

Saturday 27 July
"I know it's not the right attitude," Maurs says on the way to POW's workshop, "but with the chemo due again on Monday I feel as if tomorrow's my last day of freedom."

What is there to say, knowing Maurs is facing at least a week of nausea, constipation, and whatever else these drugs precipitate in her increasingly energy-depleted body?

Maurs has a pretty positive attitude to the chemo, all things considered. She seems to be approaching it with her working-class humour intact. Even if her strength is being undermined a bit more each time. The chemo is lethal, and not just towards the cancer.

Maurs has been telling people she's convinced she doesn't have cancer any more. That this is just adjuvant treatment to make sure all the cancer cells are gone. I hope the CAT scan that Maurs is due to have in a couple of weeks' time confirms that.

Monday 29 July
The third (small) c-for-chemo day. Now that we know what to expect, it's easier in one sense and yet dreaded in another.

It's raining. I've got the radio tuned to 3CR so I don't miss "Left Opinion" (about being a lesbian grandmother, this time). I need to get my head around all this again because it seems a bit unreal compared to my total absorption in the cancer industry.

Or maybe I'm just getting some more realistic balance. I am less fearful about what is happening with Maurs (now that I know so much more about it), and can balance it with what's going on for me in other areas of my life.

Being squashed into the small temporary room in the newly renovated oncology ward at the Royal Women's is a bit disorienting at first. I have my knitting with me, as usual, and Maurs is delighted that the telly works so she can watch the Olympics. As the new ward is open for inspection, I score a glass of red wine and bring back scones, jam and cream for Maurs.

Maurs dozes for most of the day, waking to talk, have her saline/chemo bags changed, comment on the time it's taking, and trying to hurry the process along. Not that the nurse on duty needs much prompting. She seems determined to speed through everything efficiently and as quickly as possible.

Maurs and I leave with three bottles of barium meal and an appointment the Wednesday after next for the all important CAT scan at the Children's Hospital, where all such procedures are done. The thought of drinking this thick white goo makes Maurs want to vomit.

On the way out of the Royal Women's, I ask at the front desk just in case Kristi might have checked in to have the baby while we were unable to be contacted.

Tuesday 30 July
"Isn't she marvellous!" one of the nurses enthuses.

Who am I to disagree? I glance across the crowded oncology outpatients' waiting-room to where Maurs is squatting down next to a couple of womyn to explain why they might like to consider attending the next series of Living With Cancer starting the following Thursday.

Maurs and I agreed to come in this afternoon to help promote this new venture at the Royal Women's. Maurs, in her usual inimitable style, has no trouble getting right into it. I watch as she pulls off her blue beanie every now and then to stroke her bald head. It is so appropriate in this setting: no-one blinks an eye.

Wednesday 31 July
I like this back bedroom of Maurs' at Bruce Street; it reminds me of my old sleepout when I was a kid, the wind moaning through the fly-wire screens, moving the almond tree against the roof and flapping the outside blinds.

I'm out and about because it's dole form day. I lunch with a friend, visit Shrew Women's Bookshop (rumour has it that Shrew is closing) and the artists' space, Roar Studios, wander all the way down Brunswick Street, browsing in the bookstores, before going into the city to suss out baby clothes, all without buying anything.

As I haven't heard from Kristi, before catching the tram home I ring the Royal Women's from a public phone in Bourke Street. I nearly drop the receiver when the receptionist casually tells me that Mrs Giselsson is in the labour ward although the baby hasn't arrived yet!

I quickly ring Maurs to tell her the news and get down there by tram as fast as I can. I rush up to the second floor, race along to Ward 24, ring the bell. And wait. At last a dryly humorous sister lets me in and informs me that the membranes have ruptured but that nothing much else is happening.

Kristi has just been examined and there's hardly a twinge to speak of. If she doesn't go into labour herself, they'll induce the baby within twenty-four hours. When it doesn't look as if anything is going to happen in a hurry I leave them to it. It's exciting to think my daughter is about to go through this most monumental of experiences, and that Maurs and I are poised to become grandmothers.

Thursday 1 August
Kristi is on a mattress on the floor. There is a drip into her left arm, and a band around her swollen belly attached to a machine that is monitoring the contractions and recording the baby's heart-beat. I settle in to do whatever I can, passing her drinks of water in between contractions.

When the contractions become stronger, Kristi gets back into bed. The doctor on duty, who has moved from the oncology ward to the birthing centre, arrives at six to do an internal. Dilation of the cervix is only a couple of centimetres, he tells her; still a way to go. The doctor is as startled to see me as I am to see him. He was one of the doctors who had treated Maurs, and he asks after her. Seeing him there doctoring Kristi as he used to do for Maurs makes me feel I've become too much a part of this place over this past year.

Kristi asks for Pethidine and settles in for strong, regular contractions, breathing loudly each time and feeling spaced out in between. Dan comments that I'm breathing in time with Kristi. I feel as if I'm going through this with her.

I go home and am sitting up in bed reading yet another murder mystery when Kristi rings.

"Congratulations," she says, "Sean Daniel was born at 8.46 p.m." only forty-five minutes after I left! "He weighs 3470 grams, which is about seven and a half pounds, I think. He's beautiful, and I did it all by myself without an epidural, after all"—she'd been considering one when I left. "And without either a doctor or an episiotomy." As Kristi proudly points out, "The midwives did an amazing job."

"What a clever womyn you are, Kristi." I'm as pleased as Punch that it has all gone relatively easily and more importantly, that both my daughter and grandson are well and healthy.

I ring Nana Maurs and tell her the good news. She's as thrilled as I am. "Kristi says we can visit tomorrow," I say, and arrange to meet Maurs at the Royal Women's tomorrow afternoon.

Friday 2 August

I write "grandmother" across the bottom of the self-portrait I started weeks ago but haven't had the emotional or creative energy to get round to finishing lately.

As soon as I get to the hospital with Dan first thing in the morning, Kristi places the baby in my arms. He's awake and just lies there quite content. I'm rapt. It's all so exciting I stay alternately holding the baby and chatting for about three hours.

I leave, have lunch, and then meet Maurs in the foyer as arranged to visit all over again. Just to see Maurs' face as she's holding Sean is a treat. As Maurs says, "He's not even twenty-four hours old yet. I've never held a brand new baby in my life before," and smiles down at him.

I'm impressed that Kristi is able to breast-feed him already.

"Two baldies together," Maurs says, as Dan takes photos of us having turns to hold Sean. It's true. Sean has about as much hair as Maurs at the moment.

As we pass the nurses' desk on the way out, Maurs spots one of the doctors we know and calls out, "We're grandmothers now."

Saturday 3 August
I can't stop crying.

I'm not sure whether it's because I'm a grandmother, perimenopausal, my shoulder (which is still not entirely fixed up), disappointment about not being there for the birth, love and pride in my daughter for going through the whole birthing process so well, worry about Maurs who is still not well from the chemo, or wonder and delight in this new baby boy, Sean Daniel. It's not every day I become a grandmother.

"You know how you used to say that having us was the best thing that ever happened to you, Mum?" Kristi says, gently holding Sean to her breast as if she's been doing it for years.

There's nothing else I've ever done with my writing, travelling or political activism that comes anywhere near comparing to giving birth to Geoff and Kristi.

"I could never understand why you used to say that," Kristi goes on, "but I agree. It's the most incredible experience I've ever had."

I used to find it strange when my mother said the same thing, before I became a mother myself.

I head across to Footscray for the POW workshop. With my shoulder much improved, I have a great time doing double balances, receiving congratulations, and generally getting back in touch with myself again.

I meet Maurs in the foyer of the theatre for the opening night of Donna Jackson's play, *Car Maintenance, Explosives and Love*. Maurs is still not well, a bit worse if anything, but determined to see this play that has been several years in the making.

Wednesday 7 August

After my physio appointment, I meet Maurs at the Children's Hospital. "How did the CAT scan go?" I ask, when I finally track her down through the maze of corridors.

"Pretty good. I went into this cylinder while they took all the X-rays. Except that when they were injecting the iodine, the table had to move and the boy who was doing it let the needle come out of my arm so it had to be done again. Talk about stupid. None of us were impressed. But after that it all went well."

"And the barium meal, how did that go this morning?" Maurs had had to drink one of the bottles at seven, one at eight, and the third one at nine in time for the CAT scan at ten.

"It was vanilla-flavoured and not too thick, so I managed. With the first mouthful each time I felt like heaving but I didn't." Maurs will get the results next Tuesday and is confident they will show that she's positively free of cancer.

After the treatment both of us have had this morning, we drive to Carlton to have lunch.

Thursday 8 August

I realise I've been missing Maurs lately. Mainly that Maurs hasn't been well and has preferred to be in her own bed by herself. However, I've managed to get quite a bit of archiving done at my place while Maurs has been watching the last of the Olympic events over at her house.

I stay overnight at Maurs' place, and after we've made love, she drops me back at my place on her way to the Royal Women's for her ten-day blood count—the blood test taken ten days after the chemo to monitor the cell levels to see how much damage the chemo has done.

Pat Rooney rings to let me know that the biopsy results on the lump they took out of her breast last week show that, as she suspected, she doesn't have cancer. She says, it's a relief to know for sure, even if it did take them eight days to get round to telling her.

She goes on to tell me that a womyn we hardly know, who had ovarian cancer, died a couple of days ago. "I don't think you should tell Maurs, it will only worry her."

I give the suggestion a passing thought but I have no intention of not telling Maurs. She'll hear this from someone else, and what is there to be done about it anyway?

I'm in the middle of some more archiving when Maurs turns up unexpectedly. She had vomited after lunch at Lynne Bryer's, she explains. "I'm going home to rest. I don't think I ought to go to meditation this evening."

"Of course not, darling. Are you sure you're all right to drive? Is there anything I can do?"

It's probably just the aftermath of the barium meal, we reassure ourselves. We hug and Maurs heads off again. It's a worry, although not entirely unexpected. And really, Maurs has had a far easier time with the chemo than most.

Tuesday 13 August

After waiting for two hours at the Royal Women's to see Dr Kirk, we discover that the results of the CAT scan are not there.

There has been some kind of a mix-up with the Children's Hospital. Dr Kirk gives Maurs an internal examination and it seems there's nothing obviously wrong there. He agrees that, all being well, five chemo sessions ought to be enough. Only two more to go! We go around the corner to Faraday Street for a celebratory pie and soup.

As it's top of my concerns (and also to let my interstate friends know what's happening) I send the first couple of pages of the story that I think of as *The C-Word* to be included in *Lesbian Network*,[1] the national lesbian quarterly magazine.

Friday 16 August

Now that my shoulder is (almost) healed, I'm starting to sleep through the night. What a bonus. Except I do miss sleeping with Maurs. This third chemo treatment has definitely knocked her around a lot more than the others. So much so, she'll skip the training workshop tomorrow. "I miss it though," she says miserably.

Soon after Maurs leaves to get her blood count done and to pick up a script for the anti-nausea tablets from the doctor, I get a phone-call from the Anti-cancer Council to say that my poem, "My Darling Is Wearing a New Blue Hat", will be on display during Daffodil Day Week. I'm rapt and ring Maurs to give her the good news.

Then someone from the *Melbourne Star Observer*, a gay and lesbian newspaper, rings to let me know that my review of Donna's play is in this week's *SpinOut*. Today, in fact. (Madame Zora on "Not Another Koori Show" on 3CR said Friday would be my lucky day, too.)

---

[1] No. 48, September 1996.

I've just put the forequarter of lamb in the oven to roast and am pulling the tops off enormous hybrid strawberries when Maurs arrives. While she was at the Royal Women's she started vomiting for no obvious reason. Unless it was the fish she had for lunch. Or the chemo. She's decided not to stay for dinner.

"You'll miss seeing Sean," I protest, the ostensible reason for having Kristi and Dan here for dinner tonight.

It seems to me that Maurs has withdrawn a great deal over these past few weeks. Perhaps she is conserving her rapidly depleting strength to keep going. Or perhaps she feels the aloneness of her condition, which no-one else can really appreciate or share with her. Or perhaps it's fear of where she goes from here now that the long haul is nearly over. Or she's simply had enough of all this treatment.

I can't seem to reach her or get close to her in the way we were only a couple of months ago.

"Barb rang the other night, and when I told her how I feel she said she knew exactly what I was talking about. It's hard to explain to anyone else," Maurs says, at one stage.

Maurs needs someone like Barb Anthony who shares her condition to talk to when it gets too much to bear. This is where the lesbian cancer support group would have come in handy. Maybe I was wrong not to have started one. I have to keep reminding myself that I just don't have the necessary energy to contemplate it, despite my feminist missionary zeal.

Ordinarily Maurs is such a lovable, kind womyn, such a joy to be with, such a delightful and wise companion, such a right-on lover, that it's hard. I hug her goodbye and she's not there.

Saturday 17 August
I find myself going through the motions at the POW workshop without my usual enthusiasm.

When I get home after seeing Donna's play again, with the POW womyn, I ring Maurs. "You know what it's like. If I said to one womyn I had to say it to several dozen or more that you were just not up to being there today." The Tech Crew Coordinator of the Women's Circus had especially said to give Maurs her very best regards. "Everyone, but everyone, hopes you're getting better and said to say hullo." I'd begun to sound like a cracked record by the end of the night.

Not that I begrudge passing on news about Maurs, but it does tend to get to me after a while. I start eating the halva I bought this morning and end up eating the entire block.

Sunday 18 August

As it's raining and cold outside, I ring Maurs and suggest that we meet at the Nova Cinema. Since it's not far from my place and shows a wide range of alternative films, we may as well make the most of it. We decide on two Australian films, *Love and Other Catastrophes* and *Shine*.

"There's an article in yesterday's *Age Extra* you might be interested in," I say, "about a womyn who's just put out a book of poetry about her experiences with ovarian cancer and how it later metastasised in her bowel." I read out a few more details, fold the paper to the relevant page and leave it next to Maurs' side of the bed for when she's next here.

Later, we're sitting in the foyer of the Nova, I'm eating a choc-top ice cream, when Maurs says, "I'm really afraid. Everyone I know has had cancer a second time and I'm afraid it's going to happen to me too, that the cancer will come back again."

Now that the end of the treatment is in sight, I suppose it's only natural that Maurs would start worrying about this. The womyn in the paper this morning (I'll have to be more circumspect in future), as well as other womyn we know, have all had the cancer back again. And have had to go through a second bout of treatment.

"I don't want to go through all this again. I couldn't stand it," says Maurs, her face strained with the worry of it all.

"Think of the womyn who've got better," I suggest, realising that I am worried too, although not in the same immediate sense as Maurs. "Like Barb Anthony, Geoff's ex-lover, Margaret Taylor, Moss' ex-lover" I run out of names. "Heaps of womyn, when you think about it." No point even thinking about those we know who've died.

The films are excellent and take our minds off our fears.

Monday 19 August
We are off again to the Royal Women's for the fourth (and, all being well, the second-last) chemo session. It gets harder each time for Maurs and especially this session when she's not feeling at all well.

It takes courage to return for treatment knowing it's going to make you feel a whole lot worse before it gets anywhere near better.

"Maybe part of what you're feeling has to do with not getting the CAT scan results last Tuesday," I suggest, as we get off the tram at Grattan Street outside the hospital.

"Do you think so?" Maurs is unconvinced.

"Well, maybe it will set your mind at rest once you know for sure there isn't any more cancer," I suggest hopefully.

As soon as Maurs is settled in, I head off to Melbourne Central for the launch of Daffodil Day Week. There is my poem, newly typed and laminated, stuck up on the wall with a number of others.

I feel odd being here on my own while Maurs is at the hospital attached to the intravenous line dripping the red Epirubicin and the clear Cisplatin into her right hand.

"Dr Kirk's been and he said the CAT scan didn't show any cancer," Maurs tells me when I get back.

It's a relief to have it confirmed officially. Maurs' usual cheeriness and humour are not in evidence today at all, and she snoozes through most of it. The sun coming in through this west-facing window is warm on my back.

Just before we go one of the nurses washes and massages Maurs' feet, which makes her smile. As Maurs missed afternoon tea she gets a chocolate milkshake to finish off the day.

5

End of the Year

Tuesday 20 August

"Do you realise," I say to Maurs as we're lying together in the aftermath of our lovemaking on this cloudy morning, "that everyone I speak to these days says to pass on their love to you. Hello Jean, they say, how's Maurs?"

While I might sometimes wish it were otherwise I don't mind. It's the way it is. And better that womyn are aware and informed about what's going on than not.

Before Maurs hops in the shower, I clipper her hair back to number two again. It's taken on that fluffy, patchy chemo appearance and looks better shorn back almost to the scalp again. Although, because it does seem quite bald now, Maurs gets quite a shock when she looks at herself in the mirror. And groans as she turns away. I'm surprised by her negative reaction because I'd thought she'd got used to the baldness by now.

The short story I start writing for the the *Melbourne Times* competition practically writes itself, about cancer and birth. The returned manuscript of *Death Happens*, a murder mystery I wrote some time ago, arrives in the mail from Naiad Press.

Thursday 22 August

Dan is going back to Papua New Guinea and Kristi is moving into the front room with Sean on Sunday. Maurs and I have dinner together by ourselves.

"I'm so sick of all this," Maurs says. "I don't want to have any more chemo. I just want it all to go away. I hate feeling like this all the time." And she starts crying quietly, almost to herself.

If Maurs cries she's feeling very bloody terrible. What can I do? I put my arms around her and hold her tightly. "It's all right Maurs. You don't have to worry about it now. There's only one more to go. And that's nothing after all you've been through already."

What do I know about what she's going through?

Such annihilating treatment, this chemotherapy. I don't even want to imagine what it must be like to voluntarily allow all those poisons to run into your veins. In the way thousands of other womyn have.

Maurs' courage impresses me immensely. I'm in awe of all that she's going through.

Monday 26 August

Maurs is a star! We go over to Maurs' house to watch Petrina Smith's video of POW Circus which is being shown on Bent TV's "Queer Zone". It's great. The excerpts from *Still Revolting!!!* are interpersed with bits of the rehearsal and parts of the interviews where Maurs talked about having cancer in the middle of it all.

Wednesday 28 August

I dream that I have cancer and I'm going for the final treatment, in the form of a small custard pie with fruit through it (the delivery womyn apologises that the cherries on the top have been eaten by her children in the car on the way over). I ask the womyn in charge if I still have cancer and she assures me I don't, that this is just to make sure.

The dream is probably related to Maurs saying that she doesn't want to have the last chemo. Her attitude scares me.

Even worse, Maurs is pulling away from me at the moment. Maybe it's to do with Kristi and Sean being here and taking up most of my energy, so she feels neglected after my attention has been focused on her for so long.

With that in mind, I cancel my dinner date with Kristi over at Geoff's tomorrow night in favour of having Maurs here for dinner. Just the two of us.

Monday 2 September
Kristi has an appointment at the Royal Women's in preparation for the small operation she's booked in for. I take Sean along for his first triple antigen and Hib injections this morning.

Even though I can see the sense in it, I'm not comfortable. As the needle goes into his little leg, Sean lets out an almighty bellow. Afterwards, I rock him and croon, "There, there, Sean, what a brave little boy you are, it's all right now." I'm as much in shock as he is.

Kristi arrives back. "They said that if they have to cut my cervix more than they expect it could cause an incompetent cervix." I don't know what that means so Kristi explains. "If I become pregnant again, the cervix could split and cause a miscarriage or premature birth."

Maurs rings. "You forgot to ring me last night," she says.

Is it any wonder, with everything that's going on? I apologise and ring her back. "I've decided not to have any more chemo," she says, sounding more definite and as if she really means it this time.

It's no surprise. This is the worst Maurs has been with the chemo, nauseous all the time and no end in sight. But I try persuading her to think about it some more. She says she will, but only for another day.

Then I have to ring back again to say I didn't mean to make it more difficult for her. The fact is, I'm scared that if she doesn't do everything possible, if she doesn't have this last chemo and the cancer comes back again, then we'll both regret it. Whatever Maurs decides, I'll abide by her decision and deal with my fears on my own rather than putting more pressure on to her.

During a break in the POW meeting that evening I discuss my fears about Maurs' decision not to have any more chemo with Barb Anthony. Having been through it all herself, Barb is very calm as she tells me that she also stopped after her fourth chemo session. She says that Maurs would know when it was time to stop and it was best to go along with that. She reminds me that the doctors don't really know how many sessions are effective and just make up the numbers as they go along. As Barb is looking so well these days, this discussion makes me feel a bit better.

When I get home I ring Maurs. "Guess what! We've decided to do our next show at the end of this year!" This is in response to the decision by the Women's Circus to post-pone their usual end-of-year show to March or April next year.

"That means I won't be able to do it," Maurs replies.

I'm shocked. "But it's still a few months away. The show's not till the end of November and we won't even start rehearsals till October." While I'm saying this, I wonder if maybe Maurs has been affected by the chemo much more than I realise.

Tuesday 3 September

Maurs rings and straight away lets me know that she has definitely decided not to have any more chemo. I'm relieved. In the past twenty-four hours I've come round to Maurs' way of thinking about this. Talking with Barb last night helped to put most of my fears to rest.

"We could have a big celebration and thankyou party for your fifty-first birthday," I suggest. "Maybe a barbecue, what do you think?"

Maurs thinks it's a good idea. After all this long time the treatment ends, not so much with a bang as a whimper.

Wednesday 4 September

Kristi feeds Sean and heads off to the Royal Women's at seven in the morning, leaving us two Nanas happily holding the baby. He seems perfectly content to just lie here against my breast, breathing together, all warm under the doona.

After all the trauma of the past few months, all the fears and insecurities and downright sheer bloody terror, the birth of this baby takes us out of ourselves to another place altogether. Thank goodness. The birth of our first grandchild has balanced out the exacting experiences we've had with cancer and the treatment. And I'm very grateful.

Now that I'm into grandmothering I make sure Sean is changed (Maurs refuses to have anything to do with nappies except to hover and offer advice) and bottle-fed with the breast milk Kristi expressed yesterday and left in the freezer.

Maurs is exhausted. Even after holding Sean for a few minutes and telling him stories about bears and whales and elephants it's obvious she doesn't have much strength left. I have no doubts she did the right thing cancelling the last chemo. The red blotches on her face and back are worse, if anything. The doctor says they're a result of the chemo, so they can only improve from now on.

Later that afternoon, Kristi arrives back with her brother Geoff. The operation was successful. They only had to take off a small section of her cervix rather than having to do another cone biopsy like last time. What a relief. The biopsy results will be available next week.

How often have I heard those dreaded words over these past few months?

Friday 6 September
Maurs has a big lump on her right forearm, the same arm that had the intravenous drip in last time, so it could be connected with the chemo in some way. Something else to worry about.

Maurs calls in after seeing Dr Patricia. "She says it's an infected vein," and she has given Maurs a prescription for antibiotics. "She also said that if I have any reaction at all to the drugs, which I could after the chemo, that I'm to ring her immediately. It's so sore. I've never had anything like it before." She touches it gingerly.

I've started to write little stories about Sean Daniel, Nana Jean and Nana Maurs. I'll type them and send them to Kristi for Sean as he gets older.

I suspect that Maurs is smoking again and is not game to tell me. I'm pretty sure I almost caught her in the backyard the other day. I'd prefer that she wasn't smoking, but it's entirely up to her. At least my house is now a smoke-free zone.

Monday 9 September
Dad turned eighty-nine yesterday. He's holding his own for someone who's such a grand age, especially with all the afflictions he has.

Maurs probably wouldn't have had her fifth chemo today

anyway, with her arm the way it is. But it is wonderful we didn't even have to consider going in. Already the chemo sessions seem like a long time ago. The first one was exactly twelve weeks ago, the day before our sixth anniversary.

Maurs rang her decision through to the oncology unit towards the end of last week and spoke to whoever was on duty. As he told her on the phone, he had to say he wouldn't advise her to stop the chemo at this point, but on the other hand it was entirely up to her.

It might have been better if Dr Kirk hadn't been away on holiday so Maurs could have talked over the decision with someone she knows well and trusts implicitly in the medical sense. Then again, he might just have persuaded her round to his way of thinking, which would have made it difficult the way Maurs is at the moment. She tires easily, has no energy for or interest in doing anything very much, and is generally fed up with this whole business.

Dr Patricia has suggested that Maurs' arm needs to be massaged to help get rid of the lump. I carefully stroke up the arm, trying not to hurt it any more than I have to. It's improved after the couple of days of antibiotics, but still quite swollen and inflamed.

Saturday 14 September

Maurs is fifty-one today! Party time! There are still some things in life worth celebrating and her birthday's come at the right time to do it.

Tiddas is playing on the CD and the familiar harmonies lift our spirits. The laundry trough is full to overflowing with bunches of purple irises. Kristi is in the front room (where it's warm) feeding Sean. The chops and sausages are sizzling on the barbecue in the backyard, the chicken wings and the huge chocolate ripple cake I made are on the dining-room table. Geoff and his partner, Anita are watching *Return of the Jedi* with the kids, while the rest of us sit out under the back veranda and chat. As more people arrive, Maurs shows off Sean, claiming him as our grandson, and passes his photos round to be admired.

Maurs makes a speech thanking everyone for their support and giving thanks that the treatment has been successful and that the cancer is gone. We're both far too tired to do any serious raging. But it's certainly what we need, to be surrounded by friends and family members whom we love and who love us.

Monday 16 September
After Kristi heads off to take Sean for his next lot of injections (which I don't really want to think about), Maurs comes back to bed.

She is embarrassed because there's hardly any hair at all left on her cunt. I go down to take a look. Sure enough, it's as smooth as the proverbial baby's bottom. Not at all as unpleasant as Maurs is making out.

"It looks quite wonderful," I say, meaning it. "I don't know what you're upset about."

"I don't like it," Maurs states categorically. It reminds her too much of when she was a child. With the loss of this status symbol of her grown womynhood, she is bereft in some vital way.

I only hope, if it does turn out to be a permanent condition, that she gets used to it and doesn't continue to mourn the loss indefinitely.

When we discover that she's losing the hair under her arms as well, her misery knows no bounds. "I used to be so proud of having hair under my arms, too," she mourns. What can I say?

Thursday 19 September

Kristi and Sean leave on the early-morning flight to Brisbane to connect with the international flight to Port Moresby. I am devastated. Because of Dan's job, flying planes for Missionary Aviation Fellowship, they live in a place that is practically inaccessible and expensive to visit (it's cheaper to fly to Europe than it is to Vanimo) and dangerous for their health, and I don't know when I'll see them again.

"Perhaps you'll be able to save up enough money to go and visit them in April or May next year before they go to see Dan's family in Sweden," Maurs comforts me.

Perhaps.

As we leave the airport, I tackle Maurs about my suspicions that she's smoking again. She doesn't deny it. Even though her smoking makes me nervous, it makes life a lot easier, for both of us, that she can be open about it.

I'm so depressed about Kristi and Sean leaving that I don't even try to talk myself out of it. The only advantage I can see is that I have my house back again. Just me and the archives. I'll probably just wallow for a few days till I feel able to surface and take up the threads of my life once again. No sense pushing it.

Tuesday 24 September

Maurs and I get to the Royal Women's at one o'clock, but we don't get in to see Dr Kirk till almost three. This ridiculously outdated public health system, where patients are expected to wait for hours as a matter of course, is to be changed by the next visit, I'm pleased to hear from one of the nurses. The clinic is moving upstairs to the newly renovated wing that used to be Ward 53, and everyone will be given an appointment time.

"Although," the nurse says, "I just hope womyn keep their

appointments under this new system because the doctor's time is too precious to waste if they're late or don't turn up."

As if our waiting for two solid hours is worth nothing. As if appointments are a new thing. As if doctors, even with an appointment, aren't always running late anyway. As well as implying that patients are incompetent into the bargain. I have to choke back an equally outrageous reply. It's another reminder of how little patients' needs and comfort are ever taken into account in the overall medical scheme of things in big public hospitals, and one of the reasons I gave up nursing all those years ago.

Maurs has her list of questions ready which Dr Kirk answers in his usual kind and caring manner. He decides, when Maurs asks about the discharge from her vagina, to do a Pap smear test, just in case. Everything else seems to be in order.

He didn't know, however, till Maurs tells him, that she'd stopped having the chemo at number four. Which is rather strange. This information must be clearly recorded in Maurs' file, which he has right there in front of him.

"It seems you took advantage of the fact that I went away," he murmurs. He is not about to have a go at her, but is seemingly nonplussed by the unexpected news.

"One thing I forgot," Maurs says. "I used to get Jean to bring me in Bounty Bars while I was having chemo because they were my favourites. And now I can't stand the sight of them." We'd been warned about not eating favourite foods during chemo sessions for this reason. "Even coming in here today I felt nauseous as soon as I entered the building."

Dr Kirk refuses to tell us, when Maurs asks him, where the particular cancers that Maurs has had are likely to manifest again. He dismisses the query on the grounds that we ought not to be bothered by metastasis as it will only worry us unnecessarily.

Maybe we are being unnecessarily inquisitive. But why not? What is there to be afraid of? If we're asking, we're prepared to hear the answers. But we don't pursue it.

He does say, however, that Maurs has a very good chance that the cancer won't come back. Whatever that means. But it's a comfort to hear it anyway.

Wednesday 25 September
Thirty years ago today my third and last child, Michelle Jean, was born at the Queen Victoria Hospital late on a Sunday afternoon. The placenta came away too soon, so she was blue and unconscious; she died three days later in a humidicrib.

Her death was the very worst experience of my life.

Sunday 29 September
We get to the Fringe Festival's Brunswick Street party in time for the opening event, the waiters' race. And don't get home till early evening.

This is the first time in many long months that Maurs has been well enough and had sufficient energy to stay out like this for hours at a time.

We're delighted. Progress.

Thursday 10 October
A breakthrough. After months of thinking about it, anticipating that my circus days are coming to an end, I attend my first tai chi class. It's an entirely new discipline and, while I'm not brilliant at it, I think I'm going to like this more relaxed and much slower approach to keeping fit.

Monday 21 October
Maurs and I arrived here at Barb Anthony's beach house late yesterday afternoon. The beach is windswept and deserted,

we discover, as we clamber through the rocks to stroll along the white sand arm in arm in our heavy coats. We intend to walk on the beach every day, laze in bed till all hours and relax on the back porch.

With Dad in the Alfred Hospital (he started getting really breathless, because of the lung cancer, I suppose, and called an ambulance), I wasn't sure whether I ought to leave Melbourne. He seems to be improving despite the wheezing, and will probably go home in a week or so. Besides, Maurs and I are very much in need of a break.

As we make love, on this our first relaxing morning in bed, we discover that the hair on Maurs' cunt as well as the hair under her arms appears to to be growing back again. Maurs is rapt.

However, Maurs does not seem as cheerful as she ought to be, on our first time away together for years. I can't help wondering if it's to do with hearing from Barb Anthony last Friday, that her breast cancer has metastasised, on the rib cage this time. Barb is hoping that the operation that she's likely to have in the near future, plus weeks of radiotherapy, won't damage the butterfly she's had tattooed over the scar of the original mastectomy.

I was fully expecting Barb to drop out of POW's workshops as she did last year. I was utterly surprised, as well as relieved, when she arrived for the rehearsal on Saturday with every intention of doing POW's show, *Every Witch Way*, after all. Maurs, who has barely recovered, is in there doing balances and whatnot at the workshops with everyone else. And now Barb. I am humbled by these womyn and their courage and strength to keep going despite the terrifying odds stacked against them.

Wednesday 30 October

It didn't take long for the relaxing time away to fade. We arrived back in time for the Reclaim the Night march and dance afterwards. I'm pleased that while I was away I completed a draft of the POW script for *Every Witch Way*. I did eat a bit too well at times. I've been over-eating for months to compensate for my grief about Maurs having cancer, exactly as I did when I knew Mum was dying of cancer back in 1970.

For years I have seen my father only every two or three months; it's only in recent years that I have developed a less antagonistic relationship with him. I have decided to visit Dad on a more regular (weekly) basis from now on. My decision is triggered by the realisation, now that he's home from hospital and I see how debilitated he is, that this could well be Dad's last few months. Then again, he might live for another ten years (his oldest brother died aged ninety-nine), but I'm not prepared to take the risk. There are questions I still need to ask. And I want to be there for him if it does turn out that he doesn't have all that long to go.

Friday 1 November

We've just been to see Club Swing, a dynamic group of womyn whose aerial performances are awe-inspiring and humorous and erotic, perform *Appetite* at Southbank overlooking the Yarra River. We're sitting at the stop outside the Victorian Arts Centre waiting for a tram. I open the latest copy of *Lesbiana*[1] and read that Jenny Dodd, who ran the AIDS awareness course, died from breast cancer three weeks ago, just before her forty-sixth birthday. I'm shocked and it takes me a while to grasp the implications; I can hardly believe what I'm reading. I start to cry. It's all too much.

---

[1] No. 52, November 1966.

We'd heard she had breast cancer, but also that she'd successfully dealt with it by alternative means. And now this.

Saturday 2 November
Last night, at Ursula's ceramic exhibition opening at the Artists' Garden gallery in Brunswick Street, we caught up with Marianne Permezel who has been keeping a low profile since her mastectomy. She's now finished the chemotherapy, and she looks quite stunning with her head completely bald.

That is why we find ourselves in the darkened back room of one of the local hotels at the Moreland Hotel tonight at the late (for us) hour of almost midnight, listening to Arcane, that is, Marianne and Jane on guitars, plus the drummer, as they blast their way through their repertoire of songs. Marianne is one of the quietest womyn, and one of the noisiest musicians I know.

Heavy metal is not our favourite choice of music by any means. But after having seen Marianne last night for the first time since the diagnosis (I've rung a few times and talked to Jane), we felt it was the least we could do to show our support for what she's been going through.

Sunday 10 November
Because Maurs has been open about her involvement with cancer and the various treatments she's had, she is invited to run a workshop about cancer at a women's festival weekend of activities called The Cheerful Amazon, organised by the Active Health Group.

Maurs starts the workshop by talking about everything that's been going on for her, which leads everyone else to say why they're there. Some of us have had cancer, some have parents who've died of cancer, some have been carers of friends who've had cancer.

All the womyn who attend, apart from a womyn from Women's Information and Referral Exchange (WIRE), are lesbians we know. So we manage to get a good discussion going around our various experiences, which I find very supportive. Especially given this is the first lesbian-oriented discussion we've ever had about cancer.

I'm delighted at the end of the session when everyone agrees that we need to start up a lesbian cancer support group. A date, place and time are set before we leave. After all this time and many discussions on the topic we're going to have the kind of group that would have been most beneficial at the beginning of this year.

Still, better late than never.

Tuesday 19 November
Unfortunately, even though Maurs has an appointment at 1.15 p.m. to see Dr Kirk, the renovations in Ward 53 aren't finished yet, so we're still down at the same oncology out-patients clinic under the archaic system of first come, first served. I'm furious that Maurs wasn't informed about this. Anticipating another two-hour wait, I head for the counter in high dudgeon to write a letter of complaint.

They must have seen me coming. One of the nurses heads me off with apologies. I calm down sufficiently to go and sit quietly with Maurs, who is resigned to the inevitable, waiting until her name is called. Sure enough, it's three o'clock before she gets in to see him.

Dr Kirk tells Maurs that as he's leaving soon to set up an oncology unit somewhere else, this will be the last time she sees him. It's sad because, however imperfect these doctors might be, Maurs has got to know and trust Dr Kirk a great deal. Even I don't think he's as bad as some I've met in my travels.

Maurs reiterates the point that, no, she doesn't want to take progesterone, mainly on the grounds that it stimulates the appetite and she doesn't want to put on any more weight, if she can help it. She is prepared take her chances as far as osteoporosis is concerned.

Maurs has another internal examination and Dr Kirk tells her that her last blood test showed she is still clear. Before she leaves, he asks if he can hug her goodbye. Maurs, being a great hugger, says yes.

Tuesday 26 November

I finish and run off several copies of "The Adventures of Sean Daniel" (by Nana Jean) to give to Maurs and my family; I book my return passage on the *Spirit of Tasmania* ferry to go to the Lesbian ConFest in January next year; and send off three short stories to the Women's Library competition in Sydney. Not that I'm obsessed; only two of the stories are about cancer.

I talked to Dad about his will which prompted him to do something about it. It was drawn up by Ruth Harper and duly signed and witnessed ten days ago. Not that he has much, but how he's reached the age of eighty-nine without a will is beyond me.

I'm not much better. I made a will when I bought my house back in 1976 and have been meaning to update it for ages. As lesbians we're always talking about how important it is that we have our affairs in order before we die so that our wishes can be carried out and not just claimed by (sometimes) hostile relatives. And yet I'm just as reluctant, when it comes down to it, to do the right thing.

The opening night of *Every Witch Way* is a mere two days away. This time next week . . .

Sunday 1 December

It's all over bar the shouting, and we had a great time!!

From something that started as a suggestion back in 1994, POW Circus has become not only an energising and creative exercise for a lot of womyn but also a political and social statement about what older womyn are capable of doing.

Barb Anthony managed to come to most of the rehearsals and do all three performances, and at the same time have the op to cut out the lump as well as several weeks of radio-therapy afterwards. To top it off, she was fearless on the stilts. The part called for her to fall on her stilts on to the stage each night. With her long legs emphasised by a beautiful, shimmering gold skirt, she always looked even more graceful than usual. We all held our breath and watched as she fell forward, completely vulnerable. She was nothing less than magnificent.

Maurs managed to be the inimitable clown she always is; she participated as a strong base in the double and group balances, and coordinated all the tech work. It was such a relief to know she was capable of performing after all she's been through this year.

Monday 9 December

At last. The first Lesbian Cancer Support Group meeting is held at Maurs' place. We all bring food to share, and sit around the dining-room table talking about ourselves and working out what kind of a group we want in order to meet our various needs.

We tentatively decide that it is important to support lesbians in the group who are recovering from cancer. That we perhaps want to be advocates for lesbians who are having trouble coping with the medical system. That we might also want to be available for anyone who rings with a problem or for support. That we do want to continue meeting on a regular basis each month.

I think it's wonderful that we've got together and can see some long-lasting and far-reaching benefits for lesbians with cancer, as well as carers, out of this dedicated group.

Wednesday 11 December
I finish word-processing the twelve-minute script I wrote last week and post it off to Out Cast Theatre for consideration. The title is "Waiting for Chemo".

Thursday 19 December
Making the effort to visit my father every week has its compensations. Today I ask Dad how to spell his birthplace, Donaghadee, near Belfast in the occupied six counties of Northern Ireland, for a review of an anthology of Irish stories called *Wee Girls*, (edited by Lizz Murphy, published by Spinifex Press), that I intend writing. He sang a song he'd made up about Ireland. It had the tears spilling down my face.

It seems Dad is coming to terms with the fact that he probably doesn't have all that much longer to live.

Saturday 21 December
In full clown gear and make-up, Maurs and I are busking at the Queen Victoria Market. Maurs is wearing the baggy multi-coloured outfit she adds to each year, topped by her characteristic black hat complete with sunflower. We do our plate routine and toss diabolos to one another. I do all the talking. Maurs gains the empathy of the audience with her antics. She has them laughing in no time and utterly fascinated by what she might do next. I had a hard time keeping a straight face. I'm just there as a foil to Maurs' clowning antics anyway.

Tuesday 31 December

The last day of the year, and what a year it's been. There was a bizarre incident on Christmas Day over at Dad's place. As we were leaving, Maurs noticed through the wire-screen door that the man in the next flat was lying face down on the floor. When we called the cops and an ambulance they discovered, after breaking the security door open, that he was dead. This all took some time and after several pleasant hours of eating, talking and drinking our way through Christmas dinner with Dad and Victor, it came as quite a shock.

Now, Dad's back in the Alfred Hospital and there's talk of shifting him to Bethlehem Hospital out at Caulfield for palliative care. He's very frail. It's just as well he organised meals on wheels and support services with the Royal Freemasons' Homes of Victoria when he did, because there's no way he can do everything for himself any more.

To give thanks for her recovery and continuing good health, Maurs has a barbecue at her place to see in the New Year with our lesbian friends.

6

1997—Interim

Monday 22 December

Having just heard from Maurs about the results of the latest CAT scan she had last Friday morning at the Children's Hospital, I think this is a good time to recap what's been happening over these past twelve months.

I started the year by going away to Tasmania for the Lesbian ConFest at Koonya. Maurs seemed to have recovered and, knowing Dad would be well looked after at the Bethlehem Hospital, I could relax and enjoy myself.

I was gone three weeks in all. I had a great time sailing there and back on the *Spirit of Tasmania*, and at the ConFest itself. I initiated an early-morning hour-long meditation session plus half an hour of tai chi prior to breakfast, and met one of the organisers of LezCan, the Lesbian Cancer Association of Australia based in Sydney. After that I travelled along the east coast and caught up with friends.

When I visited Dad the day after I returned, I found that he'd not only settled into Bethlehem but was a damn' sight better than when I'd left. He went back to his flat in the first week of February. Quite a remarkable achievement all round, considering he'd been more or less at death's door over New Year.

In the meantime, I started back at my tai chi lessons for the year (the only one of my class to do so), and Geoff returned from his holidays in the Americas. I was determined to make a concerted effort to shift the archives within the next few months. I just wanted them out of here and my house back again.

The womyn I'd met at the Lesbian ConFest visited on her way back to Sydney and suggested that the newly formed Lesbian Cancer Support Group (LCSG) might like to be an associate member of LezCan. I brought up this suggestion at the LCSG's first meeting of the year on 10 February. It was agreed not to make any decision till we got more information about LezCan's constitution. News of the group had spread and there were some new members at the meeting which was heartening.

After her abominable experience with the internal radium treatment at the Peter MacCallum Cancer Institute last year, Maurs absolutely refused to go there any more and told them so. Despite which they kept sending her appointment dates for January, which she ignored because she felt that her regular check-ups at the Royal Women's were more than sufficient.

Even so, on 18 February she was a little nervous about meeting the new doctor for the first time, regretting the loss of Dr Kirk. He seemed okay; only time would tell if he was trustworthy or knew what he was doing. It was a comfort to know that Maurs was still remembered, as we stopped and chatted with the various nurses and other medical staff on the way through.

It was a year for travelling as far as I was concerned. I was invited to Lismore in New South Wales for ten days over International Women's Day to speak about the NGO Women's Forum in Beijing. Next I was off to Papua New Guinea to visit Kristi and Sean and Dan in April and May. As a result, I missed the POW gig at the Midwives Conference (although I managed to do the script and was there for the first rehearsal), and more importantly, I wasn't there for the launch at the State Library of the book I'd been working on for the past three years, *Women's Circus: Leaping Off the Edge*.[1]

It was more than compensated for, I have to say, by being with Sean and Kristi for those five wonderful weeks. I didn't do much for the entire time I was there, apart from play with Sean, chat with Kristi, and get to know Dan a bit better. I gave a hand with shopping and washing and the like. But all I wanted to do was be around Kristi and gaze fascinated at our grandson as he did all of those things that nine-month-old babies do which are only of interest to grandmothers.

In between times, two of my paintings were on display at the Brunswick Mechanics Institute for the Women 1998 exhibition for International Women's Day; I shifted the Women's Liberation Halfway House archives into storage (they'd been at my place for ten years); and I went to the National 10/40 Conference in The Basin in the hills outside Melbourne over the Easter weekend.

When I got back from Papua New Guinea and realised that the main bulk of the archives had nowhere else to go, I finally decided to get my head around the fact that they were not about to move from my place in the immediate future and that was that.

---

[1] *Women's Circus: Leaping Off the Edge*. (1997). Edited by Adrienne Liebmann, Deb Lewis, Jean Taylor, Louise Radcliffe-Smith, Patricia Sykes. Melbourne: Spinifex Press.

Maurs did not really need me to go along to her appointment with the doctor on 20 May, but I felt these three-monthly visits kept me in touch with what was going on so I didn't become too complacent about the deadly potential of this disease. Going to the Royal Women's didn't improve my mood any, because it brought up all the shitty time we had last year which had more or less faded into the background and been overlaid with more interesting and less stressful experiences. But I still wanted to be there with Maurs.

As Maurs was convinced she didn't have cancer any more, for her these visits were merely a formal necessity. But the doctor always did an internal examination and Maurs had a blood test done.

The entry I put in for the Daffodil Day competition was quite different to the one I'd written the year before, while I was still very much caught up in the pain and terror of the diagnosis and treatment. At around the same time I sent in three stories to the Royal Women's competition, only one of which was on the theme of cancer. I wrote a story for the Not Another Premier's Literary Award that was based on my experiences in Papua New Guinea. I was starting to move on.

The June LCSG meeting was again at Maurs' place. Sabine Gleditsch, who'd had two bouts of cancer—a melanoma on her right ankle operated on about four years ago, and some time later, a recurrence in the lymph glands in her groin—joined the group for the first time. I'd known Sabine since she first came to Australia from Germany in the mid 1980s.

As she told us that night, after two years, she'd decided to stop having the chemo treatment she'd been taking since the operation to remove the malignant lymph glands. Even though it wasn't as severe as the chemo Maurs had had, it still made her feel off-colour most of the time, so despite her doctors' recommendation that she take it for a further twelve months, Sabine said she'd prefer to improve the quality of her life.

I was interested to learn that she administered the chemo herself by regular injections. It didn't surprise me that Sabine had decided to stop the treatment altogether and take her chances. Three years is an awfully long time to be taking any kind of deadly drug, even though she'd been able to continue working at SBS Radio throughout the treatment.

At about this time Maurs was starting to have considerable pain in her left hip, which she took to be either a recurrence of the sciatica nerve pain she'd had off and on for the past few years or a strained muscle of some kind. Except this time it wasn't going away. Dr Patricia referred her for an X-ray of her hip, which indicated it might be the onset of arthritis.

For our seventh anniversary, on 18 June, I gave Maurs the first small watercolour picture I'd painted, of a chair. I had used the paints she'd given me. A couple of days later Kristi rang from Sweden, where they were visiting Dan's family, and told me that Sean had four teeth and was walking already. At ten and a half months.

During this time I was writing another story about my experiences in Papua New Guinea. I was also busy typing up *The C-Word* story and considering what to do next about a book on the Women's Liberation Centres and Buildings in Melbourne, which had been written some time ago and needed tidying up before I considered sending it off to womyn who might be interested in having a copy. And at the POW meeting on 23 June, I committed myself to directing the next POW performance, based on Susan Hawthorne's prize-winning *Unstopped Mouths*, about our lesbian cultural heritage, to open at the end of October.

This year there seemed to be many more events and exhibitions during National Aboriginal and Islander Day

Observance Committee (NAIDOC) week in July than usual. It seemed imperative, with public figures like Pauline Hanson mouthing off, that non-Aboriginal people be seen to be in solidarity with Aboriginal and Torres Strait Islander people.

I'd been visiting Dad every week all year and he was looking increasingly frail. When he became quite breathless again at the beginning of July, he decided it might be a good idea if he went to Bethlehem Hospital for a few days to build up his strength. He wasn't eating well and had lost a lot of weight, as well as suffering from intermittent constipation and diarrhoea and the effects of a painful hernia.

I visited Dad on Thursday, 17 July, the day he was admitted, and he seemed to have settled in. When I went in on the following Monday, he had me laughing as he jokingly described the various things he'd got up to. Definitely the best place for him.

On that same day, because the pain in Maurs' hip was getting worse, she had another X-ray done. This time it was of her spine, to see if there was anything that could be done to relieve the agony she was in every time she had to walk any distance.

A couple of days later I received a phone-call at about eight o'clock in the morning from the sister on the ward to say Dad had deteriorated and that I needed to go in straight away. Before I had time to get ready, she rang back to say he'd died very peacefully at about 8.40 a.m. This was Wednesday, 23 July.

My son Geoff and my brother Victor were already at the hospital when I arrived. We were able to see Dad as he lay in the hospital bed where he'd died and say goodbye for as long as we liked. Dad had prepaid his funeral. We organised a simple service for Friday afternoon and he was cremated the following Monday. Being able to arrange it all ourselves and speak at the ceremony made it all far less stressful than it might have been.

We three spent the next couple of weeks clearing out his flat, paying his bills, returning the equipment he had borrowed, letting his family in Belfast know, and generally finalising his affairs. As executor of Dad's will, I started the process of applying for probate, something that took a bit of doing. I immediately wrote a story about Dad's dying and his easy death and sent this and other memorabilia off to Kristi and Marg so they could get a sense of what had happened, seeing they couldn't be here.

It was hard to credit that Sean was a year old already. This time last year, 1 August, Maurs still hadn't quite finished the course of chemotherapy and we were beside ourselves with excitement about becoming grandmothers.

The following day, Maurs went to Adelaide to stay with her friend Joan Russell and her partner Judith for a few days before they headed off to the snow and left her minding the house and the dogs for two weeks. I waited till after I'd read a paper and run a circus skills workshop at the Lesbian Community Feminist Futures Conference before I joined her for a delightfully relaxing week together doing nothing more strenuous than reading lots and walking the dogs at sunset.

I had to be back again by late August to begin rehearsals for POW's show, *Unstopped Mouths*, and Maurs returned a few days later. .

A week after Princess Diana was killed and the day after Mother Theresa died, Molly Donovan, a feminist activist I'd know since the 1970s, died on Sunday, 7 September, of cancer, aged 73. I was sorry I hadn't got round to visiting her in the last few weeks of her life. At her funeral the following Thursday, we were able to pay tribute to her long record of activism in the Women's Liberation Movement and her fondness for dancing.

I didn't get to the September meeting of the LCSG, but I heard from Maurs that Sabine Gleditsch had decided to start treatment again because her recent CAT scan had shown that several tumours had metastasised all the way through her body. A terrible thing.

Maurs saw the doctor at the Royal Women's on 9 September and when she asked for stronger painkillers for the incessant pain in her hip, he gave her a script for Panadeine Forte. Maurs celebrated her fifty-second birthday with lesbian friends and another barbecue in the backyard.

A couple of days later I decided, during meditation, that I was going to take a year off from all my activist commitments. The following year I wouldn't do any more Women's Circus or POW, no more collective meetings, no more anything at all, if I could possibly help it. After twenty-five years of feminist activism I needed a break.

Except for tai chi every Wednesday evening. And the archives were still stubbornly hanging in there for some reason I was unable to fathom. Apart from those two things, I would have time for my writing and anything else that came up.

I went to the opening of the Lesbian Art Exhibition at the Brunswick Mechanics Institute on Friday, 10 October, where I'd submitted a couple of paintings. Beforehand I visited Helen Robertson at the Royal Melbourne Hospital. Helen had found a lump in her breast, which was diagnosed as cancer, and had had a lumpectomy all within a couple of weeks.

I found her quite well, considering it had all come as a hell of a shock. I said I'd keep in touch and would probably see her at the LCSG at some stage if and when she was interested.

She was at the next LCSG meeting the following Monday. After we'd gone around the circle and heard how everyone was, including details about Helen's recent diagnosis and subsequent surgery, we also had an update on Sabine Gleditsch, who couldn't be at the meeting because she was driving up through Central Australia with her new lover.

By midnight on 1 November, we were partying after bumping out the fourth of POW's performances, that is, taking down all the lights and restoring the props and everything else to their original condition. Even though I'd enjoyed it, and it had been fun, my heart wasn't in it as much this time. Maurs did a great job as a clown. Despite the continuing pain in her back and hip, which no-one seemed to be able to fix, she did all three performances and co-ordinated the technical side of things, as usual.

We were both exhausted by the end of it. Especially Maurs, who had already started doing tech work for the Women's Circus show, *Pope Joan*, before POW had finished. The way her back was still playing up after all these weeks, she was beginning to realise she had to start taking things a lot easier. Although it didn't look that way at first, as Maurs was on site night and day during the rehearsal period.

I was glad when we front-of-house womyn had our first meeting so I could get involved and see Maurs occasionally. It was hard not performing for the first time in the seven years I'd been a member of the Women's Circus. But I managed.

At the next LCSG meeting at Maurs' house in November, I was shocked by Sabine's appearance. Because of the drugs she was taking, her face was so swollen that she was almost unrecognisable. Both she and Helen Robertson were also quite bald by that stage as a result of chemotherapy.

As Sabine explained, she had become too ill to continue travelling up north, so she and her lover had gone to Wilson's Promontory in Victoria instead. Her lover had returned to Germany and intended coming back again in January. In the meantime, Sabine's tumours hadn't responded to treatment and were larger, if anything; it seemed she might not have much longer to live. The logo she'd designed for the group was tentatively approved that night, subject to full agreement at the next meeting.

At the LCSG meeting and the Matrix meeting the following night as well as the POW evaluation meeting a couple of weeks later I made the announcements that I was taking time off from all my activist collective commitments for the next twelve months.

Wendy Averil, one of the members of the LCSG, who'd taken on the job of coordinating a roster of carers for Sabine when it became obvious she was no longer able to look after herself, rang me early on the morning of 18 November to see if I was available to relieve Sabine's friend who had lectures to attend that morning. Sabine had said that she wanted to die at home, so the LCSG had agreed to make sure she had someone there twenty-four hours a day. Not a problem.

When I got there, I helped Sabine have a bath. Afterwards, Sabine cried as I held her. She knew she was dying and was frightened it would hurt. "It's very peaceful," I said, recalling what the hospital chaplain had said about my father's recent death.

"How do you know?" Sabine demanded, "How does anyone really know?"

She had me there. "When the time comes you will know, and there'll be no reason for you to be in any pain," I answered, knowing how effective painkillers usually were for people with cancer.

As I was leaving I kissed Sabine and said I'd see her on Tuesday, which was my next rostered shift overnight. In the meantime, Maurs had been flat tack doing the teching for the Women's Circus and hadn't had a chance to catch up with Sabine. Now that the show was up and running, Maurs made time to see her on Sunday afternoon.

We both talked with Sabine for about an hour. She was extremely pleased to see Maurs and interested in what we'd been doing. "Given how bad things are, they couldn't be better," she repeated several times. I was so intrigued by these words I wrote them down for future reference.

As she put it, all her needs were being met, her wish to die at home looked like being fulfilled, she didn't have any pain, she was surrounded by lesbians who were catering to her every whim, and her parents had rung to say they loved her after years of neglect. She would have liked her lover to be there, but as that was impossible she was quite philosophical about it. There didn't seem to be anything more that needed to be done.

As we kissed and hugged her goodbye, I reiterated that I'd see her again on Tuesday. However, Sabine went into a coma at about four o'clock early Monday morning, less than twelve hours after we'd been speaking to her.

Maurs had yet another X-ray later that same Monday, for bone density this time, because the pain was so consistent as to be well nigh unbearable and the Panadeine Forte that Maurs was taking regularly only dulled but didn't stop the constant soreness.

Wendy Averil rang me at about 7.00 a.m. on Tuesday, 25 November, to let me know that Sabine had died at about five that morning. I said I'd be over as soon as possible to see her and say goodbye. As I'd done a few short months ago when my father had died, I trammed across to the other side of the city with my whole being focused on this final chance to say farewell.

When I arrived I was shocked to find that Sabine had already been picked up and taken to the funeral parlour. I went into the bedroom, closed the door and cried out my grief for her death and my upset at not being able to see her one last time.

However, Wendy Averil drove me to the funeral parlour so I was able to see Sabine, but under the most bizarre circumstances. She was still on the trolley, and after the attendants had peeled the sheet away from her face and roughly wiped it clean, they started to paint her face with a jelly-like substance till I told them to stop. I couldn't help contrasting this with the unlimited amount of time we'd been allowed to say goodbye to Dad at Bethlehem.

Still, I was grateful I'd been given this small opportunity at least and waited while the funeral arrangements were made.

That afternoon, not surprisingly under the circumstances, Maurs asked me to go with her when she went in to see Dr Patricia for the results of the bone density scan she'd had the previous day. It was the first indication that Maurs was worried that the cancer might have come back.

Dr Patricia was able to assure her that the scan had shown her bone density was quite normal. This was excellent news but brought us no closer to knowing what was causing Maurs so much pain.

Sabine's funeral started from Elwood beach at ten on a sunny Monday morning, and everyone who wanted to speak did so. It occurred to me just before I spoke that I'd perhaps known Sabine longer than anyone else who was there.

It was a long drive out to the Macclesfield cemetery but a beautiful spot for Sabine to be buried in. Both Maurs and I helped to carry the coffin and after the small ceremony to lower it into the grave. Afterwards we shared food and champagne and reminiscences about Sabine down by the lake.

The next day, as she had been doing for months each time she saw a doctor, Maurs requested yet another prescription for Panadeine Forte. The pain was now so bad that Maurs could hardly walk for more than a few yards at a time and couldn't stand still without either bending over or squatting down to relieve it.

The doctor checked Maurs out with an internal examination; when he couldn't find anything wrong, he recommended that she see the physio. On the way downstairs to make an appointment, Maurs had her usual blood test done. We discussed the possibilities, now that the circus was nearly over, of Maurs seeing an osteopath and whoever else to get on top of this.

We started on the round of end-of-year parties, beginning with the first year celebration of the LCSG; then the POW end-of-year celebration; drinks with the rest of the contributors of *Lesbiana* at Café Rumours; and the meeting-cum-celebration and swim with the Matrix Guild.

In the middle of this, Maurs went to get another prescription for Panadeine Forte from the all-night doctor (as she said, she was taking them like lollies). He gave her an examination and she nearly jumped off the couch when he pressed her pelvic area, so there was obviously something very wrong the other doctors weren't picking up.

Maurs duly went to her appointment with the physio at the Women's and rang me afterwards to say the physio had bluntly suggested that the pain was probably due to cancer. Not only that, when Maurs had run into the doctor afterwards, he'd told her that her CA125 blood count was up and promptly booked her in for a CAT scan first thing Friday morning at the Children's Hospital.

We decided that we would just have to postpone worrying about it till we got the results and knew definitely what it was. We didn't even tell Geoff that Maurs had had the CAT scan done that Friday morning before he flew out in the afternoon of 19 December, to live with Anita in Barcelona for the next six months. He left Maurs with his car, a definite bonus.

Monday 22 December
Which brings me up to the events of today.

Even though we have agreed Maurs will contact the doctor while I am with her, she rings me in tears to say the results show the cancer has come back and that she has to have chemo again.

This is shocking news. But not totally unexpected. I'd been more frightened by the first diagnosis. And we certainly knew a lot more this time round about the possibilities of treatment and what to expect.

But neither of us really imagined, or else couldn't bear to face it, that the pain in Maurs' hip and back was the result of cancer. I am numb with shock at the implications of this recurrence. Maurs comes round and we cry together.

"I'm not having any more chemo," Maurs says firmly, as I hold her. "I'm not going through all that again. I couldn't bear it."

It feels as if I've been preparing for this for a long time.

Tuesday 23 December
We're at the Royal Women's first thing with our list of questions. The doctor tells us that the lymph nodes following the aorta are definitely enlarged; that the cancer is likely to be ovarian rather than endometrial. Surgery is not an option. Because Maurs has already had a full course of radiotherapy a second dose is not recommended. Chemo can be started as soon as possible, probably Monday or Tuesday, six lots every three weeks with the usual symptoms.

He goes on to say that, because of the tumour, it's highly

likely that her left kidney is no longer functioning. He reassures us that the other kidney will take over automatically so that's not a problem. He tells her that tumours are very likely pressing on a nerve and causing the pain she's been having in her back and left hip over these past six months, and that morphine can be prescribed immediately.

The worst news is that there can be no cure. Even if the tumours are reduced this time round, they'll come back again. It might be months, it might be years. There's no way of telling, it all depends on how Maurs responds to treatment.

Maurs has to collect her urine over a 24-hour period to make sure her one kidney is functioning properly. She gets and has filled out the prescription for morphine. What a relief that's going to be.

As we reiterate on the way out, at least we still have each other. We agree that we'll just take all this one day at a time.

Unlike last time, I'm seriously thinking about clippering my own hair back to number one in solidarity with Maurs, as she will no doubt be doing once her own hair starts falling out, yet again, with the chemo.

Wednesday 24 December
Our friends have been ringing in with sympathy and any-thing-they-can-do-just-let-them-know, all day. Bless them.

Even though the prognosis doesn't augur well and it will probably get worse before it gets better, there's nothing else I'd rather do, nowhere else I'd rather be, except be here with Maurs and do my writing. That's all there is to it.

Thursday 25 December
As it's turned out, recent events have quite overshadowed the grief I'd thought I'd experience because it's the first Christmas without Dad.

While we're waiting for the roast pork to cook, we sit outside in the backyard and discuss what Maurs wants for her funeral and who she wants to leave what to in her will.

Victor arrives with the pudding and cream. We open the presents and amongst other things I give Maurs a recap of *The C-Word 1997* which I'd written straight onto the computer!

The absentee family members ring in: Geoff and Anita from Barcelona, Spain; Marg from India somewhere; and Kristi from Wewak, Papua New Guinea. We had already decided, what with the time delay and the echo and everything, that we would not mention what's happening with Maurs. I figure it's better to do it by letter.

Friday 26 December
They're not easy letters to write, by any means, but the act of writing them does in some way help me come to terms with the prognosis.

Afterwards we head across to visit a friend, Thelma Solomon, who I've known since the early days of the Women's Liberation Movement, with me driving Geoff's car. It's the first time I've driven a car for a couple of years. We figure that I'd better get used to driving again so I can drive when Maurs is too ill from the chemo to do so.

As Maurs has already rung and told a number of dykes about the cancer, there're not too many at the Boxing Day party that don't know about it. It seems a good chance for our friends to see that Maurs is nowhere near being at death's door and is still quite capable of being part of community events.

One of the things I'm a bit anxious about is that Maurs doesn't miss out on seeing Sean when they arrive for their holidays in July next year. I'm prepared to ask Kristi to come earlier if it comes to that. As my first priority is being with Maurs next year, it's also possible that I might miss out on going to the 10/40 in Perth at Easter time. I won't want to leave Maurs if she's not well.

Saturday 27 December
We've borrowed a video camera, and as this is the only day we have free to do it before Maurs starts the chemo we get stuck into it after lunch.

We're out in my backyard and start with Maurs talking about her background, her family, the cancer and, while she's putting on her make-up, about clowning with POW Circus. We then go on location: to the tram stop round the corner, to the terminus outside the University of Melbourne (in order to include the old W-class trams) and finally to Methven Park where I get some great shots of Maurs running and playing on the various pieces of children's equipment.

We go back to Maurs' place to see what it's like. Considering I have no experience, and that I just stopped and started as we went along without any editing afterwards, it's not too bad. With more to come in the months ahead, now that I've got the hang of it.

Maurs spends most of her nights either on the couch in the loungeroom at her place or on the mattress on boxes in my front room. I realise with a pang that not only haven't we slept together for ages, because Maurs finds it far too painful, but if this keeps up we may never sleep together again. This thought catches me unawares and I cry.

Monday 29 December
As Maurs is driving me home she says, "I was thinking this morning that I'm probably doing everything for the last time." Which may or may not be true but just makes me even more determined to make the most of whatever we do from now on.

We talk about the things Maurs hasn't had a chance to do yet: like sky diving. The motor-bike ride doesn't sound nearly so dangerous to me (even though it probably is) and is certainly achievable.

Tuesday 30 December
We're not the first to arrive in the newly renovated chemo room that is next door to where it used to be in the old Ward 53. Two other womyn are already seated and another womyn arrives while I'm down getting Maurs' by-now quite thick file which we forgot to pick up on the way through. I sign for it as Maurs' partner. No-one so much as blinks.

They find a suitable vein with some difficulty and Maurs is finally hooked up to the machine with the saline dripping through in preparation for the chemo which finally arrives from the Children's Hospital a couple of hours later.

Maurs makes jokes about keeping the nurses off the streets while she's in here. And we both settle in for the long haul. Me putting dates in the new diary Maurs got me for Christmas, Maurs reading and dozing.

Dr Jarvis calls in. Maurs tells him we're heading off to the Lesbian Festival in Daylesford for ten days in the new year. He tells us there's a womyn's health conference coming up in the middle of next year which we might want some input into. Maurs tells him about the Lesbian Cancer Support Group. He says that because of Pap smear tests they've reduced the deaths from cervical cancer. But deaths from ovarian cancer haven't changed in the last twenty years.

Given that it's taken several doctors six months to pick up that Maurs' ovarian cancer had metastasised again, I'm not surprised. As we experienced last time, the nursing staff are as caring and considerate as we could ask. However, once again we are the last to leave.

Wednesday 31 December

My New Year resolutions, which I always write up in my journal at this time every year, amount to little more than being here for Maurs and doing my writing for these next twelve months.

When a friend rings unexpectedly to say she's down from the Mountain (part of the Women's Lands in New South Wales, which used to be called Amazon Acres), and can she catch up with both of us, we make time in the afternoon for her to come round. We don't want to miss these opportunities. Who knows if they'll ever come again.

After several New Year's Eves together, where we've either gone out to the womyn's discos or had barbecue parties at Maurs' place, this year Maurs and I go out by ourselves to a couple of local pubs for Guinness, champagne and counter teas. All very quiet and what we need. Although I can't help wondering if we have any friends at all if we can't get an invitation to even one dyke gathering on this significant last night of the year.

I stay awake, do my Motherpeace Tarot for the new year, then wake Maurs just before midnight. We lie on the couch together, kiss and wish each other happy new year before I head off to bed. Maurs stays in the front room where she's more comfortable.

1998

7

January, February

Thursday 1 January

We make love, as we've been doing lately, so Maurs doesn't have to lie on her sore left hip, on the opposite side of the bed to the one either of us has been used to. I don't mind because I get to use my right hand by way of a change. I'm just grateful that after seven and a half years both of us still want to make love at least once a week.

Maurs hopes to see in the new millennium. I say that if we don't get to the millennium together we'll just bring the millennium to us. As it's a made-up concept, it shouldn't be too difficult. Or as Joko emphasises in her book, *Nothing Special: Living Zen*,[1] we need to get to that place where all hope, that life will be anything other than just exactly what it is from moment to moment, is abandoned.

Because of the chemo and morphine Maurs is badly constipated. Besides the coloxol with senna she's been taking

---

[1] Charlotte Joko Beck. (1993, 1994). *Nothing Special: Living Zen.* (Edited by Steve Smith.) New York: HarperCollins.

every day, she inserts a suppository. We want to cut our hair before going to the Lesbian Conference and Celebration in Daylesford in Central Victoria, but we can't find the electric clippers anywhere. In the midst of all this, and just to add to our list of woes, my right ear blocks up. Where now is my spontaneous sense of fun and good humour? I think to myself, as I pack.

I've gone the whole gamut over these past few days: from imagining that I'm the best carer Maurs could possibly have at a time like this, to realising that I might be the worst and she'd be much better off without me.

Tuesday 13 January

My son Geoff rings from Barcelona to say he got my letter (the day after he'd heard the news on the phone from my sister Marg) and to offer his love and sympathy.

We have returned from the National Lesbian Cultural Celebration and Conference in Daylesford.

Maurs was in so much pain from the chemo the first couple of days that she almost went home again. However, with the morphine tablets she is now taking a couple of times a day, the pain Maurs has been experiencing for months was reduced so dramatically that she was able to walk around without having to stop and bend over every few steps.

Anxious about Maurs and with my ear still blocked, I arrived at the site still very much in a state of shock and under considerable stress but determined to make the most of it.

We both went to the workshop facilitated by Lesbian Cancer Support Group on the first day, entitled The Deadly Serious Syndicate. I was moved by the stories each member of the group told, particularly Julia's. She spoke about how hard it is to watch someone you love go through as much as her lover Jacqui has over these past six years of combating cancer.

Maurs went to the second cancer workshop on Thursday morning while I chose to go to a massage workshop instead, which proved to be a perfect way to spend the time. Both the cancer workshops were very successful with the participants seeming to get a lot out of them, and a few Melbourne womyn agreed to join.

We showed the video I'd taken of Maurs and got lots of positive feedback. We watched Marie Andrews perform in Eva Johnson's one-womyn play, *What Did They Call Me?* about the traumatising effects past government policies of removing children from their Aboriginal parents had on everyone concerned. Maurs went in to Ballarat on Thursday for her ten-day blood test without me because I didn't want to leave the space. I went to the spa that evening without Maurs because she didn't want to put herself at risk of infection in that enclosed heated pool with so many others.

We cried together about something that had happened. That brought up everything else we had to cry about.

I was involved in four items in the final concert: the music and movement *Birds of a Feather*, the tai chi class demo, the circus skills workshop's performance, and my own song, poetry, plates and diabolo.

I sat every morning at 6.30 a.m. for an hour, followed by an hour of tai chi instruction, which pretty well set me up for the rest of the day. I also did half an hour of tai chi before dinner by myself. I put a few of my own self-published books out for sale on market day and sold most of them. I got quite a bit out of all three of the workshops I ran: the Racism Awareness Game, the Personal is Political is Spiritual, and the circus skills workshop.

Maurs told me in passing that being at the festival was the best thing she could have done. And Maurs did one of the things she'd always wanted to do: ride a motor bike. She borrowed leather gear and helmet and went off to Daylesford one afternoon riding pillion with someone who has an 850-cc bike. They had coffee, and rode all the way back again.

"Why didn't you tell me how fantastic bike riding is?" Maurs accused me afterwards, still full of the excitement of it all. I could vaguely remember I used to think that too before I broke both my tibia and fibula riding the bike I used to own, so that I was in plaster for eight very painful months back in 1973.

Anah and I were asked to give Marie Andrews a hand doing the Aboriginal smoking ritual of all participants with smouldering branches of gum leaves during both the opening and closing ceremonies of the festival. A definite honour. I was able to catch up with a number of my interstate friends in particular, and made some unexpected connections with dykes I've known for a while but haven't really appreciated before.

Not only did Maurs and I have a double bed, but because the pain had been reduced by the morphine, we were able to sleep together and I slept really well every night. And the food! Vegetarian lasagnes and casseroles with plenty of salads and spicy dressings. As always, I took along a packet of ground coffee beans and shared them with a couple of others who also preferred real coffee to instant.

As I said at the plenary session on the final day, the fact that it was a live-in conference over ten days was a highlight for me. That and the phenomenal support Maurs and I got from the organisers in particular and generally from all the participants. By the time we left, I felt a whole lot calmer and I now have quite a different perspective on this whole business. Taking it one day at a time.

Everyone is astonished by my new haircut. Soon after we got back from the LezFest, Maurs' hair started to fall out. At her suggestion, I clippered her hair back even further this time round, so that it looks just slightly longer than a shave. It's great.

As I stood before the mirror, I took one last look at my shoulder-length grey hair before cutting it with the scissors, then did the first strokes with the clippers myself. To begin with, Maurs was a bit nervous about using the clippers, but she got into it after a while and is as delighted with the result as I am. It seems to me as if we're Amazon warriors gearing up for the battles ahead. And I have no regrets.

Maurs and I made love both mornings this last weekend, finding it amusing that we had to be careful about moving our hands under the bedclothes now that Fran has given Maurs a kitten, Vintage, who is ready to pounce on anything that moves. Making love has always been such a pleasure between us. If it gets to the stage where Maurs finds it too difficult this will be a significant and painful departure from our usual loving connection.

Monday 19 January
Having come to the conclusion that doing *The C-Word* every day makes me too depressed, I'm going to jot down the relevant points as they come up and do a summary every now and then.

Like today, c-for-chemo day.

Once we get settled into the newly renovated Ward 51 at the Royal Women's, I'm so exhausted, for some reason, that I doze in the chair almost as much as Maurs does. In between, I'm reading a book about carers and finally conclude that I don't much like the word carer, nor the role it implies. I'm still very much Maurs' lover and partner and don't see any reason why this needs to change.

Maurs has lost weight. She was down to 78 kilograms

compared to 83 not so long ago. I've noticed she hasn't been eating nearly as much as she usually does. Because she's not hungry, she says. Her bottom has hollows it never had before.

A distinctive symptom of cancer, reduced appetite and losing weight. Not a good sign. There are also the side-effects of the chemo to contend with: a tender scalp, numbness in the tips of her fingers and toes, the aches and pains in her joints, constipation, nausea and hair loss. Her pubic hair is almost gone again, we noticed at the weekend, and the whiskers on her chin have receded as well.

We're told, after the event, that the extreme aches and pains Maurs had in her joints a few days after the first treatment are among the symptoms of this particular chemo.

Towards the end of the afternoon Maurs is asked by the drug company to give a videoed report about chemotherapy from a user's point of view. There she is, with the intravenous line still in her hand, answering questions about the symptoms she's been having, both this time and last. She deserves the two huge bunches of colourful blooms she's given afterwards for being such a star.

Soon after we get home Maurs heads over to Helen's for the LCSG meeting. It's gratifying to know all the groups, POW Circus as well, are continuing without me and especially to see Maurs so involved in things that are important to her despite this latest development.

Just when we're beginning to feel we've got a grip on this chemo business, Maurs wakes me with the news that she vomited last night's dinner at about four this morning. I try not to panic, but as Maurs points out there's nothing to be done about it.

Painting a small watercolour of a chair for Ursula's fortieth birthday, doing the drawing for my first acrylic painting, and getting up to speed, as they say, for this book helps keep my mind occupied for the rest of the day.

Before the pains from the chemo (as opposed to the cancer) get too bad, Maurs manages to get along to help facilitate the lunchtime workshop run by the LCSG on Thursday at the Lesbian and Gay Health in Difference Conference at the University of Melbourne. Although it isn't well attended, they manage to advertise the group.

Maurs bought some trevally at the Queen Victoria Market on Friday, which is delicious. But immediately after eating she vomits the lot. I can't help feeling anxious when this happens, although for Maurs' sake, I try not to let it get to me too much.

Afterwards, we lie together on the couch in the front room and Maurs holds me while I cry. I find it hard to believe, when Maurs is here now and looking relatively well and so alive, that she's not going to always be here.

Ursula's fortieth birthday party on Saturday is a rage with no less than four womyn's bands, including Sticky Beat, reconstituted especially for the night, with Ursula beaming away on the drums and Marianne slaying us with her flute.

Maurs sits on a banana lounge covered by a rug, holding court as most of her friends come up to see how she is and stay for a chat. At one stage I hold Maurs while she has a cry on my shoulder when she realises she doesn't have the energy to dance with me.

It's a jolt seeing Maurs admit her condition so publicly like that—as if she has already slipped into the role of an invalid in need of care.

It's amazing, now that I'm no longer cluttering up my

head with all the feminist activist nitty-gritty or worrying about POW, how much my mind has been freed to deal with other things.

Like getting back into writing *Behind Enemy Lines*, the book I've been doing since goodness knows when, about the Women's Liberation Movement in the 1970s. And enjoying it. Like not getting too upset that I am missing out on things, like all the Dance Cat fundraisers held to get these ballroom dancers across to Amsterdam to participate in the Gay Games, because I'm choosing to be with Maurs instead.

Patience is my word for this year, I've decided.

Monday 26 January
A week since the last chemo and Maurs is feeling not too badly this morning. We make love before she drops me back at my house on this cold rainy day.

The pattern seems to be that Maurs has a couple of days of respite directly after the chemo before the aches and pains in her joints start. She was so bad by Thursday evening that she finally rang the Royal Women's to ask if she could take more of the morphine because the extra tablets she'd been given weren't working at all and she knew she wouldn't get any sleep that night. The morphine tablets have become a lifeline.

The kitten was also driving her to distraction: she had no patience to look after it, and it was scratching her head, which is extremely sore and tender and almost bald on top at the moment. She rang Fran, who agreed to look after the kitten for as long as Maurs wanted.

Our friends ring in every now and then to make sure we're okay. Helen Robertson rings to say she's still having chemo with radiotherapy to follow. Someone else comments that both

Maurs and I are very brave. I mumble something to the effect that you do what you have to do. After I get off the phone I realise that it's Maurs who is brave, going off to have chemo and coming to terms with dying. Not me.

Cutting my hair like this has given me more insight into what it must be like for Maurs to have her hair suddenly all fall out and not a thing she can do about it. The main difference is that my hair continues to grow at a rate of knots while Maurs has grown even balder, with hardly any hair on top now—I notice when she picks me up after tai chi on Wednesday—and very little at the back.

"It looks good, I like it," I say. And I do. It's the closest Maurs has ever got to a shave without actually shaving it. I'm so impressed that I keep on chuckling every time I look at her for the sheer joy of it.

"I really like these early-morning rituals," Maurs says to me, as she brings my second cup of coffee to me in bed. It's something she's been doing for years now.

As I'm saying goodbye to Maurs, with my face buried in her neck I say, "I've just thought of a sick joke. Do you want to hear it?" Maurs nods.

"You know how we've always said we'd never talk about being together forever or till death us do part?" As feminist lesbians that whole patriarchal notion is anathema to us. "Well, it's very much beginning to look as if we are going to be together forever and till death us do part, doesn't it?" I'm making light of it because it does strike me as funny after all our protestations to the contrary.

Fortunately, Maurs sees the funny side of it too.

After Maurs drops me off for my appointment to have the wax syringed out of my ear, I feel shithouse for the rest of the day. Mainly because when I ask Dr Patricia about ovarian

cancer so I can have an overall idea of what's involved (I'd
checked with Maurs that it was okay for me to do this), she
tells me that ovarian cancer usually metastasises in the abdominal cavity and would likely go to the liver in due course.

I don't want to ring Maurs and worry her with my petty
complaints. Then that evening, when I ring her as I always do
when I get into bed, it all comes pouring out and I'm sobbing
down the phone before I know it.

"I didn't have anyone else to talk to," I apologise.

"You must always ring me," Maurs insists.

Lesbiana arrives in the mail with my article entitled "Given
How Bad Things Are They Couldn't Be Better",[1] the quote
from Sabine just before she died.

As I'm getting my ear syringed yet again, I suggest to Dr
Patricia that my ear is blocked because I don't want to hear
that Maurs has cancer. She's noncommittal.

On the one hand, I know Maurs is going to die sooner
rather than later. On the other it seems incredible that she's
not going to be here. And what am I going to do then for
comfort and love and all the things I rely on Maurs for?

Face the suffering with integrity, as my brother Victor
reminds me. "What's integrity?" I ask him. He doesn't know.

I'm finding that I desperately need my own work as a
balance in my life.

While Maurs goes off to the the first Women's Circus
information day for the year on Saturday afternoon, I spend
the time out in my sunny backyard reading the *Age Extra*.
Hearing all about it when she gets back is more than enough.

---

[1] No. 65, February 1998.

Sunday 1 February

Before we make love this morning we both have a good cry. Maurs, because each time she goes to these annual events, like the Pride March, she can't help thinking it might well be for the last time. Me, because it could be the last time I go to these significant events with this womyn who means so much to me that I don't know what I'm going to do without her.

We go on the Lesbian and Gay Pride March, and even though she gets a lift in a vintage car halfway along, Maurs is exhausted by the end of it, being a marshal and selling ribbons and all. POW Circus and the LCSG march together as there are a number of us in both groups.

This could all account for the way I'm feeling at the moment. Like I'm closed off with no energy to reach out to anyone.

Maurs has been on the Human Services list for a Housing Commission flat for nearly two years now. Because her housing situation was becoming more desperate she went to see her local member of parliament on Friday, to explain her position and to get him to put pressure on the department to allocate her a flat. Blow me down if it didn't work.

This afternoon Maurs rings me with amazing news: she's just been told that there's a one-bedroom flat available immediately in West Brunswick if she wants it until a two-bedroom flat becomes vacant. It shows what a bit of political pressure can do.

This time Dr Patricia gets it right. When I go to see her she doesn't stop syringing till there's not a scrap of wax to be seen. For the first time in a month my right ear is completely clear again.

Jean Ferguson, someone I've worked with politically for some time, and who has been very supportive of Maurs, comes round to my place for dinner. I have to make an effort to keep in touch with my friends.

We go to see the ground-floor flat first thing Tuesday morning. My initial impression is that it's very small. The front door opens straight into the tiny kitchen area which flows into the lounge as one room. The bathroom and toilet open off the bedroom next door. And that's it. But as it's just been completely renovated all the appliances, including the stove and the gas heater, are brand new and everything looks very neat and clean.

"What do you think?" Maurs wants to know. "Could I be comfortable here?"

I pace out the rooms and write down the measurements. It's obvious that Maurs will have to get rid of a great deal of stuff.

"I'm taking it," she decides, then and there.

The prospect is immediately exciting. Back at her old place I roughly measure the bed, cabinet, couch and other essentials and we work out that everything Maurs couldn't possibly do without, plus her books, will fit at a pinch. Anything else she'll either give away or sell.

"I made the right decision" becomes a refrain for the rest of the day. With the rent on the flat pegged at 25 per cent of her pension, she can actually afford it.

As we head up to Woodend, in the countryside north of Melbourne, to take advantage of the prize I'd won in a raffle, drawn by Maurs at the LezFest, it feels like a celebration. We call in and have a look at Hanging Rock along the way. Maurs' weakness is obvious as we pause frequently on the short slope. The intriguing configuration of huge boulders, the surrounding bush and the view out over the plains is worth it once we get to the top.

Sipping champagne on the veranda of Woodbury Cottage, having been warmly welcomed, we toast our good fortune. We allow the quiet, the sight of gumtrees and the fresh air to restore our senses. A new flat and a holiday away together all in the same day. We feel thoroughly spoilt.

Maurs signs the lease and gets the keys to flat 16, Gilligan Court, West Brunswick, on Thursday morning. She is excited about the prospect of her own little flat and has already given away some of the furniture she won't be needing.

Over dinner with her brother Brian that evening, Maurs talks about both of us being the executors of her will. Brian is more than willing to carry out her wishes and go along with whatever she wants for a reasonably priced funeral and where she wants her goods and chattels to go.

"Make a list," I keep urging Maurs because she's already promised some pieces of furniture and I want it all to be as easy as possible when the time comes.

Maurs and I do our usual stint on the door at the Matrix Guild fundraiser, the Silk and Satin Ball, on Saturday evening. As we slowly move on the dance floor with our arms around each other, Maurs buries her face in my shoulder and starts crying. I know immediately it is because she is imagining that we might be doing this at a womyn's ball for the last time. And because I don't want to be seen to be crying by all and sundry on the floor I hold her tightly and resist my own tears welling up inside.

Maurs and I drive out to Ringwood in Melbourne's eastern suburbs on Sunday and I stay out of the way while the LCSG meeting takes place. Having so many womyn wanting to support Maurs makes me feel less guilty if I'm not there all the time doing every little thing.

That evening Kristi rings from Papua New Guinea to see how Maurs is. As Maurs says afterwards, that's all the family checked in now since I wrote to pass on the news. Kristi tells me that they've resigned from Missionary Aviation Fellowship and will be in Australia by mid-May for a few weeks on their way back to Sweden to live. Halleluiah!

Monday 9 February
Here we are again.

With Maurs having chemo and me knitting. Because I got permission to enter a soft sculpture in the forthcoming sculpture exhibition at CERES (Centre for Education and Research into Environmental Strategies), I am now busy knitting the pages of a picture book I've designed.

"It's been quite a week," I comment to Maurs.

"Too much," says Maurs. "I need to slow down."

"Going to Woodend was okay though, wasn't it?" Maurs agrees but her exhaustion just thinking about it is evident.

When Maurs comes back from the weighing machine she tells me she's put on weight, which is a relief. It's frightening to watch my lover fading away before my eyes and nothing to be done about it.

The nurses always put on a mask, gown and gloves to handle the deadly chemicals used for treatment. The glass bottle full of Pacitaxel is slippery to hold with gloves on and the nurse makes a comment about how expensive it is as she tries to get it attached without dropping it. As it takes three hours to go through we're not going to get out in a hurry. Much later in the day, the smaller plastic bag of Carboplatin is a breeze by comparison.

Maurs sleeps for most of the afternoon and wakes looking like a ghost with an extremely pale face. She disconnects the monitor and walks to the toilet, pushing the stand that holds her intravenous drip.

As Maurs is off to the veranda for a cigarette, one of the nurses makes some comment about filthy cigarettes. "Don't you start," Maurs snaps at her.

"I wouldn't dream of it," the nurse replies calmly, and asks if I'm going with Maurs.

This kind of bad temper is so unusual in Maurs but in this situation it's a wonder Maurs is as good-tempered as she is.

Maurs is given three bottles of barium meal to take home for the CAT scan appointment at the Children's Hospital next Monday.

Later, over dinner, we talk about how pleased we are that Kristi and Sean will be here sooner than expected. Maurs predicts that I'll go mad having them all staying with me for a whole month, but it will be worth it to see them. Besides, who knows when I'll see them again. Unless I travel overseas to visit.

"Don't go on any trips overseas for the next couple of years, will you?" Maurs says quietly.

I might not even go to the 10/40 in Perth this year, so I wouldn't venture overseas at a time like this.

Tuesday 10 February
I spend most of the day at the computer getting *The C-Word* up to date. Maurs rings to tell me she, Mary Daicos and Fran have shifted a pile more stuff over to the new flat.

"I've told Mary she can have my pictures of the nude womyn," Maurs says.

"Your place won't be the same without them," I comment. It's not as if they're great favourites of mine but I've got used to them.

"Not now," Maurs is quick to say. "I've told her she can have them after I'm dead."

"What did Fran want?" I ask.

"Fran didn't want to know about it."

I'm with Fran. And yet, I can't help but admire the way Maurs is being realistic in giving away her stuff and promising things to womyn for after she's gone.

I ring Helen Robertson to see how she is. Yes, she did have shingles, which was painful because it was on the left side where she'd had the surgery done, but she hadn't been admitted to the Royal Melbourne Hospital. She is also concerned that her left hand, which is swollen, might stay like that forever. I tell her with exercise and massage I don't think it's likely.

It seems incredible that, with everything that's going on, there can still be days of joyfulness. Kristi's thirty-fourth birthday has something to do with it. I suppose if I can accept that my days unfold one after another, complete or whatever (painful, heavy, fulfilling, tiring, inevitable) in themselves, all I have to do is experience their unfolding as a gift to appreciate. And I do. More than ever.

Maurs is into red meat at the moment (to build up her depleted red blood corpuscles, perhaps?), so I buy a steak for Friday night's dinner.

Our last night sleeping at Maurs' place in Bruce Street. When we get into bed I cry on Maurs' shoulder because of the pressure I feel from everyone to conform to some idea of how someone in my position ought to behave. Maybe I am too matter-of-fact, too unapproachable, seemingly not emotional enough. But I'm living it the only way I can.

Then it occurs to me that this book that I'm writing, *The C-Word*, depicting everything Maurs and I are going through, won't ever be read by Maurs in its entirety. And I cry a whole lot more.

The move goes extremely well. Heaps of dykes arrive to give a hand. I'm driven across to the flat so I can open up and say where everything is to go, while Maurs stays behind to direct operations at the Bruce Street end. It's just as well we'd worked it all out beforehand. And because I'd erred on the side of caution all the furniture fits much better than we'd expected.

By the end of it, as Maurs and I are sitting on the couch with all of the furniture beautifully in place, the roast leg of lamb hissing in the oven, and toasting ourselves and the flat with champagne, I'm ecstatic. Now the shifting is out of the way so we can relax and get on with our lives.

Two hours at the Midsumma Carnival is more than enough. We get there in time to hear Tiddas sing, and although we enjoy the atmosphere Maurs is exhausted and I'm not sorry to leave. These mixed events are still predominantly for the entertainment of the boys.

Monday 16 February
"See how one of my eyebrows has lost more hair than the other." Maurs is at the mirror in her brand new bathroom. "I look lopsided."

"Only someone who knows you as well as I do would even notice," I assure her.

Maurs left her barium meal out of the fridge last night. As she puts it, "It's bad enough anyway, but when it's so freezing cold the liquid hits your stomach like a ton of bricks."

It's raining and I knit some of the blue page of the soft sculpture book while Maurs has her CAT scan done.

"I hate having to put the tampon in," says Maurs when she's finished, "but I suppose it's a way of telling where the vagina is on the X-ray." She shudders. "Next time I'll ask if you can come in with me so you can see what happens."

As I've been there for nearly everything else I don't see why not.

Reading Joko's *Nothing Special: Living Zen* (for the third time) is helping me to work out my fears. Fear of chaos, which I try to control to mask my fears. Chaos happens. Death happens. Mum died. Michelle died, there was nothing I could do about it. Maurs will die. I can't prevent that. Much as I would like to.

I spent three blissful days in a row at the computer this week, typing in *Behind Enemy Lines*. It's the longest time I've had doing my own work like this for a long while. I have worked out, from the letters Marg wrote from Auckland, Aotearoa (New Zealand), before she left to live in Europe, that Mum had her first operation for cancer in July 1969. One letter mentions that Mum watched the moon landing while she was still in hospital.

There's no mention of where the cancer was. We, meaning my family and society generally, never discussed painful and unmentionable things like cancer. I think it was abdominal—in her bowel, perhaps? I seem to recall hearing from the doctor that it was in her duodenum.

That was a difficult and painful time. I was very fond of and close to my mother, and was in denial for months about her imminent death. I was eating cakes and putting on weight to block the pain. I busied myself with waitressing, studying for my Matric and looking after my two primary-school children so I didn't have to deal with it. And then I wasn't there for my mother at the time when she needed me most.

It astounds me now that I didn't go with her when she went to the Peter Mac for chemotherapy.

I come to the conclusion on Friday morning that I need to start coming to terms with the fact that Maurs is dying and won't be here to hold and love me for very much longer. I want to do this so that I'm clear and can appreciate these last years absolutely and utterly.

Face the suffering with integrity. (Must ask my brother Victor who said that.) Being true to myself and who I am.

I don't want to block the pain any more with all the cakes, halva and chocolate I've been eating lately. As I did when my mother was dying. I don't want to make the same mistake with Maurs. I want to be here for her.

Maurs rings Anah Holland-Moore and asks her to do the funeral service, which she is more than happy to do, of course. Anah asks what kind of music Maurs might like, which Maurs hasn't even thought about.

I'm finding that it is relatively easy not having any more sugar. Although I think I felt a bit spaced out there for a couple of days.

Carrying a list of questions so we won't forget anything, Maurs and I go up to the oncology unit at the Royal Women's to see Dr Jarvis. Maurs wants to know what to expect, what symptoms to look out for, the anticipated course of treatment, what will happen when it gets worse, and how the cancer is likely to progress. Everything except how long it's likely to take.

Maurs says she believes she will know when it's time and will die when she's ready for it. I can't help wanting to have some idea of the overall time it might possibly take. But that's just my own stuff. And none of my business.

Dr Jarvis is more than happy to answer questions. He also wants to make sure that Maurs understands that the disease is terminal. At the same time he is able to reassure Maurs that the tumour has reduced a little bit and that the chemo is doing its job.

"But you'll know that yourself," he says. "And you're looking well."

He recommends that Maurs continue with the next three lots of chemo, which Maurs had expected and is willing to do. Exactly how the disease will progress is unknown.

Ovarian cancer has a 70 per cent mortality rate, so they discuss Global Footsteps, a new group working to raise awareness about ovarian cancer. Early detection is the only way of surviving it, apparently.

We look at the CAT scan X-rays while Dr Jarvis explains what they mean. The pale blur between the left kidney and the aorta is the tumour, reducing in subsequent shots. I'm not sure if I understand it correctly but Maurs seems satisfied.

Again, Dr Jarvis advises Maurs to take progesterone because she has "nothing to lose." The hormone will increase her appetite and cause cramps and bloating, but endometrial cancer responds well to this kind of treatment because it counter-balances the oestrogen in her body. He writes the name down, Provera, so Maurs can find out more about it.

Before we leave, one of the nurses gives Maurs a photocopy of one of the chapters from *Cancer in Two Voices* by Sandra Butler and Barbara Rosenbaum,[1] a book I've been meaning to read since Maurs was first diagnosed.

Afterwards, we sit outside a café in Lygon Street and have cappuccinos. No cakes.

---

[1] Spinsters Ink, San Francisco 1991.

Maurs begins talking about her funeral. She only wants a few flowers from her immediate family; she would prefer money to go to ovarian cancer research. She wants the scattering of her ashes at Gariwerd in Western Victoria to be a womyn-only ceremony. Brian can have a few ashes to scatter on their mother's grave. Once Maurs is dead and before she's cremated, she wants me to read the ending of *The C-Word* out loud to her. Maurs figures she'll get to hear it that way.

"I want to be buried in my shorts. My shorts and singlet," she adds. I'm trying to write these suggestions down as fast as she's saying them. "And the coffin can be open. But no photographs," she emphasises.

When we're out in the backyard at my place and Maurs starts saying who is going to get what, as is her wont these days, I realise that I get anxious when this happens and demand a list.

Wednesday 25 February
I've always imagined that my anger is justifiable. Being angry has been an enormous part of my life. For womyn, expressing anger has become a feminist necessity. Womyn under patriarchy have a great deal to be angry about.

And yet Joko in *Nothing Special: Living Zen* says something else entirely.

Sitting with all this, I get a real sense of what the word compassion means. Mind you, because of my deep-seated anger towards the incompetence of the medical profession, feeling compassion for someone like Dr Jarvis makes for an interesting shift.

Compassion for Maurs. What must it really be like to be told you have terminal cancer? She's handling it extremely well, very courageously, inspirationally.

Compassion for myself, too, in this terrible situation I'm

trying to come to terms with and understand, so I can be fully supportive of Maurs and caring of myself at the same time.

I ring Helen to see how she is. She confirms that the chemo's been postponed because after the shingles she got neuralgia on top of it. I invite her round for dinner in a couple of weeks' time.

By the time Maurs picks me up from class, where we're learning the palm tai chi, I'm exhausted. It's partly the hot weather, 37 degrees, partly the hours at the computer where I've been keying *The C-Word* straight onto the disk—a major break-through for a Luddite like myself—partly the emotional highs and lows.

My brother Victor isn't sure but thinks the quote is from Joseph Campbell. I've never heard of him before.

Victor's philosophy, so he tells me, is "Face the suffering with suffering."

When Maurs goes to see her on Friday, Dr Patricia suggests that it might be better to leave having the progesterone till she's finished the chemo.

Afterwards we go to the Nova Cinema to see *L A Confidential*, which features Australian actors in the two lead roles. My friend Moss and her partner, Heather have given us tickets to the Nova. It's a good bit of light relief. Maurs went to see *The Road to Nhill* on Wednesday.

Joan Russell, Maurs' friend, rings from Adelaide. As I listen to Maurs explaining to Joan what is happening with her, I marvel at how far we've come in terms of accepting the inevitable. It's still all rather strange, but I'm impressed with the way Maurs can say that there's no cure without being sentimental about it.

8
March, April

Sunday 1 March
Wendy Averil rings and asks Maurs to go in with her to do an interview about the LCSG for the lesbian and gay station Joy Radio's last broadcasting day. At home, I can't find the right wave-length so I miss the whole thing. When Maurs gets back she says it went well. Maurs has done quite a bit of radio work now for POW and other groups.

As we're going out the door to the Brunswick Music Festival street party in Sydney Road I ask Maurs does she have sunblock on. Then quip, "I don't suppose you're too worried about whether you get skin cancer or not these days."

We don't do much. Just walking around to watch the entertainment tires Maurs out so much that she isn't able to dance to the African band at the finale.

First thing on Monday morning I sit with my fear of Maurs dying and my anger towards others.

I am very fearful about Maurs not being here any more. I'm angry about my helplessness either to prevent her death or to stop her being hurt. I need to sit with my anger, sit with my fear, till the right approach comes up.

As Joko says: the anger is to do with being frightened.

Another all-day stint in Ward 51. The veins in the back of Maurs' hand are getting worse. The womyn tries twice, unsuccessfully, before she gets the needle in place. The day goes very quickly. Maurs sleeps for most of it.

I miss Dr Jarvis at lunchtime again. Probably not a bad thing. Maurs tells him that she's decided not to take the progesterone till after the chemo. His comment to the nurse is, "Maureen doesn't trust me."

But as Maurs says to me, it's the medical profession that she doesn't trust, not Dr Jarvis personally. She needs to make her own informed choices about what she wants done with her body.

Maurs has every intention of going to the POW meeting tonight, but halfway there she starts getting the shakes so goes back to her flat instead and rings in her apologies. No sense pushing it. Chemo is chemo, after all. Me? I'm exhausted and in my own bed by 9.30 p.m.

Not knowing how much more time we have together, I'm very reluctant to leave Maurs even for two weeks to go to the 10/40 in Perth. As far as getting away is concerned, there will be two or three weeks in August looking after Joan's place and the dogs in Adelaide that Maurs has already arranged, like last year. And much as I enjoy the 10/40s, I can miss one or two without it being any big deal.

A womyn from Global Footprints, the ovarian cancer group, visits Maurs on Friday morning. She's pleased that the LCSG wants to take part in this campaign and she will go to the next meeting on Tuesday to talk about what she's doing and how the group might become involved. As she says, because not many lesbians have children, we are in a higher risk category for ovarian cancer.

That evening, Maurs bravely struggles all round the International Women's Day exhibition, Woman '98, at the Mechanics Institute, catalogue in hand, to be there with me for opening night. I am extremely grateful. I am also very glad to see my portrait of Maurs on the far wall of the main room.

As we sprawl on the couch together, her legs spread across my knees and me playing with her feet, Maurs says, "My toes are numb, I can't feel them properly." It's the same with the tips of her fingers. Another side-effect of the chemo.

"I told Fran the other night when I was over there that she could keep Vintage," Maurs goes on to say.

I'm shocked because I'd completely forgotten the kitten. That's the way my head is at the moment, only concerned with the immediately obvious.

International Women's Day. As soon as I get up, I switch on the radio to the 24-hour broadcast of womyn's programs on 3CR.

Maurs is still not feeling well enough to go on the march. I leave her with the assurance that if she feels up to it she will meet me afterwards for the festival at Trades Hall.

"Are you marching on your own today or are you part of a collective?" a young womyn asks me as we're waiting for the rally to begin.

"No, I'm marching on my own," I tell her. For the first time in years I do not have to carry a banner, hand out a leaflet, do a performance, or staff a stall.

As usual with large gatherings of womyn, I have to answer the inevitable questions about how Maurs is. I'm pleased our friends enquire after her, I keep telling myself as I repeat the same phrases over and over, "Maurs is not so well today . . . she had chemo on Monday . . . she's here in spirit . . . thank you, I'll tell her that . . . pass on your regards, thank you."

I've noticed I've been feeling a bit distanced from others lately. Partly because I have distanced myself. All I'm really concerned about at this time is my own work and Maurs.

That evening we watch the film *Nell* with Jodie Foster on television. At one point Nell is afraid and Maurs says, "I'm afraid too. I'm afraid of what is going to happen to me."

Monday 9 March
While I sit first thing, I take delight in the sound of the magpies under the trees outside the window of Maurs' flat, those most melodious of birds that remind me of my country upbringing.

Maurs is still not well. We've been unable to make love this weekend. I am torn between staying with her in her wonderfully sundrenched flat and keeping her company. Or coming back here to my house and bringing *The C-Word* up to date. Always a dichotomy this, between being available for Maurs and doing what I need to do for myself.

"I think I'm getting a cold," Maurs says when she picks me up after tai chi on Wednesday evening. Her nose has been running like a tap all day and her voice sounds a bit husky.

"I want you to come into the hospital with me tomorrow, if you wouldn't mind." Maurs is due for her ten-day blood test and fully expects that by that time the cold will have developed enough that she'll need treatment for it.

The next day, when Maurs takes her temperature it is still normal. She's come to the conclusion that it's probably just her sinuses, so I don't need to go with her the hospital after all. "I was just being wimpish," she says.

"It's okay to be wimpish," I answer.

She rings me afterwards to say she's had the blood test; they've agreed with her it was just sinus and not to worry about antibiotics.

Later that night over the phone, I read out the letter I'd received from Kristi that day: "Hello! Lovely to speak with you the other day and hope you've received my letter with photos . . . How are you? How is Maurs? You both sounded very brave. I know that sometimes you must feel very bleak and it must be very hard. It will be lovely to see you again and be with you for a few weeks."

Maurs is as excited as I am that they'll be arriving sooner than expected. "You'll be well and truly finished your chemo by then too, all being well," I say, "so you'll be able to take Sean to the zoo, no worries." That is something we grand-mothers are looking forward to immensely.

"I get the feeling I'm not being told everything and I need to know," Maurs reiterates over dinner at the East Brunswick Hotel. "I want you to make an appointment to talk to Dr Jarvis about all this, and I want you to speak up as well. I haven't got the energy to do this by myself, and you have as much right to know what's happening and have a say about it as I do."

"Okay, but we'll have to work out how to do it properly." This will take some adjusting to: I haven't done this before except as back-up, to prompt Maurs if she forgets anything and to take notes.

Afterwards, as we're listening to those great Islander singers Vika and Linda Bull in concert at the Town Hall for the Brunswick Music Festival, Jean Ferguson asks me, "Are you going to the 10/40?"

"No, I'm not," I say, conscious that this is the first time I've actually said this out loud to anyone. It seems a decision has been made, and I haven't even got round to telling Maurs yet.

As we're leaving, Maurs lights up a cigarette.

"Should give those up," someone comments, in passing.

"What's the point?" Maurs replies.

We have nothing to do at all on Saturday. We spend some of the morning in bed making love. "You'll tell me when this gets to be too much, won't you?" I say, making sure.

"So long as, if it gets to the stage I don't want you to make love to me, you'll still let me make love to you," Maurs replies.

Tuesday 17 March

Maurs and I have a couple of Guinnesses at the pub for St Patrick's Day, toasting Dad and shedding a few sentimental tears when the Irish pipers begin to play.

I'm asleep when Kristi rings at 11.15 p.m., thinking it's just after 10.00 p.m. Which it is in Papua New Guinea without daylight saving.

"How's Maurs?" she asks the inevitable questions. "How are you?"

As I'm asked this all the time, I give the usual details about being between the fourth and fifth chemo, how tired Maurs is because she's anaemic but she's quite well, considering.

As for myself, "Some days are better than others," I say. Now that I'm over the initial shock and accept, to a certain extent, that Maurs is dying of cancer, it's become part of my life. And because I'm living with it daily through all the ups and downs, it's not so frightening any more.

Kristi tells me that when they leave Papua New Guinea

for good they're thinking of settling either in Sweden or Europe somewhere. "You can come and visit."

"Not while Maurs is still having treatment," I reply, meaning while she's still alive.

On the way over to the Royal Women's in the car on Thursday, Maurs mentions that the pain she's had before is intermittently back again in her left hip and she is experiencing another different kind of pain, an occasional burning sensation, at the back of her right hip as well. I don't like the sound of it, and it definitely needs to be mentioned to Dr Jarvis on Monday.

The visit is an eye-opener for me because, even after all this time, I've never accompanied Maurs to have any of her blood tests. The test is done quickly and efficiently, three lots of blood in different syringes while the needle is left in the vein in Maurs' right elbow, which she jokingly tells the nurse she always saves for just this purpose. That is, she doesn't have her chemo into this particular vein at all.

When we go upstairs a doctor is not only available to talk with us straight away, but she also locates the relevant computer printouts and explains them to us.

We're given the last CA 125 (Cancer Antigen) printout, and a printout and full explanation about the ten-day blood count as well as what levels everything has to be before Maurs can have chemo. The platelets, at 78, are much lower than the recommended 100, but they ought to have improved by today's blood test in time for the chemo on Monday; otherwise it would be postponed. We're told that a blood transfusion will be given if Maurs is symptomatic with the anaemia, that is, if she feels dizzy and is fainting, but it won't be necessary this time round.

I'm impressed that the doctor is able to do all this so

quickly and efficiently that we leave feeling a whole lot better about the process. We are far less anxious than we have been, about the CA 125 in particular.

When a friend rings from Perth and I tell her I'm not going to the 10/40, it occurs to me afterwards that I'm not going to miss the travelling I do every year at Easter. I'm on a bigger journey with Maurs. And this particular journey has my full attention.

At the library I borrow *Bringing Them Home: The Report of the National Inquiry into the Separation of Aboriginal and Torres Strait Islander Children from their Families*. It does not make easy reading.

Torture, beatings, punishment, rapes, slavery, starvation, deprivation, racist taunts, forced labour, and cruelty of every unimaginable kind were perpetrated on these children after their forcible removal from their families, communities and cultural heritage. And perpetrated too, by ordinary Australians. Let's not pretend.

This report is essential reading for every Australian so that we can begin to address the implications of living with this level of sadism underlying our national psyche.

Monday 23 March
We're settled into Ward 51 by 10.00 a.m., Maurs with her intravenous drip inserted, me reading *Bringing Them Home*, and Tiddas playing in the background.

Because I missed him last time, I postpone having lunch till Dr Jarvis arrives. Maurs tells him about the pain and he says that maybe she needs another CAT scan. And that maybe three pinpoint radiums can get rid of whatever is causing the pain.

Mary Daicos arrives, so I go off to lunch. One of the

nurses tells Maurs that she's doing a paper about a lesbian with cancer for her La Trobe University course. Maurs tells her about her video and says she's welcome to borrow it. I have the details of *Cancer in Two Voices* written down in my diary and pass them on to the nurse as well.

The doctor finds the results of the last two CAT scans in Maurs' file, photocopies them and gives them to us. The medical language is difficult, but after several readings I understand that Maurs has growths near both kidneys and in two locations in her small bowel. The most damning bit is the conclusion on the second scan that there's only a "slight reduction in the size" of the tumours after three chemos, so it's unlikely that another three sessions will make a great deal of difference, it seems to me.

It's raining, so Maurs gets a voucher and we catch a taxi home. Just as we're getting ready to go to bed, Maurs discovers blood in her urine. Panic stations. However, when she rings the Royal Women's they seem quite unconcerned and say she can either be admitted straight away or wait till the morning when the oncology unit opens and go in then. As there are no other symptoms, we decide to wait.

While we're lying in bed reading before we go to sleep, I keep glancing at Maurs and wondering what this latest symptom might mean. It's only another month till Sean arrives (heaven forbid she won't make it). I still can't grasp that this vibrant and articulate womyn won't always be in my bed next to me like this.

I'm dreaming that there's blood on the crutch of my knickers when Maurs wakes me at 4.00 a.m. "I'm sorry, Jean, but I've just been to the toilet and I'm still bleeding. I think I need to go into the hospital because it seems to be worse and I'm worried."

Maurs is worried that if her one remaining kidney ceases to function then that's it. And she's been warned, with her blood count depleted, not to bleed, if she can possibly help it.

The hospital is only a ten-minute drive away and we can park right outside at that hour of the morning. The nurse in Emergency takes three samples of blood and a mid-stream urine test. The doctor gives Maurs what turns out to be a very painful internal examination (even with a small lubricated speculum) just to make sure the blood isn't coming from the vagina.

We go home a bit at a loss that no-one else seems to be taking this as seriously as we are.

We're back at the hospital by 11.00 a.m. We're told that we'll have to wait because the oncology doctors are doing rounds and won't be available till 1.00 p.m.

"No way," says Maurs. "I want to see someone and get the results, now."

An hour later, we're being told that the tests show that the blood is not from the kidney. The platelet count will be available later that day and the urine test results not for a day or two. As the rest of the blood count is normal we can go home.

I can hardly believe it. "You're telling us that even though Maureen is still bleeding that there's nothing wrong and she can go home?"

That's exactly what she means. At home we're still stunned by the implications of this, trying to figure it out. Maurs rings the oncology unit for some reassurance. Fortunately, she's put through to a nurse who relays to Dr Jarvis in the background that Maurs is bleeding and being given the runaround downstairs. He immediately says to come in.

Within the hour we're in his office (with two female students sitting in) while Maurs, once again, goes through the whole sorry tale. Dr Jarvis says the bleeding could be caused by a low platelet count (in which case a transfusion might be necessary) or an infection, but not in the kidney.

Knowing he has it in hand is a relief in itself. Maurs decides to ask all our most pressing questions then and there, so I get out the list.

When I ask him where the tumours are exactly and the extent of them, he draws a diagram for us. "Sometimes the growth is in a clump and at others like birdseed scattered throughout the area," he says, as he marks the diagram.

"When it says that there's only been a slight reduction in the tumours, what are the implications of that as far as continuing to have chemo is concerned?" I ask. We'd been under the impression that the chemo would eradicate the tumours entirely this time round. Not so. The chemo isn't going to get rid of the cancer but hopefully it will slow it down, and there are other options when the tumour starts getting bigger again, like more chemo and small doses of radiation.

The cancer will more than likely manifest again in the kidneys and/or the bowel. Perhaps the liver. And the lungs are a possibility.

Then comes the big question. "I don't want to put you on the spot and I know you can't give me a definite answer"— I'd been wondering if Maurs was going to do this today— "but I'd like to have some idea of the approximate timing on this."

Dr Jarvis leans forward. "It could be longer, it could be less, but I'd say twelve to twenty-four months."

This is both more and less than I'd been imagining, depending on my mood. It's a relief to hear something at long last.

"I want to die at home," says Maurs, and mentions Rosemary Mann's lover who wasn't allowed to go home to die when she wanted to.

"I'd like to see them try to keep you here," he laughs.

Even though the urine test won't show if Maurs has an infection till the following day, "It won't hurt to take some antibiotics just in case," he says, writing out a prescription.

I've spoken more at this meeting than ever before. I feel almost tough, and certainly less vulnerable than I usually am. I was able to hear it all without flinching.

It's been quite a day.

Maurs rings me on Wednesday morning to say that the bleeding has stopped and that as the antibiotic she'd taken last night had made her feel nauseous she is not going to take them any more.

It feels like yesterday was some kind of a turning point.

A nurse rings Maurs from the Royal Women's to say that the urine test shows there is no infection and to eat lots of red meat and eggs to build up her platelet count.

After tai chi that night Maurs says that she hopes for my sake that she doesn't die on a public holiday. "My mother died on Good Friday and every Easter since has been a painful reminder of the day she died." Maurs hadn't been told that her mother was dying. Maurs wasn't allowed to see her mother after she'd died.

The effects of the chemo have hit Maurs badly by this time. Up till now she's been able to keep the worst of the shooting pains in her joints and throughout her body at bay with extra painkillers. Now she decides that she'll see if she can get something stronger for next time.

When one of our friends, Maureen Gie makes her weekly phone-call to see how Maurs is, she says that because not enough womyn have registered for the 10/40 it might have to be cancelled. Maybe it's appropriate that I decided not to go, after all.

On Friday, because Maurs is looking so ill and seeming so weak, I ask how bad it is.

"Let me put it like this," says Maurs. "See that toe, the pain in it is so bad I could cry, and I get sudden pain like that all through every part of my body off and on." Oh.

And yet, despite the pain, the constipation and her generally weak and debilitated state, Maurs insists on going with me to take the painted chair and the knitted book across to CERES, where they are hung on the veranda of the café under the vines as part of the sculpture exhibition, much to our mutual excitement. In that setting of vegetable gardens and farm animals we admire some of the other sculptures as they're set up at different strategic points of the grounds.

For the opening of the sculpture exhibition on Sunday afternoon. I'm pleased to be able to share this whole experience with Maurs. It has always been like this. Maurs has been the most supportive and least critical of any lover I have ever had, or any person I know, for that matter, as far as my work is concerned.

Having her support and encouragement for all of my artistic and creative efforts has done more for my sense of self over these past years than I can say. I have never had to argue for time to write or space to create. She has always given me room to move and be myself, without complaint.

Monday 30 March
"Now, if you need to ring me or come over or anything at all, I'm here. You know that, don't you?" I say, as Maurs is preparing to leave.

We saw *Philadelphia* on telly last night and I'm still affected by the film's emotional impact, specifically the scenes of the gay man affected by AIDS pushing his intravenous stand, and the agony his partner went through knowing his lover was dying. Maurs wasn't very well all this weekend and I'm not sure that I ought to be leaving her to her own devices like this.

I'm glad Maurs is going to the POW meeting tonight, that she is still taking an interest in the Women's Circus Tech Crew, even though she couldn't get to the meeting on Saturday, and that the LCSG meetings and activities are still important to her. I'm glad because I want Maurs to have interests in life that will keep her going. I don't want her always to rely solely on me. I'm sure she doesn't; it's only my own guilt, this feeling that I'm deserting her whenever I come back here to do my own work.

Maurs has a couple of students around, asking questions about her experiences with cancer and the treatment because, as part of their academic work, they're doing some publicity for Global Footprints.

Wednesday 1 April
After sitting I realise that all I really want is for Maurs to have as positive and pain-free time for these last couple of years as possible.

Maurs is tired after attending the Breast Cancer Forum at the Queen Victoria Women's Centre all day Saturday. Barb Anthony, Helen Robertson and Heather Chapple are also there, and Maurs is able to mention ovarian cancer and get some ideas for political strategies as well as talk to other womyn with cancer.

In answer to the note that was sent out with the last

Matrix Guild minutes, Maurs has received money to help pay for some hands-on reiki or whatever else she might need. It's a generous response from half a dozen members and friends who want to support Maurs at this time.

"I'm not coming back to bed this morning, if that's all right with you?" Maurs comes into the bedroom on Sunday morning as I've just finished the *Lesbiana* article. "I'm not feeling well enough." Of course. Sex is not an urgent part of my agenda these days.

   Because she isn't feeling up to anything much, all we do is go for a walk in the park opposite and rest for most of the day.

Thursday 9 April
I post my entries in the Daffodil Day literary awards: a poem and a short story. The social worker at the Royal Women's rings, and Maurs gives her permission to take a copy of the video of Maurs, which she'd seen and liked.

On (Good) Friday morning, I finally cry out my disappointment about not being at a National 10/40 Conference, over and above that the fact that there is no 10/40 to go to and might not ever be again. What do dykes over forty do over this four-day holiday when they don't have a 10/40 to go to?

I make a plaster cast of Maurs' head in two pieces, her smoothly bald scalp and her beautiful face which I'll join together later. Last week I drew the charcoal outline of her bald head in profile preparatory to painting it in oils. Am I obsessed?

(Easter) Sunday, the fourteenth full moon after my last period in March 1996, is the official acknowledgement of my menopause, as far as I'm concerned. That evening we celebrate that salient fact with a bottle of champagne.

The only thing left to say about this past week is that, for the first time in the weekend prior to chemo, Maurs is not in the mood to make love. We still kiss and cuddle and sleep together though, and I'm glad that I'm not as sexually obsessed as I used to be. I don't really want to think that Maurs and I won't ever make love again.

Tuesday 14 April
Number six; the final chemo day. At long last.

However, even as I buy my all-day ticket on the tram on the way into the hospital, the day, or my reaction to it, starts falling apart. The conductor hands me an information leaflet with the words, "From tomorrow you won't be able to buy an all-day ticket on the trams along here." It's the end of an era. First the W-class trams, now the connies. So instead of having a conductor on each tram to help older people or mothers with prams struggling to get on or off the tram safely, or point lost tourists in the right direction, ticket dispensing machines are going to be installed. It seems like a cynical exercise to inconvenience the people who use public transport as much as possible.

As a former connie and tram driver myself, I am even more devastated. I know how much the workers in particular, but all of us here in Melbourne, are losing.

When we arrive at the hospital, Maurs weighs herself. The machine indicates 81 kilograms. "I've put on weight," she says.

"It'll be your coat," I suggest. Maurs is wearing her heavy leather jacket today because it's freezing cold outside.

She takes it off and tries again. "You're right." It now shows 78 kilograms.

As we enter the chemo room, the half-bottle of champagne on the locker next to Maurs' chair, and a similar one for the womyn on the other side of the room, are symbols that this is their final chemo. They congratulate each other.

After the intravenous needle goes into Maurs' right hand and before the saline is attached, some blood is sent for another blood count to make sure it's safe for Maurs to have the chemo today, as she's determined to do.

We overhear the nurse on the phone. "The platelet count is still 66," Maurs relays to me. Maurs won't be having the chemo today after all. Damn.

The nurse gives Maurs the news—"Dr Jarvis doesn't want you bleeding to death, which is fair enough"—and goes off to find out what happens now.

"Do you want the good news or the bad news first?" the nurse asks when she returns. She goes straight on. "The bad news is you won't be having chemo today. But you already knew that. And the good news is that you can start having the blood straight away." She begins disconnecting the bag of saline preparatory to connecting the blood. She hands Maurs the first bag of blood to place under her shirt, to begin warming it up from its near-frozen state.

"How long will all this take?" Maurs asks, because we still have no idea.

"Each bag takes about two hours," the nurse explains. "You have to have four lots, plus flushing it through each time, which takes about fifteen minutes, so about nine hours maybe."

It's now after twelve. "You'll be through by about ten tonight," I calculate.

Soon after Dr Jarvis strolls in with, "I hear they're trying to kill you?"

I'm so het up with events so far that I don't trust myself

to speak. Maurs talks to him. "Has the Taxol already been ordered?" he asks. Of course. It's a lot of money wasted, as he makes no bones about pointing out. As if we're not under enough stress as it is.

"Can't it be kept till I have it next week?" Maurs suggests.

"Taxol only lasts for twenty-four hours," Dr Jarvis states. A lot of taxpayers' money down the drain.

Maurs hands her champagne back to the nurse till she can legitimately claim it again.

Maurs is not going to be well enough for Sean's visit and that's all there is to it. Given a choice between dying earlier and being well for Sean, maybe I wouldn't be prepared to take the risk either.

At 5.00 p.m. we trail round to a room in Ward 51 for the evening with her bag of blood hanging from the stand.

"All the best." Maurs and the womyn opposite say good-bye to each other.

It's been a hell of a day. No-one seems to care that, after all our expectations that this was going to be Maurs' last chemo, we're really disappointed it hasn't happened.

I'm carrying on about Maurs bending her elbow where the needle is situated and Maurs is getting irritated. "I think what I might do is go back home, do tai chi, have the leftover stew for dinner and drive back here to pick you up," I suggest.

"Don't forget to ring in my apologies about not being able to get to the meeting tonight," Maurs reminds me about the LCSG meeting.

It occurs to me, as I sit in the tram trying to make sense of the muddle in my head, that what I'm trying to achieve with this Zen sitting practice Maurs already knows because she's dying. We're all dying, I know that, but Maurs knows it in a way the rest of us, who haven't been told we have a life-threatening illness, don't.

By the time I'm driving back to the hospital, I've got the dramas of the day into a slightly better perspective. Maurs is still dozing, so I put my feet next to hers on the bed and read till the last bag of blood is finished and flushed through.

Once we're home, I'm so exhausted all I can think about is going to bed. When I feel her climb into bed I press my warm bottom against her cold one and am instantly asleep.

I get another letter from Marg. My sister has written, "That letter I wrote in response to your news about Maureen was one of the most difficult I've had to write in my life."

The day before, sitting in the sunshine, I'd made a start on the painting of Maurs' bald head, "I just hope you like it," I say to her. I'm hoping it might be accepted for the Daffodil Day art exhibition.

Maurs rings me to say that she's heard that her platelet count has gone down still further, to 56. This means no chemo this Monday either. Maurs was also advised to go off the old painkillers entirely and just take the new 12-hourly slow-release tablets. On no account is she to cut herself or start bleeding, otherwise she'll be in serious trouble.

Saturday is my fifty-fourth birthday. Kristi rings in from Anguganak, Papua New Guinea, Geoff from Barcelona, Spain and Moss from Footscray. I do my usual introspective look at where I am in terms of my New Year resolutions. It seems I'm on course. All I really planned for this year is to be here for and with Maurs. And to do my writing.

It seems to me that Maurs' condition has got a lot worse. We really do need to talk to Dr Jarvis about her situation in terms of adequate pain control, as well as whether to have the final chemo considering how long she is taking to recover from the last one.

On Monday, Helen Robertson rings. She's going in to be measured for her radiotherapy today and will start the six-week course on Thursday.

Because Dr Jarvis is not available we go in to the Royal Women's and talk to another doctor. She reassures us that it's not possible to overdose on morphine if it's taking care of pain. This is an interesting phenomenon and it clears up our fears about taking too much. The main thing is to get the pain under control. There's no need for Maurs to feel any pain at all.

The doctor also says it's up to Maurs whether or not she has the final chemo. It is agreed that any decision about the chemo can be postponed till after Maurs has had her blood test on Thursday.

I'm dropped back at my place to do a bit more of the painting of Maurs' bald head (which Maurs really likes) and some more typing on this book while Maurs drives back to the flat to make a start on getting rid of the pain.

Tuesday 21 April
Maurs rings and tells me that Linda McCartney, who had breast cancer, died recently of cancer in her liver. She was fifty-six. This news makes me sad.

Just as I'm finishing off Maurs' portrait (looking good), she rings me again to tell me that she's just heard that as Global Footprints had just received $20,000, they've decided to pay the $95 registration fee so that Maurs can go to the Women's Health Conference in June. Fantastic!

I have been too distracted to take much notice but over the past weeks there's been a major political crisis down at the wharves with the sacked waterside workers getting a lot of support for their picket line. Maurs rings again to tell me the courts have ordered Patrick Stevedores, the employer, to reinstate all the sacked waterside workers, which is a major victory for the Maritime Union of Australia (MUA here to stay!). As I don't have a telly, I rely on Maurs at times like this to keep me informed and up to date about popular culture.

I print another twenty-two pages of this book to give to Maurs tomorrow evening when I see her again.

Before we get into bed Maurs asks me, "Would you mind driving me in to the hospital, tomorrow, please? I'm not sure I'm up to driving all that way myself and I think I need you with me." Maurs usually goes in for her blood tests on her own without any worries.

At the Royal Women's Maurs picks up some more morphine from the pharmacist, and some advice about constipation, itchiness and nausea, all caused by the morphine. Then she has another blood test.

The decision about whether or not to have the sixth lot of chemo, and risk not being well enough for Sean's visit, is still to be made. I come back here to put some more of *Behind Enemy Lines* into the computer. Then Maurs rings to say that her platelet count is up to 102, excellent news. Maurs can have the chemo if she wants to.

Probably because I've calmed down enough about it, I've thought of a crucial question. "Maurs, if Sean wasn't coming, would you have it?"

Unhesitatingly, Maurs replies "Yes."

"That's your answer then," I say. To my mind there is no doubt Maurs has to have the chemo for her own sake. Never mind if she isn't all that well for Sean: she has to do what is right for her, and the rest of us will fit in around that as best we can. She says she'll sleep on it.

On Friday morning Maurs rings to book herself in for chemo. Later on, she rings me to say that she's been vomiting most of the day. It doesn't matter what she eats or drinks—coffee, even water and finally spaghetti for tea—she hasn't been able to keep it down.

"Don't keep telling me I have to eat." Maurs becomes exasperated with my anxious enquiries. "It doesn't help."

We agree that, in case my runny nose is a cold rather than the sinus trouble I've had in the past, Maurs won't come over to my place this evening. "I can't afford to get a cold before the chemo on Monday." No.

By the morning, I have what looks suspiciously like a cold, even though my nose has stopped running. I feel a failure. I've been letting the stress get to me more than usual, perhaps.

And Maurs is a lot worse. Even I have to admit that. She is vomiting everything she swallows. She is losing more weight too, I suspect, judging by the hollows in her bottom that are even more pronounced. She is in consistent pain. Even though she is taking the morphine tablets twice a day plus extra in liquid form for breakthrough pain as needed, the drug is just barely holding it.

It has taken five weeks to recover from the last chemo sufficiently to even contemplate having this next one. And she is not what you'd call robust, and hasn't been for some time.

When I haven't heard from Maurs by midday, I start to worry, so I ring and wake her up, much to our mutual surprise. She'd been vomiting so much the day before, she tells me, she'd wet herself. And just before going to bed she'd noticed blood in the toilet bowl again.

"I don't care whether you've still got a cold or not. I miss you and I want you here, now," Maurs insists. I can't wait to get over there.

Monday 27 April

As the nurse struggles to find a suitable vein, she advises, "Next time, if there is a next time, you need to insist on permanent access—what's called a port—which means a tube is inserted up here on the chest wall," she pats above her left breast, "and you can tell them I said so, too, if you like."

Dr Jarvis calls in, still in his theatre greens. "How are you, today?"

"I'm feeling not too badly, all things considered," Maurs answers.

"And then you come back in here and we knock you down again," he jests. After what Maurs has been through the past fortnight I am in no mood for his humour.

I stay well out of it as they go through the list of queries. Yes, Maurs can have more morphine for the pain, and extra whenever she needs, it's up to her. Yes, she can have another blood transfusion if she needs it, to ensure that her time with Sean is as comfortable as possible. And yes, Maurs can get statistics about ovarian cancer for the Women's Health Conference.

Maurs is hooked up to the Taxol just as lunch arrives and I go off for my usual wander along Lygon Street. At five o'clock the chemo ward closes, so we're shifted with all our goods and chattels, plus the half bottle of champagne, to a room in the oncology ward. The nurse has already gone home with our grateful thanks for all she's done over the past months.

It's getting late, so I decide I might as well do my half-hour of tai chi while we wait for the Carboplatin to drip through. No-one seems to mind as I embrace tiger and punch tiger's ears in the corridor.

Finally, finally, finally Maurs has the last bit of chemo, it's flushed through, the needle is pulled out. We're free to take advantage of the taxi voucher for the ride home.

We're not long out of bed when Maurs checks the last needle site to get rid of the swab and notices it is swollen, black and bruised-looking. When Maurs rings the Royal Women's, they say a doctor needs to see it to make sure. In we go with our books to read while we wait in Emergency for a doctor to tell us to go home and not to worry, it will be all right.

"I'm sorry it took so long," Maurs says as she brings me in my first cup of coffee for the day. "I had to have a shit first."

"Congratulations!" It's a new take on life when having a shit is a major achievement.

We buy and attach a spring-release bolt in the back of Geoff's car for Sean's car seat, I bought at an opportunity shop for $5. That done, Maurs heads back home to wash the seat, including the sheepskin cover. What we grandmothers have to do.

I post the photo I'd taken of the painting of Maurs' bald head in profile, "I'm in Love with the Smooth Baldness of Her Scalp", for possible inclusion in the Daffodil Day art exhibition.

Maurs is off at the LCSG meeting and I'm in bed early.

It's been a hectic couple of months and it's good to know that with the chemo out of the way we can now start preparing ourselves for Kristi, Dan and Sean's visit.

9
May

Friday 1 May

Maurs rings me late in the afternoon to say she's been sick, yet again, and is fed up. I say to ring the hospital whereupon the doctor suggests that Maurs is probably dehydrated and requires a saline drip. Needing no second bidding, Maurs picks me up and in we go. Maurs tells them that she feels like "six pennorth of god help us".

Well, we get there at about 6.00 p.m., I stay till after 9.30 p.m. and there is no sign of a drip then.

Maurs tells me on the phone the next morning that at 12.30 a.m. she'd wandered down to Emergency, "How busy are you? If I bring my file down here can I see a doctor to get a drip put in?"

She was told they were flat out, but "nice try," they said.

It wasn't till 1.00 a.m. that a doctor finally put the intravenous line in so the saline drip could commence.

One of the things I do on Saturday before going to visit Maurs is buy a cask of wine at the liquor shop across the road.

"How's your friend?" he asks me.

"Not the best." I'm a bit startled by the enquiry. I didn't realise that he even knows Maurs is not well, let alone cares enough to ask. "She's in hospital at the moment."

"All the best," he says, sympathetically, as he hands me the change.

This has me crying all the way home.

It's good to see Maurs sitting up in bed with the drip in and looking more like her usual self. We chat, read our murder mysteries and I write some more of the next *Lesbian Network* article to while away the hours.

So I can be with her while she has a cigarette, I accompany Maurs all the way downstairs to the small smoking room at the back of the hospital with her intravenous stand and the needle in situ.

"I'm going to be torn between wanting to be with you" —even more so these days—"and wanting to see as much of Kristi and Sean as possible." I voice what has been a concern of mine lately when I think about trying to be in two places at once over these next few weeks.

"No," Maurs says firmly. "You're to spend as much time with Kristi and Sean as you need because I'll still be here after they're gone. Okay?"

I ring Maurs early on Sunday morning. "I can go home," she announces, straight away.

As we're leaving, Dr Jarvis says the vomiting is definitely caused by the medication. He has decided to try morphine patches instead. This will mean another overnight stay to monitor the patches for twenty-four hours in case Maurs has a reaction.

We have a restful, if slightly impatient, afternoon waiting till it's time to meet Kristi, Dan and Sean off the plane from Papua New Guinea. It's exciting to see them all at long last. The car seat that Maurs has cleaned works beautifully: Sean is strapped into it without so much as a murmur.

Monday 4 May
I get not one but two letters from the Project Manager of the Daffodil Day awards to the effect that both the short story "One Day at a Time" and the poem "Till Death Do Us Part" have "been selected for consideration for publication in our Daffodil Day publication *Together Alone 1998*".

I figure the operative word is "consideration", but am pleased.

It's certainly hectic with a 21-month-old toddler in the house. But what did I expect? It feels as if they've been here for days instead of just a few hours. Sean's still a bit shy but hopefully that will change.

After an afternoon sleep, Maurs escapes back to her place. Kristi has a full-on cold and it's too dangerous for Maurs to be around for any length of time, particularly this week. And Maurs needs to have a rest in her own little place after the past couple of days, and before she goes back to the Royal Women's first thing tomorrow morning to have the first patch put on.

It's International Midwives Day, according to the notice in the lift at the Royal Women's. The patch, a rectangular piece of transparent plastic about the size of a fifty-cent piece, is attached to Maurs' left upper arm in the afternoon and will start working properly in twelve hours.

As we sit at the front of the hospital while Maurs has a cigarette I notice that her eyebrows are down to mere wisps of hair and her eyelashes are similarly almost nonexistent. I stay for a while and do my half-hour of tai chi before going home to cook tea. Being in two places at once is tiring work but it's also quite satisfying in a weird kind of way.

There was blood in Maurs' urine again this morning, an indication her platelets are down, perhaps. But we're not too concerned. Just a matter of keeping an eye on it.

I go back to Maurs' flat to cook us both tea before tai chi class. Maurs still isn't feeling well.

As she says, "It feels like I'm never going to be well ever again." All I can do is sympathise because it has been a long time now since Maurs was anywhere near well.

By Thursday morning Maurs has diarrhoea. "My stomach is in shock with all the food that's gone into it," Maurs says, referring to the first decent meal she's been able to eat for ages.

As Maurs drives me home on her way to have her ten-day blood test and pick up some more patches, I say, "I've decided that all I'm going to do while they're here is either be with you or Kristi. Everything else will just have to go by the by." As I'm hardly going to anything much these days anyway, it isn't a big deal.

"Just remember that I'll still be here when they go," Maurs repeats.

"I'm not going to not see you, my darling, okay?" Apart from needing to be with Maurs, I couldn't be with the family twenty-four hours a day, anyway. It's a struggle to find a balance between these two essential parts of my life.

As we're lying in bed I reach up to twirl Maurs' chin whiskers, as is my habit, and realise. "Maurs!" I say, shocked that they are not there any more. While the hair has been growing back on her head (we were still not sure if the last chemo might make her lose it again before it grew back properly) the hair on her face has practically disappeared.

Monday 11 May
I drive Maurs to the Children's Hospital today, in all the cold and rain, and go in with her while she has the CAT scan done.

The machine has a donut-like hole and a bench for Maurs, tampon in situ, to lie down on. The bench then moves in and out of the hole as the scan is taken in a revolving motion round her body. I stand outside and watch Maurs' bones, her spine, pelvis and hip joints on the screen.

Next, the injection of dye, two big syringes of thick, clear liquid. It takes four attempts and two doctors to find a vein in her left elbow that is working sufficiently to take the liquid. All of this hurts so much that I hold Maurs' hand to comfort her as they fiddle and faddle, leaving bruises covered in gauze and sticky tape as they go. Once the liquid is in, Maurs has to lie with her arms above her head and breathe whenever the recorded voice (American female) tells her, as the bench moves backwards and forwards through the hole.

This time the images on the screen show the soft abdominal organs, with various parts in white that I'm unable to read. And I'm not sure I want to know whether and how much the tumours have regressed—or not just yet, anyway.

Maurs is shaking so much at the end of it that we go downstairs and have a drink and something to eat in the coffee shop (avoiding the McDonalds in the main foyer, bizarre!) while she recovers enough to go home and have a sleep.

An hour or so later I'm lying on a couch at the Red Cross having an intravenous line put into a vein in my left elbow so I can donate blood.

On this day, back in 1962, I got married. Good grief. Am I old enough, as I say on the phone to Kristi's father when he rings this evening to talk with Kristi, to have been married 36 years ago today?

Wednesday 13 May
Maurs rings me to let me know that the LCSG meeting at Helen's went well last night. The Telstra Gay and Lesbian Staff Association, Crossed Lines, has decided that the LCSG is one of their designated charities for any money they raise over these next twelve months.

Maurs also says she rang the Royal Women's for a copy of the CAT scan results. When the nurse asked for Maurs' fax number she seemed uncertain what to do with it if she couldn't fax it. What's the world coming to? Maurs is going to ring later today to see if she can get stronger patches as the pain has increased dramatically.

The CAT scan results arrive and say in part that the tumour is now 5 centimetres in diameter, an increase in size since the last scan. It is affecting the left psoas (the muscle which attaches to the lumbar vertebrae and the femur, according to my old nurses' dictionary) and para-aortic areas (near the aorta) and has eroded part of the vertebrae, which is also a new development.

This is a shock but not surprising given the way Maurs has been feeling lately. Dr Jarvis adds that, while it isn't good news, he thinks radiation might relieve the symptoms.

While Maurs is in having her blood test done she gets stronger patches to see if that will do the trick.

On Friday afternoon, while Kristi and I are having lunch together at Southgate, overlooking the Yarra River, I tell Kristi that it isn't easy living with the pain of Maurs dying and her and Sean leaving the country indefinitely.

When Maurs arrives to pick me up to go to the Queen Victoria market later in the afternoon, she looks so terrible I'm frightened that something drastic has happened. Maurs reassures(!) me it's because she vomited on the way across from the flat after eating too much at lunch.

As we're lying in bed that night, with Maurs sitting up to sleep as the pain is too severe to lie down properly, I notice that the huge bruise from the last lot of chemo, has faded to a dirty yellow. The five little ones (four CAT scan, one intravenous saline) are still there.

I'm tempted to do my usual rave about the inadequacies of traditional medical practices. Except as soon as I start Maurs pulls a face.

"You can't see them but they're up," Maurs says, in relation to her eyebrows, making me laugh, as she still can, which is one of those things that made me fall in love with her in the first place.

By Saturday, the 50-milligram patch is not holding the pain. Maurs starts taking four morphalgin tablets to cover the breakthrough pain instead of two. They work. Even so, Maurs is not full of energy, exactly. The disease is taking its toll and then some.

I'm very aware that some members of the dyke community haven't so much as rung to see how we're going. It highlights for me, yet again, that I don't really have any close friends I can call my own, despite all my political work over the years. It makes me question what I thought I was doing all those years.

"Look at all this stuff pouring out of me," Maurs says, as she's sitting on the toilet.

"What stuff?" I ask, somewhat alarmed.

"This stuff out of my vagina." It is probably just the body getting rid of the chemo in any way it can, but I don't get out of bed to check.

First thing on Monday morning, Maurs rings the pharmacist at the Royal Women's, about the unbearable pain. She advises Maurs to add one of the spare 25-milligram patches to the 50-milligram patch. A simple solution. "I don't know what I'd do without you," Maurs says to this pharmacist who has always been willing to pass on information and advice whenever Maurs asks.

I lose it on Tuesday. For starters, we're told we have to be at the Peter MacCallum Cancer Institute by 8.30 a.m. to discuss the CAT scan results and to make arrangements for the very necessary, as we saw it, pin-spot radiotherapy. We arrive and are told no appointment has been made. We wait two hours and end up seeing one of the radiologists. He tells us, in no uncertain terms, that the cancer is in the vertebrae and without radiotherapy Maurs won't last six months.

He strongly advises Maurs to have a Positron Emission Tomography (PET) scan initially. This is a more sensitive imaging procedure and will show if there is any more cancer than has already been indicated by the CAT scan.

If there is more cancer elsewhere then it is still advisable to have palliative radiotherapy, as it will certainly reduce the painful symptoms Maurs is having. However, if the PET scan shows that the largish tumour situated around the aortic lymph glands is the only site, he recommends what he calls curative radiotherapy. This involves larger doses over a longer period, similar to the treatment Maurs had in 1996. He says that the chemo isn't very effective in cases like this: radiotherapy is certainly the way to go.

Stunned by all this, we reel up to the PET scan department to arrange an appointment, and then go to the Royal Women's to get more patches. By the time I've been round the block three times looking for a parking spot I'm furious and tell Maurs to go up without me.

Maurs is sitting in the corridor when I get up to Ward 51. Dr Jarvis and entourage arrive and they discuss the need for stronger patches. The pharmacist says she'll order 100-milligram patches the following day; and in the meantime Maurs can take as many of the morphalgin tablets as she needs for the pain.

Before we leave, we're told that it is probably time for Maurs to start having regular visits from the Melbourne City-mission Hospice Service, a non-denominational Christian welfare agency. I can't help feeling it is one step closer to the inevitable and too reminiscent of Dad's last few months, but it wouldn't hurt to establish some ongoing support from these outside agencies for when we really need it.

That evening, when Kristi asks me about making arrangements to scatter Dad's ashes while she's here, I have to say I'm on overload and can't deal with another issue that is going to demand my full emotional attention right at that very moment.

On Wednesday, and with such a short time now till the family leaves the country, I spend most of the day playing with Sean at the library and the playground. Maurs goes in to have her PET scan on her own. It's not the best solution but what can I do?

After the PET scan, Maurs picks up the 100-milligram patches at the Royal Women's and then calls to tell us all about it. She took off the 50-milligram patch and put on the 100-milligram one, because just lying on the couch to have the scan done was absolute agony.

She received an injection of a radioactive chemical beforehand and had to wait forty-five minutes for it to diffuse through her system. They offered her valium, which she refused. "Just let's get this over and done with," she told them. And gritted her teeth. Her back was sore from lying down, but otherwise the procedure was straightforward and not at all painful. As for the CAT scan, Maurs lay on a couch that went through a hole in the machine while the scan was being done.

After I head off to tai chi that evening, Maurs drives the family into the city to catch the bus to Adelaide to visit Kristi's father.

We're just settling down to sleep for the night over at Maurs' flat when Maurs flies out of bed and into the bathroom to be sick into a bucket.

"That feels much better," Maurs says, as she gets back into bed. This is becoming par for the course.

Thursday 21 May

The family is away for a few days, and I am about to relax with Maurs, just the two of us for a change and no conflict of interests. But, before I'm even out of bed, Maurs is on the phone to the Royal Women's because the pain is not being controlled even by the stronger patches.

"Yes," I hear her saying, she could be in there this afternoon and is quite prepared to stay overnight to have a driver attached if that is what's needed.

The driver is a battery-operated gadget that releases liquid morphine in small controlled doses over a 24-hour period straight into the body. It is the most effective method for controlling extreme pain.

So much for our time together. A doctor rings from the

Peter Mac to say that the PET scan shows that there are no more tumours anywhere else, which is something. The cancer is definitely in the spine though.

Because the driver reminds me of the time a friend of mine, Anne Stafford had a driver during the last couple of months of her life back in 1988, I was initially nervous about Maurs having one put in. It seems like a last-ditch stand. And it is so restrictive having to carry it around.

It was Anne's decision to die at home being cared for by her family and friends (of which I was one), that has been a benchmark for me as far as being in control of our own processes and dying with dignity. A very empowering experience.

The needle of the driver is attached into Maurs' left thigh with a long tube so that the battery-operated syringe casing can be carried in her pocket. It's all quite neat, now that I'm getting used to the idea. And if it really does mean that Maurs can be relatively pain-free after all this time, then it will be worth it. Maurs is shown how to press the button on the side whenever she needs a top-up.

As I drive home I reflect on the kind of life I'm leading at the moment. Between being with Maurs as much as I possibly can, spending time with my precious daughter and grandson before they leave, coming to know Dan more, I haven't had all that much time for my own work these past few weeks. Now this is my own work, all of it, one seamless way of being.

When I arrive, one of the nurses is helping Maurs fill out the application to the Melbourne Citymission Hospice Service to make sure that Maurs gets support with the morphine for the driver after she goes home. She confirms that I'm down as Maurs' partner. "But you don't live together?" the nurse asks, puzzled, as she takes down my different address and phone number.

Well, we do live together, in a manner of speaking. We just have separate living areas. She enquires whether I'm also getting the support I need. I suppose I am; it's a bit hard to tell.

We're both surprised when the nurse mentions that Maurs has to stay overnight again to make sure that the driver is doing its work and to continue to monitor the level of morphine she will need.

"But we were going to see a play tonight," Maurs protests. I'd managed to get our names on the waiting list to see *Who's Afraid of the Working Class?* by the Melbourne Workers' Theatre.

"You can still do that," says the nurse, even more surprisingly.

One of the other nurses demonstrates how to draw up the morphine, dilute it with water and set the syringe in the driver. She leaves Maurs with an extra set so we can practise doing it ourselves. Even though it's thirty years since I gave up nursing, I can still remember what to do.

Because she is now on so much morphine that it's unsafe for Maurs to drive, I drive the car round to Trades Hall. Maurs has the driver in her pocket and is pushing the button every now and then. The play is excellent and we don't get back to the hospital till 11.00 p.m., feeling like kids who've sneaked out without anyone knowing.

The next morning as we're heading home, Maurs with her driver attached and enough morphine to keep her going for the next couple of days, someone jokes that we could now go out and sell it on the street. Adding, not that we'd get much for it.

Maurs doesn't want to put the driver in her pocket because it's uncomfortable. But each time she stands up, she forgets it is resting on her lap. After it has dropped to the floor for the second time, I yell, "That's it! Put it in your pocket. Now!" I'm terrified it will break, and then where would Maurs be with the pain the way it is?

Then when Maurs vomits the meal I've just spent time preparing, I snap, "I won't cook for you any more if you're just going to be sick afterwards." This releases the huge well of tears I've been carrying for days.

"I don't want to lose you," I sob.

Maurs wakes on Sunday morning feeling really well. She is pain-free for the first time in weeks and we're looking forward to a quiet day together. First I must drop the car at my place so the family can use it.

I'm delighting in seeing Sean again and hearing from Kristi that they had a good time with her father in South Australia, when Maurs rings to say she has vomited twice and has rung Helen who has agreed to drive her to the Royal Women's.

By the time the family drops me off on the way through, Maurs is sitting up in bed. "They're going to put my name on the door," she jokes. Another anti-nausea drug, Droparodol, has been mixed with the morphine to see if that will be more effective.

Helen, who is still having radiotherapy, suggests that we have a cup of coffee together in Lygon Street while Maurs sleeps. It's good to chat with someone who understands what we're going through.

The family picks us up in the car at about 6.30 p.m. and we all go back to Maurs' flat for fish and chips and the video, *Paradise Road*.

As this is their last week here, I'm spending every night at my house to be there for Kristi and Sean in the morning. After breakfast with Sean, one of my delights, I drop the family off in Coburg for Sean's triple antigen and Hib injections. Then I head over to pick up Maurs to be measured for radiotherapy at Peter Mac.

The womyn from the Citymission has arrived to draw up syringes both for the driver and for breakthrough pain.

"This is Lola May," Maurs introduces us.

"I knew your father, Jean," Lola says, much to my surprise. "A real gentleman. We really liked nursing him. And so fiercely independent, wasn't he?" Of course. I remember Dad speaking about Lola May.

"He really liked you, too," I say, "and appreciated everything you did for him." Dad was able to maintain his independence to the end and continue to live at home, thanks to the daily visits of the Royal Freemasons Homes of Victoria, which supplied meals on wheels, cleaning, shopping and other services at an affordable cost, and the thrice-weekly visits of the Melbourne Citymission Hospice Service nurses.

At the Peter Mac, the radiologists measure Maurs and draw lines on her midriff to pinpoint where the radiation has to go. Two tiny marks are tattooed either side of her pubic bone as permanent measuring guides.

Maurs decides not to take up the offer of a lift to the POW meeting that evening. As I drive back home I realise how very tired I am.

On Tuesday, I wake up feeling, for whatever reason (and it's certainly not circumstantial) in a joyful mood. After another enjoyable breakfast with Sean, I go across to sit in on Lola May's visit. They seem to have everything well in hand; making sure that the Citymission understands that, when the time comes, Maurs wants to die at home; assuring Maurs that the Citymission will do everything they can to ensure her comfort and to meet her needs at all times.

After Lola leaves, we go into the Peter Mac where Maurs is going to stay overnight before having the MRI (magnetic resonant imaging) done first thing the following morning. Maurs is put in one of the rooms where the torturous internal radiation is done, complete with the machine in the corner. Neither of us can quite believe it.

When I go in to pick Maurs up she is filing her list of complaints with the patient liaison officer about the uncaring treatment she's received from the nursing staff. Nothing too serious, like not getting her another pillow when she asked for one, but on top of the reminder of the trauma she went through last time she was here, Maurs is not about to stand for any neglect from anyone at the Peter Mac. Good on her. Maurs is now down to 71 kilograms, and there was blood in her urine again this morning.

As Maurs explains on the way home, the MRI was an extremely unpleasant experience. Even though she had earphones on the music didn't entirely block the noise of the machine, which sounded like jackhammers. The patches across her eyes had only partially blocked off the sensation of having the cylinder completely encompass her to within an inch or two of her face. She never wanted to have another MRI ever again.

After all that, we go to the zoo. Under somewhat different circumstances (Maurs and I imagined we'd take Sean to the zoo by ourselves, but that's impossible, Maurs' health being the way it is, so Kristi and Dan come with us) and certainly more trying than we'd envisaged (we hire a wheelchair so Maurs can get around) but it is still very enjoyable. Maurs is delighted to observe Kristi's excited response to everything she sees. With map in hand, Kristi sets a cracking pace so we don't miss out on seeing any of the animals. At one point, even Sean has a go at pushing Maurs in her wheelchair.

By the end of those several hours wandering everywhere and seeing everything, Maurs is absolutely exhausted. And yet pleased that she's actually managed to be with Sean at the zoo as she's wanted to for so long.

It brings home to me, as I'm pushing Maurs around in that wheelchair, how much her condition has deteriorated in the little time Kristi has been there. If anything, this only makes me feel even closer and more loving towards Maurs. Maybe this is what loving someone means, loving Maurs as she is, no matter what.

After tai chi I go round and tuck Maurs into bed.

I take Maurs to her first radiation session on Thursday afternoon. The doctor had already rung with the results of the MRI. Part of the vertebrae has been eaten away and the muscle is also infected, but as the tumour doesn't appear to be anywhere else they are going to go for full treatment. The radiation won't be in the same place as last time, meaning it is curative rather than palliative.

Maurs has her Polaroid photo taken (which makes her look pale and sickly) and it is all much the same as last time, with a similar blue gown.

Because it is the first session and they don't want to be distracted while they set it up, I wait outside and watch Maurs on the monitor. It is over and done with quickly. While Maurs lies on her back the machine is rotated to do underneath first, then rotated back to radiate from above onto her midriff.

Maurs is having a much-needed rest in our bed at my place before roast pork dinner with the family when Kristi says she is calling out for me. I go in to the bedroom to find Maurs sitting on the edge of the bed and shaking like a leaf.

The small syringe of 40 milligrams of morphine is sticking out of the bypass tubing attached to the needle going into her stomach.

"Suddenly, I had this terrible pain," Maurs explains, "I thought I could do it by myself but I can't."

I sit next to her and slowly, so it won't sting, push in the plunger, resting every now and then, till it's all gone. It feels as if I've been doing this all my life instead of for the first time.

Friday morning, before meditation, I do the same thing. "Look at you," Maurs says, as I'm lying back on the pillows with one hand casually on the plunger. "I don't quite know why but I'm feeling very peaceful this morning," she goes on to say.

For me, the highlight of this very sad day is walking Sean to Methven Park, while Kristi and Dan are off picking up Kristi's visa. Sean holds my hand crossing the road and we take the long way round. Even though Maurs needs me too, she is content to rest in bed till I get back.

After the sadness at the airport, seeing the family off to Sweden indefinitely, I do tai chi out in the backyard to calm my shattered nerves. At least the bombshell of bedding in the front room where the family were sleeping can be cleaned up. Just in time for Lola May to visit on her way home to fill the syringes.

And before Maurs and I go in to the Peter Mac for the second radiotherapy session that evening.

I'm surprised when Maurs says that she really wants to go across to Footscray Community Arts Centre and see the dress rehearsal of the new small portable Women's Circus show, *Swimming with Sharks*, Saturday morning. I'm still too sad but go along anyway. I'm glad I do, because we enjoy the show and catch up with everyone.

Afterwards we go across to the Coburg Town Hall for the local Reconciliation Celebration—between Indigenous and non-indigenous Australians. Lou Bennett from Tiddas and Archie Roach—both well-known Koori singers—are the highlights. On the way back to the flat we call in to the supermarket and do some shopping. Or at least I do, Maurs waits on the bench outside on the concourse.

"I want to thank you for the way you've been about not making love," Maurs says. When I shrug depreciatively, because it isn't something I'm too fussed about while Maurs is so unwell, she goes on, "I just want you to know I appreciate that you've been so understanding about it."

Needing the rest, and still sad, I don't get up till mid-afternoon on Sunday. Then I do Maurs' washing, put it through the dryer, fold everything and put it away.

"I'm finding this quite difficult," Maurs comments at one stage, as I bustle around being domesticated. Not only is it the first time I've ever done any washing for Maurs, but it emphasises her increasingly dependent state. What is surprising, for me who hates housework, is that I do all this without any fuss or bother whatsoever.

10

June, July, August

Monday 1 June

The first day of winter and it's warm and sunny here today.

Lola May arrives while I'm still sitting and doesn't seem fazed when I emerge in my nighie.

"Yep, I'm bleeding again," Maurs mutters matter-of-factly from the bathroom. "I thought I was."

My shopping list reads: toilet paper, morphine, bread, coloxyl with senna, olives and fetta cheese.

Wendy Averil takes Maurs in for her radiotherapy appointment and is able to get all the appointment times over these next few weeks. She rings later with most of the roster already organised. Even though I need to be part of the process, I don't want to do every session. Or set myself up as the only one who can do anything.

As I'm leaving tai chi the instructor enquires, "How's your partner?" and "Give her our regards," she says.

Wendy Averil rings to say that the roster has been completely filled. It seems there are more lesbians willing to drive Maurs in than there are radiotherapy sessions to be covered.

This doesn't surprise me. Maurs has lots of friends and she's put a lot into the lesbian community over the years.

Before we leave the Peter Mac, because her back is hurting, Maurs asks me to give her a booster shot of morphine. It is a bizarre situation. Sitting in full view of the public, with two people on the chairs next to us, I calmly insert the syringe into the bypass valve poking out of Maurs' abdomen and push the plunger.

If I have learnt one thing these past few months it is to love someone for who they are, not how you want them to be.

In bed, as I'm falling asleep, Maurs wakes me up to say she needs a booster of morphine. I grumble and mutter as I find a swab, get the syringe out of the fridge and inject it, in no mood to be doing this when I'm so very tired. Afterwards, I apologise profusely for being so mean-spirited about it.

Halfway through our dinner of grilled steak and boiled vegies, Maurs feels nauseous. I immediately down my knife and fork, get the syringe of Droparodol, inject it, and we continue our meal as before.

Later that night, after Maurs has gone to sleep, I'm suddenly overwhelmed by how much she's changed in these past couple of weeks. It is so distressing to think about how pale and drawn and weakened she is that I start crying quietly.

Within seconds Maurs is asking why I'm crying and has turned over on her back so she can put her arm around my shoulders to hold and comfort me. This is so unexpected and so kind I can't help laughing. No wonder I love her.

Monday 8 June
It frightens me a bit, the way Maurs is nowadays. She looks so different and it's happened so quickly. Besides her bald

head and hairless face there's no hair under her arms, no pubic hair to speak of; she's much thinner and weaker, has hardly any energy.

I decide, after a restless night, that I love Maurs just as she is. Changed and all, she's still Maurs and I love every pale, hairless and fading bit of her.

Even though I tell myself Maurs will be all right, I still expect a phone-call on this, the first day of the Victorian Women's Health Conference, telling me she's had enough and to come and pick her up from the Hotel Sofitel. Not so. It isn't till after 8.30 p.m. that Maurs rings me from the LCSG meeting at Helen's to say she's ready to go home.

"I'm so proud of you," I keep saying on the way back to my place.

"What for?"

"For attending the conference, of course."

When I wake on Wednesday morning, Maurs is asleep beside me with her mouth open. This is fast becoming a familiar sight. Sometimes though, she looks so pale and so very still that I have to check to make sure she is still breathing.

The doctor at the Peter Mac gives us copies of both the PET scan and the MRI results. He also says it's likely that Maurs will always need some kind of painkiller because of the level of damage that has already been done.

The tumour seems to have got bigger and a fracture in the vertebrae is a new concept, but there's not much in the reports that we don't already know.

We call in at the Royal Women's for another blood test. "Tell the sister she did a good job yesterday," Maurs says, referring to the paper on gynaecological cancer that the sister had given at the conference.

By Saturday morning Maurs' condition is lot worse. She is so weak I take her down for radiotherapy in a wheelchair.

We're at the Royal Women's for the blood transfusion by 10.00 a.m. and we settle in for the day. Three lots of blood takes till mid-evening, before we're allowed to go home. Maurs has improved so much she's able to walk down to the car.

Not only that—when we get back to the flat, Maurs asks me to dance with her to the music that's playing. It's the first time we've danced in an age.

And we need to do something after hearing that Pauline Hanson's One Nation Party has just won ten seats in the Queensland election. Australia's racist policies, particularly towards the Aboriginal and Torres Strait Islander people, have always been amongst the worst in the world. The popularity of the One Nation Party, based as it is on denying basic rights to the Indigenous people and migrants, seems to confirm this shameful fact.

Monday 15 June
"You need to have a word with them about changing your appointments at the last minute like that," I say on the way home from the Peter Mac.

Maurs makes a joke of it. "Are you saying you don't want to take me in if someone else can't make it?"

As I'm already down for three sessions this week and I ended up going in an extra time last week, another day doesn't appeal in the least. "Not that I don't like being with you," I say, "but enough's enough."

Not only do we wait an hour for the radium treatment, but we don't get to see the specialist till almost two hours after the appointed time.

He suggests that Maurs needs something called a Boston

brace to give her back, and especially the fractured vertebra, the support it needs. He explains it will be uncomfortable, but when she's out and about it will protect her back.

Maurs receives a poem by Coleen Clare in the mail, "For the Clown with Flowers", and good wishes from some of the other POW members.

Thursday 18 June
Our eighth anniversary.

We go up to the fourth level of the Peter Mac to see the physiotherapist so Maurs can be measured for the brace.

Then we go downstairs to find out that the following day's appointment has been moved to Saturday without so much as a by-your-leave. On top of the three-hour wait the day before, it's all too much and I lose it.

If this is how they treat terminally ill patients with cancer it doesn't say much for their overall attitude, it seems to me.

While I try to get myself into a better frame of mind to enjoy the remainder of the day—it is our anniversary, after all—I begin worrying that all my complaining might rebound on Maurs and she'll be made to wait even longer in future.

Going to see the film *Mrs Dalloway* improves my mood somewhat. I have long been an admirer of Virginia Woolf's writing and Vanessa Redgrave does such a splendid job of playing Clarissa Dalloway.

I finally decide that I need to sit with my role in all this in order to get it into perspective. Getting angry and upset is not the way to handle something that makes me even angrier and more upset the more I think about it.

I get a letter from the Anti-Cancer Council to say the painting of Maurs, "I'm in Love with the Smooth Baldness of Her Scalp", has been accepted for the Daffodil Day exhibition in

August. I'm pleased because I want this image of Maurs to be part of the exhibition, as a way of acknowledging all that Maurs is going through and her courage in facing it.

Over dinner that evening Maurs asks, "Do you mind?" as she administers a dose of Droparadol to herself at the table.

"Not at all." If it means Maurs can eat her dinner without vomiting I'm all for it.

With the Boston brace on (it turns out to be a hard plastic wrap-around held in place with three velcro straps across the front) we head off to La Mama theatre and find a disabled parking place around the corner in Drummond Street.

Not for the first time I'm struck by how much wiser Maurs is about life generally. Here am I, sitting for an hour every morning to get to the stage that Maurs has already reached as a matter of course.

Maurs realises that it's much more convenient to disconnect the driver before she gets in the shower than worry about not getting it wet while she's in there.

Maurs and I go for a short walk in the park across the road. Then I do Maurs' washing, before friends arrive for afternoon tea. As Maurs is too tired by evening, we have decided to invite friends for afternoon tea on Sunday from now on.

Monday 22 June—Winter Solstice.
While we're waiting (another hour) at the Peter Mac for the radium, Maurs changes the syringe in her driver, because it's run out, in full view of everyone else in the waiting area. No-one turns a hair.

As we pull in to the supermarket, Maurs is undoing the brace preparatory to taking it off because it's hurting her under her arms. "I need to get them to cut it back," she says.

I don't think it's a good idea to take it off just yet: walking around the supermarket is precisely the time she needs it on. As we get out of the car, Maurs puts the brace firmly on the back seat. "There's no telling you anything, is there?" I say, with a grin as I take her arm to do the shopping.

Helen Robertson arrives late in the afternoon for a chat. She confirms that Barb Anthony found another lump, in her other breast this time, but had kept quiet about it till after it had been aspirated and tested not to be malignant.

I shower and join Maurs on the couch to wait for Lola May to arrive. Maurs looks exhausted. "I'm so tired. I'm so sick of all this. I just want to go to sleep and wake up and my life will be back to how it was before." I put my arms around Maurs and we sit there, enduring the suffering.

When Lola arrives, she is full of sympathetic concern. "Ring us whenever this happens again," she says, when she hears that Maurs took the needle out last night because the stopper had been lost and it was leaking everywhere. "That's what we're there for."

"It's my fault," I say, because I'd advised Maurs to wait till today.

Maurs lies on the bed while Lola reinserts the needle and reconnects the driver straight away. She also puts in a second needle for the breakthrough pain and nausea, as she explains to try to prevent the site becoming inflamed quickly. I hold Maurs' hand as the needles go in. The plastic pieces look like blue and yellow butterflies on her white thigh.

Then Maurs says, "I just want it all to go away."

"Of course you do. It's hard for you, Maureen, and Jean loves you very much, it's very hard for you both to be going through all this."

By this time I'm crying again as Lola continues to affirm how courageous Maurs is in facing everything the way she is every day.

After all the drama I sleep very well and wake on Saturday morning lying next to Maurs and feeling good as I doze, conscious of how wonderfully affirming it is to feel the full length of her warm body against my own.

"I'll ask our friends, when they come for afternoon tea tomorrow, whether they'd mind witnessing my signature," Maurs says. This will finalise her will.

The sooner the better, after the recent experience of Sabine Gleditsch dying intestate, with all the angst that entailed.

Kristi rings from Sweden (during the television series *Sea Change*) to say hullo and to see how we both are. Not having had a television myself (by choice) for almost twenty years now, I have watched more programs this year with Maurs, than I have for a long time. It seems Australian shows have improved a great deal.

Monday 29 June
I'm reading Joko when Maurs comes out of the toilet. "Nothing. Not even a piddle." I immediately think: the right kidney's blocked now. But I don't say anything.

Next I hear Maurs on the phone to Citymission. "As Lola is on holiday I'm ringing to find out who's coming this morning as the driver has just run out." Just as well we don't panic about these things any more.

It takes me ages to find a parking spot outside the Peter Mac, so that by the time I join Maurs I'm stressed. "You're here now," Maurs says, getting it into proportion.

I haven't quite recovered when we're told that Maurs is supposed to have a CAT scan today. What CAT scan? we ask, taken aback.

"You haven't been told? This is to see if it's advisable to have more radiotherapy at an adjusted level depending on how big the tumour is now."

More radiotherapy? "They're hopeless," I say, after the radiologist heads off to make the necessary arrangements.

"You can decide not to have it, of course," the doctor adds.

"Why wasn't Maurs told about this?" I want to know. He says that he hadn't mentioned any of this because sometimes if patients are told about possible treatment ahead of time and it doesn't happen, they get upset. So? It's his job to keep Maurs informed.

It's an ordinary CAT scan without injections. Maurs is positioned on the couch that moves slowly through the hole in the machine as pictures are taken. We're told Maurs can ring the doctor in the morning for the results. Afterwards we go downstairs to MI5 for the usual radiotherapy session.

That evening Maurs is picked up and taken to the POW meeting over at Claire Warren's. Maurs wants to tell them that it's unlikely she'll be able to perform in the show this year after all, although she's willing to be consulted about the tech stuff.

Maurs rings the following day to report that the doctor has told her that the CAT scan has shown some shrinkage in the tumour. She has an appointment with him next Monday to make the decision about the eight extra radiation treatments.

Wednesday 1 July
We decide on the way in to the Peter Mac that we will still treat this as the last of this lot of radiotherapy, which will give us a reason to feel Maurs is getting somewhere. Even if it doesn't really feel like it.

Wendy Averil arrives to drive Maurs to a meeting with John Thwaites, the shadow minister for health, to add a lesbian perspective to the forthcoming Labor Party policies on lesbian and gay health matters. Wendy gives me a bunch of flowers for the "one who gets missed out", as she put it.

When Maurs comes out from seeing the optometrist, the red drops she's had put into her eyes make it look as if her eyes are bleeding. Not a pretty sight at all.

These ups and downs are the stuff of our lives. Maurs is becoming weaker all the time, her face almost like a death mask some days when she sleeps.

"I think my pubic hair is growing back," Maurs announces when she gets out of the shower, "because it feels all prickly down there. Do you want to check it out?" she invites me.

Needing no second bidding, as she stands beside the bed, I peer very closely at her cunt. There are straggly hairs around the top and what does appear to be the beginnings of growth further down.

"A good thing," says Maurs, when I've made my report. "It hasn't worried me as much as it did last time, I have to admit, but I'm still glad it's growing back again."

Monday 6 July
Maurs and I are both sitting on the edge of the bed while she takes off her boots. "I'm not going to beat this, am I?" she says.

What can I say? "I don't think you are, my darling, no." I add, tentatively, "I thought you'd come to terms with the prognosis?"

"I have. It's just every now and then I hope it's not going to happen. That I'm going to be all right."

"I gave up hoping a while ago," I say. "Although if a miracle came along I'd be rapt." Maurs is so vulnerable and there's nothing I can do about it.

We sit on the couch, Maurs with her cup of Milo, me with my lemon tea, saying how exhausted we are by the day's events. Emotional exhaustion.

This book I'm writing might make for interesting reading one day, when it's finished. Then decide I don't like the sounds of that. I hope it's never finished.

Using more of the plaster of paris pieces, I join the two sides of Maurs' plaster head together. It's still not entirely right and needs strengthening round the edges, but as a shape of Maurs' bald head it's quite remarkable.

"What are you going to do with it?" Maurs wants to know. I have no idea. In the meantime it's on display in the dining-room.

When I arrive at the flat, Maurs wants to go for a walk in the park. There is no small measure of contentment in taking these slow journeys with Maurs arm-in-arm around the perimeter of the oval to the limited extent of her energy.

We go out to dinner in Sydney Road. When I suggest to Maurs she might be better off ordering the entrée-size pasta, she cracks me up by asking whether I'm trying to starve her and orders the full meal. Maurs hasn't eaten a full meal of any kind for weeks.

That evening, the major news item is the passing of the 10-point plan through the Senate to further reduce land rights to Aboriginal people. In the middle of National Aboriginal and Islander Day Observance Committee (NAIDOC) week, yet, to add major insult to terrible injury. As if we non-Aboriginal people haven't done enough already.

At the NAIDOC march on Friday morning it's interesting sorting the few dykes who are there into those who have and haven't heard about Maurs and how they respond to the news. I am feeling remarkably peaceful and don't mind answering questions and talking about what is happening with both of us at this time.

Maurs has a terminal illness and is becoming weaker with every passing day. Having to come to terms with this excruciatingly painful fact is taking all my time and energy.

Heather Chapple duly arrives for afternoon tea. Before we eat, she drills the requisite number of holes in the concrete walls and inserts screws so Maurs can hang all her pictures at long last.

During the Koori Day at the Gasworks Arts Park, I find myself watching to see how others are responding to Maurs. No-one seems shocked, though her physical condition has deteriorated a great deal. Everyone seems very caring and considerate.

We're at the Royal Women's and are told Maurs will be given her blood transfusion in the chemo room rather than her usual Room 10.

"What's the matter?" a nurse asks, "You look restless, what is it?"

"No, I'm okay," said Maurs. But afterwards we agree that being there probably brought back the unpleasant nausea-inducing memories of the ten chemotherapy sessions Maurs has had in that room.

Another womyn arrives who is looking a lot better than the last time we'd seen her: then she was bald and in the last stages of chemo after an operation. I can't help a feeling of what? distress? resentment? sadness? that she is seemingly surviving ovarian cancer a lot better than Maurs is. The contrast between the two womyn is quite marked.

Finally, finally, finally the blood is through. The nurse disconnects the apparatus, and we both give her a hug goodbye as she's leaving to work elsewhere. She is one of the most compassionate and friendly nurses I've ever come across.

Tuesday 14 July

Here I am, with a full-on cold; runny nose, aches and pains, the whole catastrophe. I have no intention of doing anything more today than writing an article for *Lesbiana*, about NAIDOC week, and getting this book up to date.

"I'm dying," I tell Maurs, "if you'll pardon the expression," and it seems like it. I feel like death warmed up and aching all over. "I'm sorry," I add.

Maurs assures me she won't catch my cold.

Maurs and I decide that we want to be together more. So, I will stay with Maurs tomorrow afternoon and at other times, whenever I can. I find it difficult seeing Maurs so weak and vulnerable, losing weight and out of it on the morphine. And yet, her dry humour cracks me up, I feel safe in her company.

It seems as if Maurs has entered some kind of final time. How long this might be is anyone's guess, but she certainly seems different somehow. Maybe this cold is an indication I'm not grieving enough. Maybe I need to face this more, let Maurs go, face what needs to be done? Then again, her spirit is still strong and I can't bear the thought of not having her here.

I have to face it though, Maurs is no longer the same womyn who's been my lover for the past eight years. She's fading before my eyes. Not that it makes any difference to my love for her, which is becoming even stronger and more tender with every passing day together.

I picked up *Cancer in Two Voices* by Sandra Butler and Barbara Rosenblum from the library on the way through to the flat. It's a new expanded edition and I'm looking forward to reading it very much indeed.

Maurs cooks a delicious tea, for the first time in ages, and then eats almost as much as I do without any nausea at all.

"I'm not ever going to get better, am I?" Maurs asks, at one stage during the evening, as we lounge around in front of the telly.

I can't answer and finally say, "The way you've been feeling lately maybe there's cancer somewhere else they haven't picked up on?" The thought is too terrible to contemplate, but how else to explain the complete lack of Maurs' usually animated self?

It's been a strange day, just the two of us in our cocoons of pain, coping together and needing each other's company. It feels quite peaceful, in an odd sort of way.

Maurs is out of the shower, naked, the tube from the site on her stomach dangling round her neck, the weight loss evident in her flattened stomach and her wasted bottom. As I have so many times over the years, I sit up in bed watching as she slowly gets dressed. The hair under her arms and on her cunt is growing back. The hair on her head has more grey in it these days, much to Maurs' delight. A couple of weeks ago Maurs was unable to get her partial plate to fit in her mouth and hasn't worn it since.

These changes only make this womyn whom I love with my whole heart more precious with each passing day.

"I was so bad yesterday," Maurs says, as she sits next to me on the bed, "that I was thinking of getting sleeping tablets and taking them. I wouldn't," she hurriedly assures me, "but I felt like it."

We're talking about *Cancer in Two Voices* when I notice Maurs is not with me. "What are you doing?" She's touching between her eyes.

"I'm seeing how my frown goes," she says.

"How does it go?" I ask.

"A big bump in the centre and little ones on the outside." I crack up.

I've noticed in myself of late that any ambition that I ever had about my writing has almost completely gone. It seems to me that if I've reached fifty-four years of age without having been published or recognised after thirty-one years of writing and twenty-two years of self-publishing, then that's the way of it and no use making a fuss. Indeed, there's something to be said for being able to get on with my writing without fear or favour, beholden to no-one except myself and what I want to do.

We're talking about the plan to stay at Joan Russell's house, while she and her partner are away on their annual jaunt to the snowfields. I'm concerned not so much about getting to Adelaide but how we'll survive once we get there. What will we do if something happens, and Maurs needs medical treatment of one kind or another, not to mention getting her morphine delivered on a regular basis?

"I know it's just my own fears, Maurs, but I think we need to be realistic about your capabilities, too," I suggest.

"We could get someone else to walk the dogs each day," Maurs decides. We could at that, but it doesn't resolve any of the rest of it.

Then, while I'm in the shower Joan rings. By the time I'm dressed, Maurs has agreed with Joan that it would be better that we don't house-sit, after all. "It's not your responsibility," Joan had said. I couldn't agree more, and Maurs says that she feels relieved now that it has been decided.

"We can always go over for a week after Joan and Judith get back from the snow," I say.

Monday 20 July
Today I drive Maurs in to have the first of the next lot of eight radiotherapy sessions. I spend some of my sitting hour trying not to let the fact get to me, because I really don't want to become angry if they start messing us about.

Then the radiologist at the Peter Mac rings to say that the machine in MI5 has broken down. Maurs can either go in and wait till it's fixed or wait till Saturday. Maurs chooses to make an appointment for Saturday. We don't have to go in today at all. A reprieve!

"Do you suffer from Mondayitis, as I do?" I ask Maurs.

"I suffer from everydayitis," Maurs answers. She cracks me up.

I get home to discover that two copies (one for me, one for Maurs) of *Hot & Bothered* have arrived from Arsenal Pulp Press in Canada, with "Essential Connections" by Emily George on page 143. In all these years it's the first time any story of mine has appeared in an anthology, let alone in a book about lesbian desire.

How exciting. I'm not so overwhelmed that I can't get back to doing *The C-Word*, however. Having a short short story published is not the be-all and end-all of my life these days.

On Tuesday I wake with a tension headache. After I've read the daily chapter in Joko's *Everyday Zen*[1] I wonder how I

---

[1] Charlotte Joko Beck. (1997, 1989). *Everyday Zen: Love and Work.* (Edited by Steve Smith.) Thorsons; New York: Harper and Row.

can begin to live with Zen awareness that also incorporates feminist and lesbian principles.

When I get home, I light a candle to commemorate the twelve-month anniversary of Dad's death. It was very sad at the time, not so sad now. In the midst of life there's death.

Sara Elkas arrives back from the Peter Mac with Maurs and stays for a cuppa and a chat in the backyard. Sara and I have known each other since the 1980s, working together as political activists, mainly to ensure the continuance of the Womens Liberation Building by helping to organise the Women's Balls. As I'm not attending any activist collective meetings any more, it's good to catch up. After she leaves we head off to visit Barb Anthony and Helen Robertson. Barb has the remnants of bronchial pneumonia but despite not being at all well is still intending to leave for the Gay Games in Amsterdam on Sunday. Her hacking cough has me worried. But nothing seems to keep her down.

Next we go to the Glasshouse Hotel to say farewell to Mary Daicos, who is going with the Dance Cats to Amsterdam.

Over dinner, POW's new director, gives us a run-down on the show POW intends to do, based on the Tarot cards, which sounds like a great idea. I feel a twinge of nostalgia for the creative enjoyment in getting a script together but don't regret missing out on all the responsibility and worry. I'm looking forward to being in the audience for a change.

It must be a lot harder for Maurs, who has had to drop out because she just can't do it any more. I have to keep that in mind.

As we're leaving I have to hold back tears as I watch Maurs and Mary together, remembering how they used to be when they did their routines in POW. As clowns they were the best, so dynamic and funny. Whereas now, Mary is excited about going on this adventure and Maurs is almost completely out of it on morphine and weak with cancer.

Either it's the aftermath of the cold or a residual sadness, but I don't feel at all well on Friday. And yet, there's a depth in our togetherness at the moment that is very satisfying, and I wouldn't trade it for anything in the world.

Before Adrienne Liebmann arrives to visit Maurs, I head off to buy our (rather expensive) tickets to three Aboriginal plays during the Melbourne Festival in October. We've hardly spent any money like this the whole time we've been together and it seems appropriate at this stage. It's forward planning too, to ensure that Maurs will still be here to enjoy them.

"We haven't seen you for a while," one of the radiologists comments to me on Saturday morning.

"It's because the roster is working so well," I say. I'm doing a couple of sessions a week, so it's not as if I'm missing out.

"I like your T-shirt," she says to Maurs. It has the slogan "I'm a thorn in Jeffrey's side", and is one of my favourites. Having Jeff Kennett as Premier of the State has been a trial and a tribulation for those of us who don't agree with his policies on privatisation of services and other hard-hitting legislation.

"Anne's in a good mood today," I say to Maurs afterwards.

"That wasn't Anne," Maurs replies.

Maybe my memory for faces is even worse than usual.

"You don't smile any more," I observe during the evening. If Maurs does smile it is very fleeting and nothing like her usual broad grin. "I've got nothing to smile about," Maurs answers.

Kristi rings from her new flat in Sweden and we both talk with Sean, who can now say "Nana Jean and Nana Maurs" as well as "bye bye" in clear tones. Very clever for an almost two-year-old.

As she does every night, Maurs turns the cassette over in the clock-radio beside the bed and presses the switch. I'm always pleased when it's Pachelbel's Canon rather than the Gregorian chants.

Monday 27 July
Another Monday.

"While I was vomiting," Maurs tells me, "I was thinking I won't get to see the plays with Jean." There is always fear at the slightest symptom in case it leads to something more drastic.

"Who's taking you in today, Maureen?" Lola May asks.

"I am." I wouldn't miss this last radiotherapy for quids.

We find a park right out the front. I help Maurs undress, and everyone is very friendly. I go in with Maurs and hang around outside watching her image on the monitor as she has her last three zaps. Then I help her get dressed again, before we go up the road for a small celebration brunch at the café nearby. It feels good.

On the way home Maurs throws me by saying that she could perhaps be driving the car by the weekend.

"I don't want to be the heavy," I say, "but I'm not so sure that would be such a good idea, just yet." Then again, how can I really tell if Maurs is capable or not?

Not wanting Maurs to feel she can't get out and about, I ask her, "What do you want to do today?"

"I don't know," says Maurs. We decide to have a think about it.

Meanwhile, I start re-reading *The Cancer Journals* by Audre

Lorde.[1] Audre was a powerful political activist and poet, and it's not long before I am moved to tears by her writing.

I realise that it could just as easily be me who has cancer with Maurs doing the caring, instead of the other way round. Cancer strikes without warning and makes no distinctions.

Maurs gets out of the shower with the cord disconnected from the driver and slung over her shoulder and slowly gets dressed. By the time she's finished, she's exhausted and breathless and lies stretched out on the couch like a rag doll, not moving.

Saturday 1 August
Sean's second birthday.

I do some archiving of the material Maurs had given me when she was moving, quite a number of scripts from all the times she did lighting for various community groups, including Amazon Theatre, Voice of the Heart and the Women's Circus. It makes for an interesting couple of hours sorting it into some semblance of archival order. As I say to Maurs when she wakes up, we've had fun times over the years working on some of these productions together and Maurs has built up a number of considerable skills as a result.

"I just wish it was over, one way or the other," she says.

I'm alarmed. "What do you mean?" There's only one way it can be over, that I can see, and I don't want that to happen.

"I'm bored. There's nothing I'm interested in. I just wish it was over," Maurs repeats. As she has very little energy I can only imagine how frustrating that must be for her.

"Do you want to see a counsellor?" I ask. Maybe talking with someone else might help.

"I don't know," said Maurs, who doesn't seem keen on the idea.

---

[1] Audre Lorde. (1980). *The Cancer Journals*. New York: Spinsters Ink.

There's a brief respite at this point because Maurs remembers, all of a sudden, that she's forgotten, once again, to change the driver.

"I have to tell you," I say, as I get the syringe out of the cheese compartment in the fridge and insert it in the driver, "that I'm not into . . . what's the word?" I can't recall it for the life of me, "helping you suicide or helping you to die before your time." I don't want to lose Maurs before I have to.

"I can't think of the word either," says Maurs.

I try to get some of these comments down on the backs of envelopes so I won't forget to include them in *The C-Word*. "I'm just jotting this down," I apologise, as I do so.

"Euthanasia was the word we were trying to think of yesterday, darling," Maurs calls out to me from the lounge-room.

"How do you manage?" I'm asked at the Women's Circus Book Crew get-together.

"By taking it one day at a time," I reply.

My son Geoff rings to tell us that they'll be home in December. "It means we've got the car for another four months," I say. I'm so grateful for the car that I thank Geoff every time he rings.

Monday 3 August

Maurs' brother Brian rings to tell her that Don, her older brother whom she hasn't seen in years, has tracked Brian down because he's dying of lung cancer and wants to make contact with them both again. He is in his late sixties, and, like Maurs, has been having treatment at the Peter Mac.

I can't help wondering how Brian must feel with both his siblings dying of cancer.

Maurs rings the oncology unit and gets her blood test results: platelets 93 (the highest they've been since before the last chemo) and haemoglobin 9.6, not so good.

"Are you going to have a blood transfusion?" I ask.

"No, I'm sick of doctors and hospitals. I just want to have a rest from any kind of treatment for a while."

"You don't seem as breathless today as you have been," I comment. Maurs will go back to taking the Kapanol pain-killing morphine tablets this evening preparatory to coming off the driver in the morning. It seems the radiotherapy has been successful in reducing the cancer because the pain is not nearly as severe as it has been. It's such a relief to be rid of the driver. Even though one needle will be left in situ for breakthrough morphine injections as needed, it's less inconvenient than living with the driver all the time.

Over dinner with my brother Victor, to celebrate his forty-sixth birthday tomorrow, he asks about Maurs. It has occurred to me only recently how difficult it must have been for him living at home, a 17-year-old student in his first year at university, when Mum was dying.

An herstorical occasion on Wednesday morning when Maurs takes the driver out herself. After two and a half months. She'll be a lot more mobile.

That evening, despite being worn out, still breathless, weak and all as she is, Maurs accompanies me to the opening of the Daffodil Day exhibition at St Paul's Cathedral, for which I'm very grateful. Maurs' portrait, hanging between two other paintings, looks great!

"You must feel a bit let down." The Citymission nurse is full of sympathy when she arrives this morning. Maurs is off the driver but still has a needle in her stomach so she can take Droparadol, the only drug that has any effect on the consistent nausea caused by the morphine.

It all seems never-ending to me. How much more so must it be for Maurs?

As I'm finishing rereading *Cancer in Two Voices*, and once again crying my eyes out at the ending, a little voice calls out from the depths of the couch, "Are you okay in there?"

Love that womyn.

Just as I'm about to start painting the chair I might enter in Window Works, an art exhibition displayed in shop windows along Sydney Road, the phone rings. "I just rang to hear your voice," Maurs says.

That night in bed after Maurs has fallen asleep, I notice that it sometimes takes her an inordinate amount of time to draw the next breath. During which I lie very still and wait, holding my own breath till she breathes again.

"I could drive the car next weekend," says Maurs.

"Maybe," I caution.

"When am I going to drive it then?" I don't know. "You just want to keep the car to yourself," Maurs accuses, but not in a nasty way.

Towards the end of the evening Maurs says she has a pain in her right side like a stitch. "It'll be all right in the morning," she adds.

Monday 10 August

By morning the pain is worse and there's also a pain in the middle of her chest. Maurs decides not to ring the Royal Women's about the blood transfusion until she's rung the Citymission and got this pain under control.

Maurs tells me the pain is a number ten. "Out of what?" I ask.

"Out of ten."

The doctor arrives. After he's examined Maurs, who tells

him it's sore to sit, stand and breathe, he decides that the pain is caused by one of two things. A hairline fracture of a rib, which can just happen, because of osteoporosis perhaps. Or another tumour on her rib. Only time will tell.

After Maurs vomits the vegetable soup we had for lunch, she says, "Well, my stomach thinks it's been fed."

I laugh and say, "I've got to get that down."

I get my latest issue of the anarchist feminist magazine *Mother Earth* in the mail. I have a tiny passing regret that I am not able to get up to the Northern Territory to take part in the the blockade against the Jabiluka uranium mine, which is on the land of the Mirrar people at Kakadu. But being with Maurs is much more important than anything else I can possibly do.

I buy Maurs a bunch of flowers, having decided to make sure she always has flowers from now on, and after I put in my dole form I drop them in to her.

Maurs is in good spirits. "I'm surprised how well I feel. I'm content just to be here in the flat."

There are no leaves left on the tree outside the window, birds rest on the bare branches and I'm a womyn on a bed, sitting with awareness.

I go back home to finalise and post the two articles I'm writing about lesbians and cancer for both *Lesbiana* and *Lesbian Network*.

While Maurs is off having a pizza with Brian, I go to hear a visiting Buddhist nun, Tenzin Palmo, speak. Helen is there too and tells me Barb Anthony is in hospital in Edinburgh with bronchial pneumonia and is having a CAT scan.

---

[1] Issue 5, August 1998.

Maurs seems so peaceful sitting on the couch with her face calm that I am moved to comment, "You look like Buddha yourself."

We're talking about Barb. "I hope Barb doesn't do a Pat," I say. Because Pat Longmore had died of cancer on holiday in London in 1992 none of us here had had a chance to say goodbye to her properly.

"Of course she won't," says Maurs.

"How do you want to die?" I ask Maurs.

"In bed. I want to go to sleep and not wake up. Also a lot older," she says, making me laugh. "I was looking forward to ninety." So was I, with Maurs.

When the Citymission nurse rings to say he will call in after work this evening, I think for one heart-stopping moment that it's Barb Anthony's son, ringing to tell us some bad news about his mother.

Di Brown rings to talk to Maurs about her partner, Kiersten, who, having been diagnosed with cancer, is now having chemo. Di mentions that she now has a much better understanding of how brave Maurs has been all these many months.

As I'm putting the latest photos in the album I'm struck by how different Maurs looks these days. She's much thinner, as is to be expected. But her whole face has a different expression. Her eyes, now framed with lashes and hooded by growing eyebrows, are more deep-set than usual but still clear and direct. Fiercely and disconcertingly so, at times.

Each time I look into that ravaged face, with the whiskers in proliferation round her chin, the fuzz on each side of her face, the deep set grey-blue eyes, the intense gaze that misses nothing, the deliberate way she moves her head, the stillness of her whole way of being, and above all the indefinite something that is still very much Maurs, I'm moved.

While I'm outside doing tai chi, Don rings. He and Maurs have a conversation for the first time in over thirty years.

Monday 17 August

We're talking about how Maurs is only now getting over the effects of the chemotherapy—her hair is almost back to normal, three and a half months down the track—when Maurs says, "I might not have any more," meaning treatment.

"How do you feel about all that?" It would be a decision to die.

"Waiting. I'm waiting. Waiting till it comes up again. Just waiting. It's always there, it never goes away. Just waiting till I have to make decisions."

There's nothing I can say or do, except to cuddle into Maurs. We're waiting together; there's that about it, at least.

As I head for home to work on *The C-Word* I'm conscious that I'm using my house as an office these days, where I do my work and not much more. My living is done with Maurs at her place.

Maureen Gie rings to tell me that she and Thelma have heard from Helen Robertson that Barb Anthony, who is now living with Deb Ball in Edinburgh, has metastasised cancer in her liver. I wait till I get back to the flat with a pizza to tell Maurs about this devastating news in person.

Maureen rings again to let us know that she rang Deb's place and that Barb seems in very good spirits, although she is wondering why this wasn't diagnosed in Melbourne when the Edinburgh Hospital picked it up straight away. It's terrible news, but at least we know.

"How are you feeling this morning?" I ask Maurs.

"I'm not sure how I feel. I haven't quite made up my mind," she replies.

My eye appointment confirms my myopia is a lot worse (it's three years since I last had my eyes tested) and I need new glasses. It feels good to be taking care of my own needs.

At my appointment to review my dole entitlements, it's established that I ought to apply for a carer's pension instead. However, I'm more concerned about driving Maurs to the Royal Women's for yet another blood transfusion.

It takes ages, all afternoon and into the evening, for two units. I'm annoyed. Maurs takes it in her stride. Afterwards, Maurs remarks that she hasn't had a cigarette all day. Which means that she's too weak to walk all the way round to the veranda.

Almost as soon as I get back to the flat, Maurs begins heaving so I fetch the bucket. "Maybe I make you sick," I joke, which Maurs doesn't appreciate one little bit.

"I want a hug," says Maurs, "I'm frightened with all this vomiting."

All I can say is that it might not get any better. "How do you feel about that?"

"Resigned," Maurs says. "I'm resigned that it might be earlier than we expected." That is what I'm coming to believe, too.

Maurs intended to go to an auction fundraiser for the Women's Circus but decides at the last minute that she isn't well enough.

I answer the inevitable questions about how Maurs is and promise to take everyone's best wishes back to her. I make a point of saying that Maurs is not at all well because her voice on the phone is a lot stronger than she is in person. I want everyone to realise this so that if they want to contact Maurs they can do it before it's too late.

"What do you want to do today?" I ask Maurs.

"Nothing," says Maurs. "I don't feel like going anywhere."

That evening I massage Maurs' feet, something I forgot to do last week. We are taking increasing pleasure in each other's company. I haven't slept at home by myself for two weeks now.

Monday 24 August
What I'm feeling right now is fear. Maurs is much worse. And to all intents and purposes we're living together. Just typing that makes me fearful because it's tantamount to admitting that the end is that much nearer.

It seems that this past week has brought the situation into sharp focus for me. That is why I'm feeling fearful, I suppose. I'm not ready for Maurs to die just yet. She's far too precious and we still have things to do together. Like see in the millennium and everything else in between.

Although right now, I'd settle for her fifty-third birthday in exactly three weeks' time. Even the tickets we have for the plays at the end of October seem a long way off. As does Geoff and Anita's proposed return in December.

"It seems more serious now," Maurs says. So it does. It feels right to confirm that we want to sleep together every night from now on, and not only because we sleep so well together.

"I hate having a shower," Maurs says, unexpectedly. "I can't stand up any more."

"That's why the seat's there," I say, wondering if perhaps

Maurs needs a bath for a change. The flat has a shower with a fold-down seat but no bath.

"I can see how much weight I've lost. I look ugly, all skin and bones." So that's it.

"Well, you've certainly lost weight but you still look beautiful." It's one of the advantages of being a big womyn to start with. Besides, Maurs will always look beautiful as far as I'm concerned.

"So long as you carry me in your heart, I'll always be with you," says Maurs.

"You'll always be in my heart," I assure her.

Later, for her check-up appointment at the Royal Women's, Maurs sees the doctor. There's not much more that can be done now, according to her, except to keep the pain under control.

As Maurs put it, "They've used up all their bag of tricks."

"I always get depressed after seeing the doctor," I say on the way back to the flat, "probably because they never have anything good to say."

Wednesday 26 August

"You're looking a lot better today," I say. Or is it me? Am I just feeling a lot better on this sunny morning? Because nothing has changed. Maurs is still breathless, weak, nauseous and in pain.

My fear notwithstanding, I have felt a lot more peaceful in myself lately. Probably because I'm inside the experience, it's part of my very existence. I'm accepting the way things are and just enjoying being with Maurs as much as I can, while I can. Although it feels as if Maurs has turned another corner, it's not the end yet, by any means.

"The reason I'm feeling better today," Maurs tells me later, "is because I don't have to go into the hospital."

I open the *Melbourne Star Observer* I picked up at the Bruns-wick Community Health Centre yesterday and there's a photo of several members of the LCSG: Jacqui, Wendy, Maurs and Heather, and an accompanying article about the LCSG. Stars, the lot of them!

As I'm picking up the seemingly vast quantities of mor-phine from the local chemist, I joke to her that I feel like a drug runner.

I've worked out that my reluctance to apply for the carer's pension is because I don't want to admit that Maurs is in need of care and also because I don't want to be making money out of her condition. I ring Centrelink to make an enquiry and am taken aback when the womyn makes an appointment for me over the phone. The die is cast, it seems.

Maurs is so breathless and it takes so long for her to go to the bank that both of us are frightened by this irrefutable evidence of how weak she really is.

Yet afterwards, Maurs says she wants to see the Australian film *Head On* that evening. So off we go to the Nova Cinema, where we get the escalator changed around so Maurs doesn't have to tackle the stairs. We meet Marianne Permezel, with friends in the foyer. She is looking extremely well if a bit tired, now that her hair has grown back since she finished the chemo.

I spend the whole day at the Malthouse Theatre going to three writers' festival sessions. A day off. I chat with friends. One of them asks, "Is Maurs living with you now?" That old question.

"I'm living with Maurs," I answer. Much the better arrangement.

"Have you heard about Kiersten?" she asks. And goes on

to tell me Kiersten has been in the Royal Melbourne Hospital these past ten weeks having chemotherapy and blood transfusions and has just been given a bone marrow transplant from her brother.

"Have you heard about Barb Anthony?" I counter.

Helen rings to tell us that Barb is starting chemo on Monday and may have two sessions before she considers coming home. She also says that Heather Chapple has painful lumps on her thyroid gland which her doctor has said are probably malignant. She's seeing the surgeon on Monday about a possible op.

"It's an avalanche!" I exclaim.

Monday 31 August

"I'm feeling much better this morning," Maurs tells me. "I can breathe without it hurting." She gives the small shuddering sigh that denotes taking a deep breath. "I can stand up longer." She does seem a bit better.

I complete the carer's pension application with something bordering on conviction. I'm still not convinced I want to do this, but there seems no doubt, with everything I do and Maurs' weakening condition, that I'm eligible.

I'm nearly finished tai chi when Ellen Kessler arrives to visit. "Could you get the Droparadol out of the fridge, please?" Maurs says, when I go back inside.

The conversation with Ellen continues as I fossick in the blue cardboard box for the syringe, and pull the plunger back to make sure it's not stuck. Flicking the syringe to position the bubbles of air, I slowly push the plunger back again till the air is all gone and a bubble of liquid appears at the top.

I pass it to Maurs who takes the stopper off the end of the tube in order to insert the syringe. We all continue to talk as if this is the most natural thing in the world while Maurs slowly administers herself the anti-nausea drug. It is getting on for dinner-time, I notice, glancing at the clock.

"I'll have to ask you to leave shortly, Ellen," Maurs says after a while, "I'm getting tired."

11

1–24 September

Tuesday 1 September—Spring

I'm woken at 5.30 a.m. by the sounds of Maurs vomiting into the toilet bowl.

"Just a little bit," Maurs assures me, as she gets back into bed.

I mix the barium meal with a litre of water and give it to Maurs in two containers for her to have at two-hourly intervals.

With Maurs in a wheelchair we head up to the first floor at the Peter Mac, where Maurs puts on a white gown that I tie up at the back. To my surprise the radiologist (a womyn I've never met before) won't let me go in with Maurs. So I wait out in the corridor and chat to the man from a farm up Shepparton way who has recently found out he has a brain tumour.

Back home, I ring Heather Chapple who tells me the surgeon seems certain the lumps on her thyroid are not malignant and that he'll operate in about four weeks' time. About the time Heather plans to shift to her new house.

Maurs receives a letter from Barb Anthony. She's "having

a great time, despite/in spite of this bloody disease" and she has started chemo "once a week for six months". Between times she and Deb "intend to do more travelling" in the van Deb bought. It sounds as if she's in the best possible place for the time being. And somehow it is no surprise that Barb is fitting in holidays between chemo sessions.

Lola May, the nurse from Citymission, arrives and advises Maurs to take the breakthrough morphine when she needs it rather than putting up with any pain whatsoever. As she says, pain is very debilitating and Maurs doesn't need that extra drain on her energy. She also says she will arrange to have a wheelchair delivered at the weekend.

Then the doctor rings with the results of the CAT scan. As he puts it, the news is not so good. The original tumour has been reduced, but there is now cancer in her liver and in the base of her right lung.

Even though we've been more or less expecting something like this, we're devastated to have it confirmed. I'm crying, of course, as we sit together on the couch and comfort each other. This latest news is going to take a bit of getting used to.

It feels like the beginning of the end.

I drive Maurs round to Sydney Road on a mystery errand and am thrilled and overwhelmed when she presents me with an Irish drum. It is a belated birthday present, she says, and to say thankyou for my support.

"You said one day you wanted an Irish drum." It's the perfect present, and just like Maurs to think of it. The wooden base and the cross bars at the back are painted dark green with gold trim and it comes complete with a black carry case. As I've had a few quck lessons from an interstate friend at various Lesbian Festivals, I'm able to give Maurs an idea of what it sounds like: deep and resonant.

"I'm not looking forward to today," Maurs says, as we're getting ready to go into the Royal Women's for another blood transfusion. I misunderstand her concern till she adds, "I think they'll give a time limit."

"You don't have to know," I point out. Anything to protect Maurs.

"Yes, I do." Maurs is adamant. "I can't be kept in the dark."

I agree. We've known this for some time. Maurs has been so debilitated and weak there had to be cancer somewhere else, "You're very courageous, you know that."

Maurs dismisses this with, "It's just how I am."

"That's what I mean. You're a very courageous womyn. It's a privilege to be in a relationship with you."

"And I with you."

After all the years of not living together, now that we are, we're doing it in the easiest possible way. That is, neither of us has had to shift furniture or work out how to share the combined space. All I needed to do was bring over a few extra T-shirts and carry on as before.

Maurs asks me to lower the shower nozzle, turn it on and put toothpaste on her toothbrush so she can have a shower. "You look cute sitting on the seat," I comment, once Maurs is ensconced in the cubicle with the water running, having assured me she is still able to wash herself.

At the Royal Women's, Maurs is taken up in a wheelchair. We're no sooner walking in than it's decided to do the intravenous line straight away. "I feel like something the cat dragged in," Maurs says.

The first (of three) units of O-type blood is being hooked up in the late morning. We will be out of there by late afternoon.

We don't get to talk to the doctor till later in the afternoon. She says that, although there's not much more that can be done in the way of treatment, the pain can certainly be controlled. Maurs can have more blood transfusions if she wants them, but they'll have limited success as time goes on. The doctor points out that these latest metastases have developed since the MRI test three months ago, so they're growing at a fairly fast rate.

What we can expect is that the liver will pack up altogether or the other kidney could stop functioning. Fluid around the lungs could cause more breathlessness. It can be drained as necessary but there isn't any sign of it, as yet. Maurs will gradually become weaker.

"How long do I have?" Maurs wants to know.

"It's impossible to say. You could die within two weeks if you were that way inclined. But you're not," she adds, confidently. "You're in control. It's entirely up to you now and how long you want to continue fighting. You'll know yourself, and eventually you'll just give in to it."

"How will it happen?"

"You could die in your sleep. Some people go into a coma. Or drift in and out of consciousness. Are you afraid of dying?"

"I'm not frightened of dying," Maurs says, "But I'm pissed off about missing out on things, like watching Sean grow up, things like that."

"Are there any issues that need resolving?"

"No," says Maurs. It's good to know. We want to know.

When we get home there are no less than eight messages on the machine. The word is out. However, all we want to do is spend the next few days with each other quietly in order to get used to this latest development and not have to deal with or see anyone else till next week. More than ever I want to be here with and for Maurs, to make these last months as enjoyable and fulfilling as possible.

I'm having trouble concentrating properly during sitting, but I persevere. Without this daily practice over these past two years I doubt whether I'd have been able to cope. I certainly don't want to stop now.

When we get home from seeing the movie *Dead Letter Office* with fish and chips, there's a bunch of yellow roses and purple irises from the Women's Circus on the doorstep.

Then Fran, who cancelled her visit this afternoon, rings and wants to come round then and there. "No, Fran," Maurs says firmly, "Jean and I just need the weekend to ourselves to work through all this stuff." She makes arrangements for Fran to call in next Tuesday afternoon.

It's pleasing to note that Maurs is still in control of her environment and what she wants to do and who she wants to do it with. That doesn't involve having to give in to everyone else's fears and insecurities at a time like this. Most dykes have known for these past eight months that Maurs has terminal cancer, and yet the moment they hear that it's worse, suddenly want to come round and visit.

They'll just have to be patient and take Maurs' needs into account. I'm prepared to protect Maurs, if there comes a time when she can't do it for herself, to allow her the peace and quiet she needs while she catches up with friends without tiring herself out too much.

Joan Russell rings from Adelaide and is very upset to hear the news. She says she'll make arrangements to be in Melbourne by the end of the week and will catch up with Maurs on Friday and over the weekend. Good on her.

"I feel contented," Maurs unexpectedly says that evening, after our roast rack of lamb dinner, "like a cat curled up before a fire."

It seems that easing ourselves into it—being together is the main part of it—is beginning to pay off.

Thinking we need a strategy, I ask Maurs "How do we want to work this?"

"A day at a time," Maurs answers.

"I knew you'd say that."

We're gradually, slowly coming to terms with this latest prognosis by absorbing it into our very beings so that we can believe, live, love, and enjoy it. We have known about it for months; but knowing is one thing, and living consciously and clearly nearer the end quite another. That is what we're determined to do.

We talk about notifying others. "We don't have to do anything about it today. This weekend is for us, remember?" Maurs reminds me.

We go for another walk with Maurs in the wheelchair. The chair is brand-new and handles extremely well. And because it allows us to go a lot further afield than we've been able to lately, we go twice round the oval. It's fun. It opens possibilities.

As Maurs is having her usual afternoon sleep on the couch. I think how very much at home I am in this flat and how much I like the way we've set it up. The furniture is just right, everything within convenient reaching distance, the familiar pictures on the walls at last. It's warm, cosy and lightfilled.

Geoff rings from Barcelona, so I tell him about Maurs' latest condition. Anita gives me her mother's phone number so we can arrange to go down and stay at their house in Torquay on the south coast to get away from it all.

Monday 7 September
"Your eyes are different," I say to Maurs. They're calmer, big and round, clear, not so intense.

"Are they?" She takes off her glasses.

"Perhaps it's because you can now see infinity," I suggest.

Lynne Bryer arrives with lunch and yet another bunch of flowers which I put into a jug as we've run out of vases. As I'm leaving to go to my place to sit in front of the computer for a few hours, Maurs reminds me, "You need to be back here by five to do your tai chi."

I walk in the door of this house that I've owned since 1976. As it's a single-fronted terrace house it's dark, and crowded with furniture, archives, pictures and photos. I've lived here off and on for the past twenty-two years with my children, friends and assorted lovers at different times, and know as well as I know my own name. It feels strange, alien, as if I don't belong here. I feel much more at home in Maurs' flat.

"So many flowers," the doctor says. The flat looks like a florist's.

Maurs tells him about the sharp pain in her lower right side that materialised this morning. After he has examined her, he says it's probably due to the enlarged liver pressing on nerves and causing the pain. The swelling in the liver was the body's response to the cancer and could be reduced by steroids which would reduce the pain. The steroids would also increase the appetite but might cause thrush.

Maurs enquires about her low haemoglobin count. He says it's like climbing a mountain, as in altitude sickness, where climbers became weaker and more tired the less oxygen there is.

"Like I'm going up my own personal mountain," says Maurs.

Thursday 10 September
I wake in the early hours of the morning. Then I hear Maurs get up for a piss. When she doesn't come back to bed I call out, "Are you all right?"

"I'm having a cigarette," comes the answer.

Maurs is only back in bed a few minutes when she asks, "Can you do me a favour? Would you mind getting me a breakthrough of morphine out of the fridge?"

Maurs has been in a lot more pain these past couple of days. After administering the dose I can't go back to sleep, so while Maurs snores beside me I read for about half an hour.

In the morning, as Maurs is getting undressed, and particularly as she is heading into the shower with her shoulders slightly bowed and shaky on her legs, it hits me again how thin and frail she is becoming day by day, so that every movement is an effort that is difficult to observe. Her bottom is so sore that when I pull the patches off it starts to bleed in a couple of places.

I ask Maurs if it could just be her and me towards the end, without others around. Would she mind?

"I'm worried about you being on your own," says Maurs.

I'd prefer it, I assure her.

"I would just like to die in my sleep," Maurs says. I don't see why not.

Back here at the computer I start the *Lesbiana* article and do the by-now-daily *C-Word*. Far from depressing me as it used to do, it's affording me a measure of relief at the moment.

I pay Maurs' bills and head back to the flat where Joan Russell has already arrived from Adelaide and is settled next to Maurs on the couch.

The anticipated visit with her brothers, especially Don whom she hasn't seen since she was twenty-one, went very well indeed that afternoon, Maurs tells us, and they are planning to do it again soon.

Joan stays for a couple of hours, promising to be back for dinner tomorrow, so Maurs gets to see the opening of the Commonwealth Games on television after all.

It's so good to see Maurs enjoying Joan's company in a way she doesn't with anyone else and relaxing into what could be the last time, although maybe not. As they've known each other for almost thirty years, this time together is essential for both of them. When Joan goes to the toilet and exclaims over the practically antique, wooden shoe-box and how much she likes it, Maurs promptly says she can have it. As Maurs explains, she's been wondering what to give Joan and this is obviously the perfect gift.

After Joan leaves, Kristi rings in tears about Maurs, having already heard the news from her brother Geoff. It gives Maurs the opportunity to chat with Sean.

In the early hours of Sunday morning I conclude that I need to be open to the pain of the full realisation of Maurs' fast-approaching death, and at the same time fully enjoy this final time with Maurs as much as possible. I want to hold both the knowledge of the imminent loss of her and the warmth of her undeniable presence at the same time.

When I finally wake, I wonder how much this is possible anyway.

Joan arrives at midday for another couple of hours before we drive her to the airport. Maurs looks a lot sadder today than for the previous two days. Perhaps because, even though Joan plans to return at the end of September, who knows what will happen before then?

Monday 14 September
Maurs' 53rd birthday!

I read in Joko's *Everyday Zen: Love and Work* that by paying attention to life as it is, rather than getting caught up in nonsense generated by my frantic thoughts, will make it less frightening. Easier said than done, I think.

I give Maurs her presents; tickets for Circus Oz, three gift voucher tickets for the Nova Cinema, a promise to pay for a hot-air balloon ride (something Maurs has always wanted to do) and, of course, a pair of the hand-knitted socks I always give her for her birthday. It isn't much: I want to give her the world.

"I'll be paying for everything today, too, of course," I add.

Maurs doesn't feel like a shower so she doesn't have one before we go out. When we get to the National Gallery I park in the forecourt and get a wheelchair from the gallery for Maurs to use.

We have a great time. We see, and enjoy all three of the Aboriginal and Torres Strait Islander exhibitions, one piece at a time: the Raiki Wara Long Cloth, the long lengths of cloth fairly shimmering on the wall with their vibrant colours and traditional designs; the Great Icons, some traditional bark paintings, statues and artwork from the northern tribal communities in particular; and the stunning paintings by Emily Kame Kngwarreye, whose artwork has deservedly received critical acclaim. We also have a look at the Wine Cask and the Recent Acquisitions exhibitions, and have a couple of drinks and meal breaks at the café.

By the time we get home, nearly five hours after we'd left, Maurs is exhausted. Added to all the other enjoyable times we've had together, this is a day to remember.

There are flowers and chocolates and a card on the doorstep, as well as more birthday cards in the mailbox and several messages for Maurs on the answering machine.

"It's very strange," I say to Maurs, that evening. "I know that you're dying, I can see you're not going to be here much longer, and yet it still doesn't feel entirely real."

Maurs still can't be bothered having a shower this morning. We start talking about the funeral arrangements. We don't speak, as we have before, as if it's something academic and in the future—as it was, back then—but as of something imminent. I imagine we'll have some kind of ceremony at the crematorium so people who want to can speak. And then some less formal occasion with food afterwards. But where, is the question?

Maurs suggests the Women's Circus warehouse space. Just talking about all this stirs me up so much that I cry on Maurs' shoulder.

Womyn are still ringing frequently. Trish Sykes, one of the Women's Circus Book Crew, rings and reads out the poem she wrote after she visited Maurs a couple of weeks ago: "I Don't Do Warm-ups". She says she'll put a copy in the post for Maurs to have. Maurs gets off the phone moved.

I go home to do some more of *The C-Word*. Then I work on the chair that I am painting, which has to be finished now that my Window Works application has been accepted. I'm not as excited about this as I might otherwise have been. I'm impressed that Maurs is coping so well, whereas I seem to be only capable of doing one or two things a day. Even little things throw me if they don't go according to plan.

I ring Di and leave a message for her and Kiersten from Maurs and myself to say we're thinking of them both during this difficult time.

Maurs has been postponing a shower for days now, so she decides to have one as soon as she gets out of bed. Her energy levels are down to nothing so this takes a great deal of effort. I lower the shower nozzle, get her toothbrush ready, and turn on the water.

"I can't even dry between my toes," she says afterwards with a catch in her voice. "Would you mind?"

I've been doing these small but essential tasks for some time now and it's no bother drying between those cute toes.

"Not so rough," she says. I notice her feet and lower legs are even more swollen this morning.

I feel very heavy, with what? Grief, I suppose, and sadness, pain is certainly one of the main components. It is not easy being this close to another human being who is dying before my eyes, slowly, day by day. And especially not easy that this person is my lover, my partner, my very dear friend and beloved companion.

I love Maurs so very much and I don't want to see her suffering like this. Nor do I want to watch her painfully slow progress or observe her wasted body or hear how breathless she is with every step. It breaks my heart. But I also want to be here with her while she's going through all this. It's the very least I can do for this womyn who has given me, and continues to give me every single day, so very much.

I love her, it's as simple as that, and I will do whatever is necessary to make these last few weeks as comfortable and satisfying as possible, to the best of my ability.

Just as we're getting into bed, Maurs realises she's forgotten to take her morphine so I get the syringe out of the fridge for her. As usual, I rub some moisturising cream into Maurs' bottom before I switch out the light. The pressure sores are no better but no worse than they have been these past couple of weeks. We go to sleep to the sounds of the Gregorian chants.

On Thursday, just as I'm about to sit, I notice a crow in the tree outside the window. Crows always remind me of Anne Stafford because they were part of her Koori heritage, and of death. As if I need reminding at the moment. Every time I leave the flat now I'm aware that Maurs might die before I get back again.

Over these past few months I've been coming to terms with how my life is, as opposed to how I thought it might have been or hoped it would turn out. One of the advantages of being fifty-four is that there's a lot to look back on and I realise that not a lot is going to change. I now accept that my writing, although it is central in my life, will not set the world on fire. I enjoy painting, and I had a great time performing and being a circus womyn and a director. I did these activities for fun, without wanting fame or glory or needing to make a profession of them.

There's some peaceful acceptance in knowing that I am as I am, pretty ordinary really, without having to make a big deal about it.

I feel very heavy and full of dread, as I have since yesterday, because it seems to me as if Maurs has moved onto another stage.

As Maurs puts it, "I think we've left the ballooning too late." I'm not ready to concede this, but I can see her point. It occurs to me that we can try to do everything we want to do before we die, but to die with some things not done perhaps indicates that life is still full of promise.

"I'm amazed I'm not depressed," Maurs goes on to say. "Before, it used to make me depressed just thinking about what I was going to do with myself till the final time comes. Now that the final time is here, I'm much more content because I know the answer."

Coffee with Moss doesn't cheer me up, but it does allow me to articulate how stressed and grieving and apprehensive I am watching Maurs become progressively weaker and knowing she is about to die. I figure that the reason I'm feeling even more wretched all of a sudden is because I'm picking up any subtle changes with my body while I'm sleeping with her.

When I get back, Maurs is sitting up in a chair cushion

that someone from the Citymission had dropped off to make Maurs more comfortable on the couch.

Because I feel comparatively peaceful on Saturday morning I am able to acknowledge my fears about being away from Maurs in case she dies when I'm not with her.

"Remind me I need to take the steroids twice a day," Maurs calls out to me still in bed; to reduce the swelling in her liver. Some hope. My memory is worse than ever.

I feel like shutting the door and going into a retreat while I go mad with grief, and out of that eventually work out who I am and what I'm supposed to do in my lonely future.

Going to see Circus Oz is an adventure. I drive to Swanston Walk in the centre of Melbourne, where I give Maurs a hand getting into the wheelchair before going off to park the car. Both Circus Oz and the Melbourne Town Hall have people assigned to watch out for wheelchairs, so we have no trouble going up in the lift and getting a special front-row seat.

Circus Oz have always been extremely entertaining and on the cutting edge of alternative circus. Some of the performances are excellent, like the aerials, the hoops and the vertical bar. My favourite act is when they make a political statement about the ticket machines replacing connies on the trams, and the "connies" do group balances.

Maurs and I thoroughly enjoy ourselves. Mainly because we are doing it together.

That night in bed Maurs says, "I'm not feeling very well. I just want it all over and done with." Her stomach is distended and I can hear how ill and frustrated by her debilitated state she is feeling.

Surprisingly, I'm not fearful going to sleep although I know that Maurs could die overnight. It isn't her death that frightens me, nor the thought of her cold body in bed in the morning. It's what happens afterwards when I am all alone without Maurs' needed and loved self to support and comfort me—that is my major concern.

Maurs is still breathing I note with relief on Sunday morning. She gets up to have a shower, a slow process, but once I get everything ready she can still wash herself. I cut her toenails and help her to dress. The effort so zonks Maurs that I ring Jody-Lee and Jude and ask them to bring the movable feast to the flat, instead of us going to them as we've arranged. Jody-Lee is the daughter of one of my ex-lovers and I've known her since she was eleven years old.

"I'm ready," I explain to Maurs, "or as ready as I can be knowing that you're going to die."

"Even though my body is very weak, I'm still too strong in myself and optimistic about the future," explains Maurs. She goes on to talk about not doing too much to conserve what little strength she has left.

"Besides," I say, "you need to save your strength to see POW on Thursday," the next outing we have planned.

"I just had a thought," says Maurs. "I want to give you money now for a diary in case I'm not here at Christmas time." As Maurs has been buying me a diary for Christmas every year since we've been together, this offer has me in tears. "Perhaps someone else will buy your diaries in future," she says, as she hands me a blue envelope with $25 in it. On the front in wavery handwriting are the words "20/9/98. To my darling Jean. Happy Xmas. I hope that your diary brings you great joy. Love always & forever, Maurs."

"No," I assure her, "that will always be yours." I am imagining that whenever I buy a diary in future it will always remind me of Maurs.

Jody-Lee and Jude arrive with a car-fridge full of food

they've bought at the Queen Victoria Market. It is all so delicious that Maurs eats more than usual. Part-way through the afternoon, hurrying to answer the phone Maurs trips and falls. With her feet so swollen and her legs so weak, she isn't steady on her feet any more, and the slippers she is wearing aren't supportive enough.

Maurs isn't hurt, thank goodness, but she is shaken. It takes a while for her to recover enough not to be nervous about walking again.

Afterwards, with Maurs in the wheelchair, we go for a couple of laps of the oval in the park across the road in the fading late-afternoon sunshine.

Monday 21 September
Maurs is up and down during the night, keeping me awake. At one point, she asks me to help her off the couch. I realise I'm cold in bed on my own.

At this point, Maurs can hardly do anything for herself. "It's almost to the stage where you need someone here twenty-four hours," I say, pretending I'm not devastated that it has almost come to that, "don't you think?"

Just as I'm finishing off *The C-Word* for the day, Jean Ferguson rings to reiterate what we've heard from others, that the Women's Circus sent love to Maurs at the end of the Circus Day at the weekend.

I buy a telephone extension cord on the way across to the flat and set it up as soon as I arrive, so that Maurs has the telephone beside her on the arm of the couch, within easy reach.

Having spent the past few days feeling heavy and depressed and as if I have no friends to see me through this terrible time, I finally mention all this to Maurs. "No-one else loves me," I say, "I feel terrible."

"Have you written that down?" says Maurs. I've been jotting everything down on the back of used envelopes for weeks now, including dialogue, so that I can refer to it when I type it into the computer. "You're stressed because it's a stressful situation."

Of course. As soon as we start to talk about it, I begin to feel easier. I'm stressed alright. My lover is close to death. I'm starting to spiral out of control, so I'm blaming my friends for not being supportive enough. Easier to blame them than deal with this painful situation.

I realise that there is no-one who can understand what I'm going through right at this moment, so I have to stop expecting there will be. It is a lonely process. Debilitated and all as Maurs is increasingly becoming, this is all we have now; we must make the most of what little time we have left together.

I complain that I'm starting to forget things, like buying another cask of riesling. I'm not even sure I have enough left to have a glass with dinner.

"Open the champagne," Maurs suggests grandly. "What does it matter if you only drink one glass." Her carefree attitude makes me laugh.

As we're going to bed I notice that Maurs has some difficulty getting off the couch, but she does manage and walks slowly into the bedroom, breathing heavily all the while.

Even though Maurs is cutting down on visitors, she's actually had five people in to see her today. That's no mean feat. Maurs is making a determined effort to see as many of her friends as she can and makes appointments every day so the visits don't become too tiring.

Today, Maurs also finalises the list of instructions regarding her possessions and the funeral arrangements.

For the first time, because the effort to have a shower or wash herself is too much, I give Maurs a wash all over while she sits on the stool in the bathroom, and help her to get dressed afterwards.

"I wonder when Anah's due back?" I say, thinking that it might be too late by the time she does return from Amsterdam to organise the funeral ceremony. We'd already heard that Anah won gold for the Dance Cats.

"Anah's back," says Maurs, unexpectedly. "She came back Sunday." Just as well someone is on the ball.

I wheel Maurs out to the car and she gets into the passenger seat with some difficulty. When we arrive at the Royal Women's I drive up to the back door and ask for a wheelchair. Maurs is taken straight to the ward while I park the car.

The sister wants to know if Maurs would like to stay for a couple of days. Maurs says she doesn't even want to stay overnight.

I feel more accepting of the situation, even though I can plainly see that Maurs is a great deal worse. She's a lot weaker and can barely walk. She is lapsing in and out of such a deep sleep I have to really rouse her on occasions. She isn't as coherent as she has been either, and yet is witty at times. Suddenly it seems as if the end is near.

As Maurs' haemoglobin is 8.1, the order is for two units of blood, but Maurs is convinced that three would be more beneficial. When the doctor comes round towards the end of the afternoon, Maurs firmly states her case. Eventually the doctor gives in gracefully and says she can have the three if it makes her feel better. I have my doubts. I'm afraid that Maurs might die while we're there and that would distress me even more because we both want Maurs to die at home. I don't mention any of this to Maurs.

I do more work on my story about Sean Daniel in

Melbourne, the only story of mine, all these years down the track, that Maurs has not read in draft form. Knowing she won't be around to see Sean grow up, it's too painful for her to read.

Wendy Averil calls in before the LCSG meeting and I ask her to put the members of the group on notice that some-time soon Maurs might need a roster of carers drawn up.

It's late, almost midnight, when I leave Maurs in the wheel-chair lighting a cigarette outside the back door of the hospital while I go to get the car. As I'm heaving and pulling to help Maurs into the passenger seat the receptionist comes out to give us a hand.

It's even worse when Maurs and I get back to the flat. Our combined efforts cannot move Maurs from the car to the wheelchair. After a great struggle Maurs finally kneels on the foot-rests of the chair and we make it to the door. When Maurs can't make it inside, I leave Maurs sitting on the concourse and ring the ambulance service. Two men lift Maurs to her feet, and she is able to walk to the bedroom with me holding her hands to guide her.

Tired as she is, once we're in bed Maurs puts her arm round me. I lie with my head on her shoulder while she holds me, as we do every evening before we go to sleep.

In the middle of the night I wake to find Maurs sitting on the side of the bed. After a while I manage to persuade her to lie down again because what she is saying doesn't make a great deal of sense. It's as if she is talking in her sleep.

Although there's been another dramatic shift in Maurs' condition since the day before, she is reasonably coherent. As I help Maurs get dressed I notice the broken veins on her abdomen due to her swollen liver. But Maurs is still able to walk to the toilet and then to the couch without too much assistance.

I put the new Madonna CD, *ray of light*, on repeat and get half an hour of sitting in before the nurse from the City mission arrives. He says that someone will call in every day from now on. Maurs' humour is intact, and at one stage she tells him to be more straightforward when he's talking to her so she can understand what he's saying.

Realising that the end is near, even though I can hardly believe it, I ring a friend and say that I won't be visiting that afternoon as arranged. When the phone rings Maurs asks me to speak to callers as she is no longer capable of prolonged conversation.

Sarah Cathcart, the new artistic director of the Women's Circus, calls in with flowers and a poster with written messages from the womyn of the Women's Circus. "Do you want a cup of tea?" Maurs offers. Sarah says she doesn't as she's only staying for a moment. "You'd have to get it yourself," says Maurs.

Realising how serious the situation is, Sarah closes her eyes and stays quietly by Maurs' side for a couple of minutes. Till Maurs wants to know why it's so quiet and no-one is talking.

After Sarah has gone I sit next to Maurs on the couch, holding her hand and telling her I love her. "I love you, too," says Maurs. It feels as if time is standing still and there is just the two of us there on the couch. Around midday Maurs tries to light a cigarette, but the effort is too much and she never tries again. She still doesn't feel like eating anything but is drinking copious amounts of water.

Mary Daicos arrives, full of the Gay Games in Amsterdam, and shows us her photos of the trip. By the time Fran arrives in tears, I'm exhausted. After they've gone Maurs begins vomiting. I manage to get the bucket to her just in time.

Wendy Averil rings to say that there are any number of womyn who've offered to care for Maurs when the time comes.

By the end of the evening, Maurs has deteriorated even further. She keeps insisting she can get off the couch by her-self to go to bed, but it is obvious she can no longer co-ordinate her limbs to get them to do what she wants them to. Although she's lost a lot of weight, with her legs so swollen, she is too heavy for me to lift her even those few feet to the bed. She is conscious, but incoherent and disoriented.

I manage to manoeuvre Maurs so that she is lying down comfortably on the couch. I cover her with a blanket, kiss her good night and go to bed on my own for the first time in weeks. I keep waking every now and then and listen to make sure she is still breathing. Convinced that she might die at any moment, I want to be there if she does.

Thursday 24 September
It's a relief, then, to wake early on Thursday morning to hear Maurs is still breathing. When I go into the lounge-room she's wide awake, not nearly as zonked as she has been. She wants to sit up, which I help her do. While she understands what I say, gives me kisses, says she loves me and can converse in a limited way, she occasionally goes off on a brief but incomprehensible tangent of her own.

I put the Madonna CD on repeat, give Maurs her Kapanol and Droparadol, and settle in for however many days or hours or minutes we have left together. I'm not going anywhere and I don't have to do anything else but be here with this womyn whom I love with all my heart.

During sitting practice Maurs calls out, "Jean," and again, "Jean."

"Yes, darling?" I say.

"Are you on the toilet?"

"No, I'm sitting."

"All right."

A pause, "I love you," I say.

"I love you, too."

Noticing Maurs' yellow eyes, purple knuckles and red face, I get a damp face-washer. "Oh yes," says Maurs, taking it out of my hands, "give it to me." She wipes her face and then sits with it folded across her forehead.

Later on, as we're sitting next to each other on the couch I ask, "Do you know you're dying?"

"Yes, I do," says Maurs.

"Do you know when?"

"Soon."

We keep kissing each other every now and then and saying "I love you," as Madonna keeps on singing as she'd done all the previous day and looks set to do again today.

Maurs is hardly drinking any water at all and is having difficulty swallowing when she does take small sips. The Citymission nurse arrives and I explain that I want to make Maurs comfortable on the couch for the day. He doesn't have a problem with that. He administers a syringe of morphine both before we move her and again after we've finished to make sure she doesn't suffer any pain.

First, I gently wash Maurs all over with warm water. It's obvious Maurs is now incontinent so the nurse goes out to buy some large pads rather than put in a catheter. He gives me a hand to stand Maurs up while I dress her in a clean set of clothes, including the pink T-shirt that says "Lesbians Are Everywhere, Especially in Brisbane 1994". He also puts more padding on the sores on her bottom, which are much worse.

I strip all the urine-soaked covers off the couch, which isn't wet underneath as Maurs had been lying on a sheepskin during the night. I place the chair cushion in the middle of the couch, and put another sheepskin on top of it. Between us the nurse and I help Maurs position herself so she's sitting comfortably. He suggests that it might be easier if we put Maurs to bed tomorrow when he visits.

When I ask about the possibility of Maurs being able to get to the opening night of POW, he seems to think that any benefits would be outweighed by the stress and effort of getting there.

I've been looking forward to seeing POW's show with Maurs for so long that I'm reluctant to give it up. As I'm having a bit of a cry about this, Maurs takes my hand and says, "It's all right."

"How much longer do you think this will take?" I ask the nurse.

"To be brutally honest," he replies, "no more than a week."

"We'd rather know," says Maurs. Just like that.

After the nurse leaves, I put all the wet clothes and bedding in the washing machine. Then I sit beside Maurs on the couch, holding her hand. We give each other a kiss now and then and say "I love you," as I try to encompass all the implications of this latest development.

I ring Brian at work to let him know that Maurs is a lot worse than when he'd last seen her on Monday. He says he'll call in.

I continue to sit beside Maurs, taking phone calls as they come in. I don't want to leave Maurs' side for a minute. It is kind of womyn to offer to do the things I can't get round to doing at the moment.

Then Maurs says, "I'm finding it very hard to cope with everyone feeling sorry." And again, when I come back from putting the washing in the dryer, Maurs wants to know, "Where have you been?"

Maurs is not as out of it as she appears. She's drifting in and out of sleep, taking small sips of water, making strange statements out of the blue, but she knows me and what is happening whenever I say anything.

Susan Paxton arrives and we sit either side of Maurs on the couch as we all talk. Susan notices a bag of licorice on the coffee table that Mary had brought the day before and asks Maurs could she have a piece.

Maurs takes the piece Susan offers her and drapes it across her knee for a while before taking a bite off the end, which she then chews and chews for a long time. She puts on a Gay Games in Amsterdam cap that Mary had given her; I think, but don't say, that the yellow peak matches the colour of her saffron-coloured eyes.

After Susan leaves, I'm still sitting quietly on the couch holding Maurs' hand when Helen arrives. Maurs greets Helen with a kiss and tells her, "You'll be happy." Soon after this Maurs lapses into such a deep sleep it gives me a fright at first because it looks seriously like the end, till she relaxes back on the pillows still breathing with her eyes partly open. Helen says she'll go and get the mail in order to give us some time together.

"I'm going now," Helen says to Maurs, "but I'll be back."

"Yes," breathes Maurs.

Wendy Averil calls in a moment later with a cask of wine and a box of tissues to say she is going with Helen and will see us later.

I don't let go of Maurs' hand, just put my head on the pillow next to hers and say "I love you," every now and then. After a while I experience something that's hard to describe. There is some sensation in my chest and I feel very much at peace. It's so strong and unexpected I lift my head to try and understand what it is and it fades away.

Helen and Wendy come back with the mail. Fran arrives and makes everyone a cup of tea. We're sitting around chatting and laughing when I notice Maurs give a bit of a sigh. I look at Fran in shock and say, "Maurs just died."

I can't take my eyes off Maurs as she gives another couple of breaths (maybe she isn't dead, after all), suddenly closes her eyes and stops breathing. I'm stunned. Not only by the suddenness of this long-anticipated death, but by how peacefully Maurs has died and how she's allowed us all just to be there with her at the end.

I'm grateful that Maurs and I had that time to ourselves beforehand and yet it is almost as if she'd waited till the others came back so I'd have company when she did finally die. I lay my head next to hers on the pillow and cry.

It's 3.40 p.m.

12

The Funeral

Thursday 24 September

Events become a blur after that. I ring Brian but he's already left work. When he and Don do eventually arrive, it is odd to meet Maurs' long-lost brother for the first time as I'm sitting on the couch holding the hand of his recently deceased sister. Don smiles at me gently and I notice how strong he looks for someone who is so ill. Even though Brian had left work soon after I'd rung and gone to pick up Don straight away, their visit is too late.

As friends ring, they're shocked to hear that Maurs is dead. After dropping Don back home, Brian comes back and we begin discussing arrangements for the funeral. Maralann arrives after work to take Maurs' clown hat along to POW's opening performance that evening. By dying Maurs has up-staged everyone else well and truly. Someone rings from the warehouse in tears to say the performance is being dedicated to Maurs.

Neither Dr Patricia nor the Citymission doctor are available, so a locum eventually arrives to write out an interim death certificate. I ring Simplicity Funerals to get a quote for the simple kind of cremation Maurs has requested. Brian is more than willing to go along with any arrangements Maurs and I have discussed together.

The POW womyn ring after the performance to say how well it went and ask can they call in to see Maurs. It seems appropriate that they have the opportunity to say a final goodbye to this womyn who'd been there at the beginning and has contributed so much to POW over the previous three years.

It doesn't take long for the first womyn to trickle in and soon it is an avalanche of womyn sitting next to Maurs on the couch, squatting on the floor, paying their respects, reminiscing, crying, laughing and telling stories.

"Maurs is our ancestor now," comments Chris Sitka, someone I've known since the 1970s.

I say how important it is for me that Maurs had been as dedicated a grandmother to Sean as I am. "More dedicated," someone points out.

Claire Warren is the last to arrive. "You're even colder than Maurs," I say, when I touch her freezing hands.

By now Maurs' hands have become alabaster white, but with everyone holding and stroking them they are still relatively warm. I had thought of keeping Maurs overnight, but when the funeral parlour suggests she might begin to smell by the morning I realise I don't want to observe her physical deterioration any further than I have already.

I ring back and two men arrive to pick Maurs up at 12.30 a.m. She is placed in a plastic bag on a trolley with her face exposed. As she is wheeled down to the car with me sobbing, everyone else sings

> "Dear friend, dear friend,
> Let me tell you how I feel,

You have given me such pleasure,
I love you so."

They form an archway for her to be wheeled through and into the van. We circle the van and do the three traditional pre-performance whooshes to send Maurs on her way.

As we're still standing on the footpath, stunned and crying, Claire notices the number plate of the van. "Oh look," she exclaims. "O-L-C, Old Lesbians Club," at which we all crack up laughing. Everyone begins writing lesbian symbols and slogans in the mist on the back window, telling the driver it can't be washed off. He wants to know if Maurs will come back to haunt him if he does. It's the moment for the van with Maurs inside to be driven away.

Everyone gives me a group hug in the middle of the road, accompanies me back inside, makes cups of tea as we chat a bit more. Finally they leave. I wander around sobbing. Everywhere I look there are memories of Maurs. The pain of her absence is excruciating. How am I going to cope without her? How will I sleep tonight and subsequent nights, I wonder, as I get into bed, still crying, still agonising over the loss of Maurs, my most precious lover, the irredeemable fact of her death.

I turn on the cassette in the bedside radio—Pachelbel's Canon, my favourite—and turn out the light. "Hold me, Maurs," I request, "hold me," and am instantly asleep.

I'm awake at 6.00 a.m. Friday morning, refreshed after a surprisingly good night's sleep, but crying as soon as I open my eyes on a day without Maurs in it and beside me. Getting used to being on my own again after all these years of such loving company and memorable times together will be excruciatingly difficult, I realise. A day at a time, as Maurs would say.

Brian arrives and we divvie up the tasks. The arrangements Maurs had typed up are simple:

1. Plain coffin so womyn can decorate it.
2. Most of my ashes to be scattered at Gariwerd (the Grampians) a small portion to be scattered on my mother's grave and some to be scattered in Jean's back-yard.
3. No photos of me in my coffin.
4. No religious service.
5. Womyn are allowed to speak.
6. Anah Holland-Moore to pull the service together.
7. My brother Brian, Geoff and Victor are to be allowed to speak if they want to.
8. Flowers.
9. Notice in the papers.
10. Articles *Lesbiana* / *Lesbian Network* / *Melbourne Star Observer* / *Brother/Sister*.
11. Music.

When I ring the funeral parlour and ask can I collect the coffin to paint it, expecting to have to argue the case, the undertaker merely wants to know when I can pick it up. As I say to Thelma Solomon when I ring to ask her to collect the coffin, "Did the world change when I wasn't looking?"

I try ringing Kristi in Helsingborg several times, to no avail. Eventually I get on to Geoff in Barcelona who is distressed about Maurs and concerned about me. I leave a message on Marg's answering machine in Munich.

When Thelma and Maureen Gie arrive at my house with the coffin I'm impressed. Even though it's made of chipboard, it's stained a warm brown, with aluminium handles on the sides and screws on the top. It looks exactly like a proper coffin complete with a plaque with Maureen O'Connor etched into it on the lid. We leave it sitting on the coffee table in the front room.

I drive back to the flat because it's where Maurs is. It's where I cry. It's here that I talk to Maurs, tell her what I'm doing, referring to her as I've always done. Her presence permeates every square inch of this flat. It's here that I know I'll do my immediate and gut-wrenching grieving.

Kristi rings first thing Saturday morning because she's heard the news from Geoff. We cry together. Over the last months of her life Maurs faced her inevitable death with courage and humour and became more herself with every passing day. She was compassionate and magnificent to the end.

By one o'clock, I'm back at my house with several tubes of acrylic paints for the painting of the coffin. I make a start by painting a large purple labrys just beneath the nameplate, and under that a red and yellow lesbian symbol. When the others begin to arrive, we rest the lid on milk crates in the backyard and sit around it to create the best-looking coffin lid imaginable.

We set the coffin up on the dining-room table and create more images, making it her very own. I begin to feel a great deal better in myself and realise this is an extremely important thing to do. We're not only actively engaged in something useful and worthwhile, but we're demystifying the processes of death and making a claim for lesbian community in our own way.

Susan Paxton arrives with her son Tsari to give me a lift to POW's closing night.What I enjoy most about the performance is that I can sit there in my front-row seat and be entertained. I just wish that Maurs had lived long enough to see it and that we could have gone together.

Back at my house, it's another beautiful sunny day. Between the womyn sitting around the coffin lid outside and those surrounding the coffin inside, the creativity starts to resemble some kind of lesbian get-together.

Almost forty lesbians call in over the two days to put their own particular mark on Maurs' coffin. This is the first time any of us have ever painted a coffin. By the end of the day, Maurs has a coffin we're all proud of. It's colourful; the images reflect Maurs' life, from circus balances to techie gear; and a great deal of love and care has gone into the painting of every one of them.

I'm awake early, remembering some of the good times we had together over these past few months. It hasn't all been pain and suffering. I used to wonder if I'd be able to last the distance. What if Maurs lingered for several weeks in a coma and bedridden? How would I cope? Would I still be able to give her the same level of love and support I was giving her now, or would I find it too much? How would I manage on my own after Maurs died? How would I cope emotionally? Would I be able to organise the funeral to do justice to her courage and her lesbian life?

I'm moving through the hours, doing what I have to do, making the motions, all the while conscious that the next main thing is organising the funeral and making sure all the arrangements are in place.

I sort the clothes Maurs will wear in the coffin: blue jeans, leather belt, dark blue T-shirt with "LESBIANS do it best" on the front, knickers, red-checked flannel shirt (one of her favourites) and the 53rd birthday socks I'd knitted her most recently. Even though Maurs had requested to be cremated in shorts and singlet, she didn't actually write this down and I find I can't quite bring myself to leave her looking so vulnerable. I also include the "Stick With Wik" arm band, a symbol of the support Maurs gave to the Aboriginal and

Islanders' ongoing struggle for Land Rights, after the High Court ruled in favour of the Wik people retaining their rights to Native Title.

When Brian and I get to my house to talk with the undertaker, there is a big bunch of native flowers on the doorstep from Kristi, Dan and Sean, and Geoff and Anita, plus a bunch of lilies from Anita's family. How wonderful! Marg rings briefly from Munich to pass on her condolences.

After Brian leaves, Helen arrives and she and I carry the coffin out to the funeral parlour van and take photos of it going off to meet up with Maurs in all its splendour. Then I sit in the backyard while Helen cuts my hair, which has grown a great deal over these past weeks, right back to next to nothing again with the electric clippers. I not only feel, but I now also look, like the grieving widow I am.

Barb Anthony rings from Edinburgh and we chat about everything that's been happening. She tells me she's been thinking of us both and grieving.

Having decided to do some more work on *The C-Word* today before I lose too many of the details of these last crowded days, it feels good to be sitting here at the computer (with Maurs in spirit). A lot has happened since I last wrote. Everything, in fact.

Anah arrives and we sit in the backyard discussing the arrangements for both ceremonies the following day. By the end of two cups of tea, we figure that everything seems to be taken care of and what isn't will, no doubt, leave room for spontaneity on the day.

Wednesday 30 September
Susan Paxton arrives to take me to the crematorium. I dislike being the centre of attention; to be the focus of everyone's

sympathy and condolences is overwhelming. But after a while I realise that with the dozens of hugs and kisses I'm actually being carried along and supported by all this combined energy.

I introduce my brother Victor to Brian and Don. The memorial cards have Maurs' photo (taken by Geoff on the day he flew out to Barcelona) and the words "A woman of remarkable courage. Generous, open hearted and loving. She gave the best hugs!" They are handed out to everyone along with sprigs of lavender. When it is our turn to go in to the Cordell Chapel, any number of womyn are ready and willing to carry Maurs in her splendid coffin.

Maralann and I unscrew the lid and set it against the wall. While I stand on the far side, stroking Maurs' hair, a long line of womyn come up and place their lavender on Maurs' chest; some cry and others murmur words of farewell. It takes me a moment to realise that her whiskers, which have been part of her appearance for so long, have been shaved off. I'm thunderstruck.

When Anah announces I will speak first, I begin by briefly thanking everyone. I include the absent family members, mentioning them all by name and saying how much they loved her and she them. I finish by placing the six flowers that I had taken from the bunch they'd sent me in the coffin with Maurs to symbolise their love.

I read a piece from *The C-Word* as Maurs had asked me to do and expand it to talk about some of the good times we'd spent together over the years and these last days in particular. The first gift Maurs ever gave me was a bunch of yellow roses for my forty-sixth birthday, I explain, as I place the roses in the coffin.

Brian speaks next, giving a humorous overview of his sister's life and a generous acknowledgement of my role as

Maurs' partner. Then Fran, between tears, sums up other aspects of Maurs' life.

Anah then invites everyone to sing "Dear Friend" as we spiral round the coffin in a final farewell. Just before we put the lid on and screw it down, I give Maurs a final kiss. Another six womyn carry Maurs out to the hearse. Outside, we form a huge circle around Maurs and the van. We give three whooshes, and then the van, with Maurs in her magnificent coffin, drives slowly down the path, round the corner and out of our lives forever.

Joan Russell and I get a lift back to the warehouse with Brian. We agree that, as funerals go, it's the best we've ever been to and that Maurs would have been pleased.

Ursula and other friends from the Circus have arranged the space beautifully with lilies, photos, burners, candles and altars. The food and drink is laid out in the other room. It's hard to credit that the last time I was here, only four days ago, it was still set up for POW's performance.

We gather in the Pit theatre space with Anah once again doing the introductions. I lead off with the palm tai chi. Chris Sitka reads out a prepared eulogy that honours Maurs as an ancestor. Then Brian speaks briefly about the need to take care of me in the same way everyone had taken care of Maurs. It's so rare for the lesbian community to get such support from a relative that he exits to (almost) a standing ovation.

The Women's Circus aerialists pay tribute to Maurs as they hang from trapezes, ropes and cloud swings and do their routines in slow motion to music.

We sing the POW song that Pat Rooney wrote for the show last year. Both Coleen Clare and Trish Sykes read the poems they'd written for and given to Maurs.

It's an open mike as womyn go up one at a time to pay tribute to Maurs and tell their usually amusing stories about their experiences with her over the years they've known her.

The fax from Kristi arrives and I read it out. "Our two-year-old grandson has also sent a fax," I say, which brings a laugh: "To dearest Nana-Maurs . . ."

It's late by the time we move outside to take a small tree in a pot down to the Maribyrnong River. I set a light to the messages on bits of paper tied onto the branches so they rise up in smoke and ashes to become part of the ether. Afterwards, we all throw dozens of flowers into the river, which are borne downstream, in a slow-moving and colourful expression of our communal grief.

I kiss everyone goodbye and Susan drives me back to the flat. We put the flowers in water: two purple, green and white bunches combined look stunning set up in the bucket. It's a creative use for it, considering the number of times Maurs used it for vomiting.

It's been nearly a week already since Maurs died.

When I wake on Thursday morning I still feel so exhausted from the events of yesterday that I take it easy for the rest of the day.

As I hang the painted chair in Savers' window for the Window Works exhibition, I feel a pang that Maurs, who always supported and encouraged my artistic endeavours, is no longer here to share in the excitement of this one. She never saw the finished product because she'd been too ill to even call into my house during the last weeks.

Friday 2 October
Helen arrives just before Fran and her partner and we head off to Geelong. We get to the crematorium and find a comfortable possie under a small tree near the dam. I set up Ursula's ceramic altar that she gave me after Maurs died,

and light the candle for the first time. Appropriate, I think. We light more candles and as the others, Jan Gladys, Chris Sitka, Anah Holland-Moore and Marie Andrews gather, we tell stories about the first time we'd met Maurs and how significant she'd been in our lives.

There has been no activity at the crematorium to speak of. We can't actually see Maurs at all, not even her coffin, but it is important for us to be here so that she doesn't make this final journey on her own.

We take a couple of flowers each and toss them into the dam, where they float in an array of purple, green, yellow and white, before being gently swept out over the water by the wind.

Two swans fly overhead. "Oh look, there's Jean and Maurs," Jan says.

We sit on the grass at the Aboriginal Cultural Centre just up the road and share Fran's sandwiches before making our way home.

That evening, after the opening of Window Works at the Mechanics Institute, I walk up Sydney Road in light rain to view the artworks in the shop windows. I'm sad that I'm not pushing Maurs in her wheelchair so we can enjoy this occasion together as we have so often before. The pain of her loss is terrible. How am I ever going to get through all this?

In *Everyday Zen*, Joko reiterates the point that to give up hope that life is going to be any way other than it is makes for good practice.

I haven't voted for years. Instead, I write political slogans on my election ballot papers before meeting Brian at the flat. When he leaves he takes his computer and a few other bits and pieces away with him. It is the beginning of the dismantling of the flat. However, once I'm on my own I find it difficult to contemplate shifting any of Maurs' precious possessions.

The Federal election result that evening with the conservative Liberal government returned for another term is the expected, dismal outcome.

When I get back to the flat later that afternoon, after having nearly completed the bare-bones draft of *The C-Word*, I play the videotape of Maurs that we filmed back in December. I'm surprised that, instead of the dread and tears that I'd expected, as soon as I see Maurs' image on the screen I'm grinning and extremely delighted to see and hear her again. How strange. I suppose it brings her back in a way nothing else can and I'm very glad to have it.

In between washing and drying Maurs' clothes, I also slowly do some more sorting and packing.

Womyn are still keeping in touch. I tell them that once everything is cleared away I'll be able to make books and ceramics and other things available to anyone who wants to have them as mementos of Maurs.

It's very hard. Wherever I look there's a memory of Maurs, and I find myself in tears at the thought of having to move anything at all. As I've run out of warm clothes, I'm now wearing one of Maurs' long-sleeved shirts.

Well, that's that, I realise after a few more hours at the computer; the book is up to date at long last. Now I can begin to consider making a start on the several articles I want to write to commemorate Maurs according to her instructions.

In the mail today, there's the galley proof of a short story, "The Definition of a Lesbian", that I'd sent to a periodical in the United States, over two years ago. It is going to be published; after all this time I'd given up on it.

Before we go out for an Indian dinner in Lygon Street that evening, my brother Victor goes through Maurs' bookcases, as she'd promised him he could do, and takes away an impressive array of books. So I give him my small bookcase for good measure. This is something about Maurs that not a lot of people realise: she has an abundance of books on an eclectic and comprehensive range of subjects, from murder mysteries to *The Recognition of Aboriginal Customary Laws*.

I still can't settle to reading anything as long as a book. I can't bring myself to go out anywhere either. All I want to do is be on my own so I can cry as much as I like.

However, I make a start on a portrait of Maurs for the Lesbian Art Works exhibition, and post the first eulogy for the *Women's Circus Newsletter*. Womyn are still ringing in to make sure I'm all right and sending cards.

On Wednesday, not only do I still feel immobilised with grief, but it's raining and I wake with the beginnings of a cold.

I'm still vacillating between wanting everything that belonged to Maurs and wanting nothing of hers. Because Maurs is dead, her flat has become a sacred place, a shrine.

At tai chi class it feels good to be moving my body to the familiar forms. As I get into bed, I finally accept that it is a humane thing that Maurs has died because she suffered a great deal all this year. Too much, between the disease itself and the barbaric treatment.

On Thursday, 8 October, International Lesbian Day, I wake feeling a whole lot better about everything. Maurs isn't suffering any more, a rooster is crowing, the birds still twittering on the tree outside the bedroom window which has more leaves by the day, and the gas, which has been cut off for days due to an industrial accident, is being reconnected this afternoon.

Then Brian rings to tell me that Don died suddenly this morning. How must Brian feel with both his siblings dead within a fortnight of each other? Yet his voice on the phone seems quite calm.

I'm crying and crying with the pain of missing Maurs when I get into bed.

I'm still finding it extremely difficult to pack Maurs' stuff. So I go to see the Australian film *Radiance* at the Nova, as Maurs and I had planned to do.

"Your friend's not with you today?" the usher comments, as she takes my ticket. Maurs and I have been to the Nova so often over the past months that I'm not surprised; indeed, I'm touched that she mentions Maurs.

"Actually, she died. She was very sick and died."

"Oh dear, and you're here all on your own." She is full of sympathy.

This has me sobbing by the time I get to my seat in the darkened and almost empty theatre.

I cannot believe that Maurs, who was always so alive and amusing, making me laugh, is actually dead. It's the terrible absence that's hardest to bear. An absence that just goes on and on, like an unrelenting horror.

It seems as if the initial shock has worn off because I feel such pain, more pain that I've felt before. As we move the furniture out of the flat, all I can do is cry. With these bits and pieces going out the door, it is as if I'm losing Maurs all over again.

I buy fish and chips and the *Age* for tea and settle on the couch with a blanket over me to write in my journal.

On Sunday I decide to stay at the flat all day as we used to do. I spend the next few hours sorting some of Maurs' papers, cards and letters, and reading an old journal Maurs kept years ago, which moves me a great deal. It gives me a broader sense of the kind of womyn Maurs was, I'm delighted she hadn't got rid of it.

I'm left feeling drained and sore by it all and missing Maurs extremely. The journal confirms that I was lucky to have been lovers with such a remarkable womyn who, despite the issues that she never really came to grips with, was a loving and compassionate lesbian in every sense.

I'm crying again as I go for a couple of laps of the oval, in the lightly falling rain.

I go through the motions, full of pain and misery. That's all I can do.

I open a new disk and a new file on the computer to recap the last ten days of Maurs' life, her death, the funeral, the cremation and whatever else to send to Geoff and Kristi and Marg and give to Victor.

All I really want to do is slowly clear out the flat, grieve, and write it all out, as much as possible.

Kristi rings and I talk to Sean.

I've been thinking of visiting them next winter for four or five months perhaps; I'll return in time for the Lesbian Festival in Adelaide in September, and have some kind of memorial for Maurs on the first anniversary of her death, which falls during those eight days.

I drive to the Fawkner Cemetery an hour early for Don's funeral to have a cry in private, because this was the last place that I saw Maurs in her coffin being driven away. I sit next to Brian in the same front row, in the same Cordell Chapel, at the same time, organised by the same funeral parlour.

I'm there to support Brian and represent Maurs, but the feelings all rush back. To my surprise, probably because I'm here in different and less emotionally demanding circumstances, I can let it all flow over me while I revisit the ceremony we'd had for Maurs. I couldn't appreciate it on the day because it was all too overwhelming.

I can sense the chapel full to overflowing with our friends, hear their voices singing "Dear Friend", see their tear-stained faces, and my own responses as I touched Maurs for those last moments in her open coffin.

The undertaker gives me Maurs' ashes afterwards, this time I am able to take her home with me.

I don't know if it's the warmer weather, or having Maurs' ashes, or that three weeks have passed since Maurs died, or being there at Don's funeral, or writing it all out, or a combination of everything, but today I'm feeling better. I'm still crying at the drop of a hat, still numb, still finding it difficult packing everything up, still missing Maurs, and I still keep forgetting things. But after all the pain of the past nine months Maurs is much better off wherever she is.

I'm still sorting, sorting, sorting because I've sent out word that the flat is an open house for the next two afternoons and I want womyn to take away as much stuff as they can.

We sit around and chat over cups of tea. Although quite a bit of stuff is taken—and there are no hassles about who is going to take what—there is still an inordinate amount of it left by the end of the day.

On Sunday afternoon, as happened the day before, everyone seems delighted with what they are taking away with them and it isn't nearly as painful to see things go as it was last weekend.

Both afternoons have been great social occasions and I seem to have more energy.

Thursday 31 December
It took me five painfilled weeks to clear out the flat before handing in the key. The only thing that no-one wanted to take was the battered old couch.

The couch that Maurs died on.

Appropriate really, I thought, as I did my final tai chi in that bare flat I'd just cleaned, facing the couch where Maurs was still very much in spirit, the tears running down my cheeks.

The following day I caught a bus to Mildura in north-west Victoria for the Lake Primary School reunion. I returned several days later to get my house into some semblance of order in time for a party to make me feel at home again.

The first of the Aboriginal plays, *White Baptist Abba Fan*, which I went to with Helen Robertson, was the most difficult because I kept thinking that Maurs would have loved it. Especially as the performer Deborah Cheetham, said that her aunt, whom she mentioned during the performance (and quite unbeknown to me), is the singer Betty Little who was billeted with Maurs during the Lesbian Festival here in Melbourne in 1990.

I bought the tickets for these plays as insurance that Maurs would still be alive to see them. I saw Leah Purcell in *Box the Pony* with Jean Ferguson, and *Stolen* with Brian at the Malthouse. Brian's kindness and consideration has been a great comfort. We intend to continue to keep in touch and have been out together a few times, as well as to see the Women's Circus show, *The Soles of Our Feet*. He reminds me of Maurs and not only because they look alike.

I didn't do front of house for the Women's Circus this year.

It seems my circus days are over. But I went to the clean-up day down at the performance space in Williamstown to leave candles and other memorabilia for Maurs, did overnight security with the Book Crew and was there for the dress rehearsal. I saw the show, which was dedicated to Maurs, several times, and had dinner with the performers and Tech Crew beforehand.

It was a very emotional time for me because these Women's Circus shows were something Maurs and I had enjoyed together since 1991. I gave myself plenty of time to grieve. Even so, on closing night I found I was broken-hearted all over again at the loss of these tremendous times —the sense of community, the fun, the creative passion— Maurs and I had shared.

I put the portrait of Maurs in the Lesbian Art Works exhibition at the Mechanics Institute and read my cancer poems at the performance finale of the Art Works a couple of weeks later.

I continued to sit for an hour every morning and to go to tai chi class once a week. I tidied up the story of Maurs from her fifty-third birthday onwards and sent copies to Geoff, Kristi, Marg and Victor so they'd know what had happened during Maurs' last days and her funeral.

I wrote and presented a paper, "Feminism the Theory, Lesbianism the Practice: Lesbians and the Women's Liberation Movement in Victoria during the '70s", at the Australian Homosexual Histories conference at the University of Melbourne. I wrote several eulogies for Maurs which were published with photos.[1]

---

[1] *Women's Circus Newsletter* (Showtime 1998), *Lesbiana* (November 1998, December 1998), *Melbourne Star Observer* (30 October 1998), *Brother/Sister* (12 November 1998), *Lesbian Network* (Summer Solstice), and *Lesbians on the Loose* (December 1998).

A growth on my neck, which I'd been picking at, got so bad that eventually I saw a doctor about it—a new doctor, because Dr Patricia had resigned. She referred me to a specialist who wanted to take it off at once and send it for a biopsy. Dreaded words. I wouldn't let him and it cleared up over the next few weeks by itself.

I was not looking forward to Christmas. But Geoff and Anita returned a few days beforehand and I didn't even regret having to hand the car back because just having my son back in the country immediately eased the pain and loss.

Barb Anthony returned from Edinburgh with Deb Ball, and I caught up with her a couple of weeks later at Jan Gladys' housewarming at Barwon Heads. She was looking good, considering her hair had started to fall out with the chemo and she's even thinner than usual.

Mary Daicos said I could have the small table she'd lent to Maurs for my backyard. I painted it with the images I had painted on the coffin as a way of keeping the images and memories alive and called it "Mo(u)rning Maurs".

I wrote three short stories about Maurs, a trilogy, and sent them off for the Women's Library short story competition in Sydney. I finished *Behind Enemy Lines*. And I started a Women's Liberation Movement activist project: a compilation of all the activist groups, collectives, conferences, books, actions and events that made up the Women's Liberation Movement during the 1970s (there had to be a reason the archives were still at my place).

I was still spending heaps of time on my own, because I wanted to, because I needed to, so I could grieve lots and be with Maurs.

Tonight, as I haven't been invited anywhere, I intend to do all the things Maurs and I did last year on our own; a counter tea and a Guinness at a local pub, and a champagne on the way home from seeing *Waking Ned Devine*. Maurs and I didn't see a film last New Year's Eve but we've seen so many over these last months that it feels right.

Life without Maurs is strange, different. There's still a long way to go.

13
1999

Monday 8 March

I realise it's going to take me a long time to get used to being on my own again, without Maurs to add substance and laughter and companionship and love to my days. I still cry every day. Usually it's triggered by something—a piece of music, an event, a memory, the thought of scattering Maurs' ashes.

I continued doing the Women's Liberation Movement activist project throughout January. It was something not too demanding and at the same time worthwhile to keep me occupied. I went to a few of the Gay and Lesbian Midsumma Festival events that Maurs and I used to attend together, like the opening night Street Party, the Silk and Satin Ball, the Lesbian and Gay Pride March and Carnival.

I wrote a short story about the day Maurs died and read it out at (Not so) Rapid Fire, a book-reading organised by the gay and lesbian bookshop Hares and Hyenas. I went to a Buddhist Summer School to learn more about Zen practice. The carer's pension ran out and I had to reapply for the dole.

I started painting another kitchen chair with images similar to the table and the coffin, calling it Maureen's Chair. When I applied to put it into the International Women's Day exhibition, Women '99, at the Mechanics Institute, the curator used the image of the chair, in bright red, yellow and blue, for the invitations. This pleased me no end because it was another memorial to Maurs.

I was saddened to hear that Marianne Permezel was diagnosed with metastasised cancer in her liver and lung, and went to the fundraiser that Ursula organised—a benefit similar to Maurs' in 1996 to raise money so Marianne could attend Ian Gawler's intensive residential retreat.

I booked a plane ticket to fly to Copenhagen on Tuesday, 30 March, to stay with Kristi, Sean and Dan in Sweden for at least three months. Realising it would still be quite cold in Sweden, I stopped cutting my hair in preparation for going away.

According to Maurs' wishes, Brian and I had scattered some of her ashes on her mother's grave in the new year. The thought of leaving the rest of the ashes behind when I left for overseas was untenable, so I began making arrangements for the womyn's ceremony at Gariwerd in western Victoria on 27 March.

I wrote to the traditional owners based at the Brambuk Centre, respectfully letting them know our intentions of scattering Maurs' ashes at Gariwerd National Park and asking if they had any objections or otherwise to let me know in advance.

Saturday 27 March
Jean Ferguson, Barb Anthony, Deb Ball and I drove up yesterday. After we'd booked into the caravan park we headed off to look at likely locations to scatter Maurs' ashes. The ranger

at the information centre told me that Burrong Falls would be a quiet and discreet place to hold the ceremony.

As soon as we got there, it seemed ideal. There was a space next to the car park with a table, a fireplace, and enough space for the twenty or thirty womyn I expected would come. The walk to the waterfall itself took ten minutes and was not too difficult to negotiate. We four spent some time there taking in the beautiful surrounds, the waterfall, rocks, bush and red flowers. I was rapt. Maurs would be happy with this final resting place. We called into Reid's lookout on the way back to admire the gold and purple sunset along the rocky outcrops and the misty purple hills on the horizon.

After a restful night's sleep we begin gathering at the Brambuk Centre at about 1.00 p.m. (where I have a wattle-tree-seed damper in the café) before we meet outside in the large stone circle, all thirty-four of us. We hold hands and remind ourselves we are on Aboriginal land.

As we drive in convoy to Burrong Falls, it starts to rain. Dressed in wet-weather gear and holding umbrellas, we form a circle; as each womyn holds the basket with Maurs' ashes, she says a few words or stands quietly before passing it on. I then uncover the ashes and the basket is passed round the circle again so everyone can become familiar with the appearance of the ashes before we go down the the falls to scatter them.

Some womyn elect to stay and scatter some ashes in the surrounding bush while the rest of us trail down in single file to the waterfall. Soon there are womyn dotted on rocks, squatting by the falls, under the trees and all around, taking handfuls of Maurs' ashes to toss into the rain-filled air. They mingle with the water as it falls to the earth, the finer particles blown back into the air like a fine mist.

We stand quietly and remember our times with Maurs in

our own personal ways. It is the company of these splendid lesbians, I can't help thinking, that is making it possible for me to be here doing this, letting go of the comfort of Maurs' ashes before I fly out in a couple of days' time. At times like this I appreciate how fortunate I am to be a lesbian and part of such a creative and diverse and supportive community.

We head back up the slope to where a fire is already blazing, and we stand around drying ourselves and keeping warm as we consume the food and drink we've brought with us. Deb Ball has been taking a video of the whole event and several others are taking photos.

On the way home, we stop off at Bunjil's Shelter. Just standing in front of this Aboriginal rock art, I am in awe of the creative conection with this land that goes back so many thousands of years. Back in the car, Jean Ferguson, Deb and I discover that all three of us, unbeknown to each other back then, had been at Greenham Common in December 1983 and took part in the protest action of holding hands round the cruise missile base along with the several thousands of other womyn. The womyn who were camped there on a daily basis were doing so under the most challenging of conditions in the middle of winter and yet there was a sense of resistance and achievement that sustained the protesters for the many years they were there.

This farewell to Maurs has been a momentous occasion, all the lesbians who've made the effort to be here for the weekend or for the day, paying our respects to the Koori people to start with, the magnificent beauty of Gariwerd, and Burrong Falls, which has now become connected with Maurs in an indelible way, the simple and appropriate ceremony that unfolded as we went along—even the rain. It has all melded into something that we can keep as a significant reference point forever.

Tuesday 30 March

I'm up early and crying as I scatter the remainder of Maurs' ashes in my backyard to fulfil the last of her requests. I fly out this afternoon. I'm looking forward to seeing Kristi and Sean and yet still emotionally engaged with the powerful events over the weekend.

Friday 31 December

The overseas trip was much more demanding and at the same time more empowering than I'd expected.

During my time in Sweden I read in the July issue of *Lesbiana* (the editor was posting them to me) that Marianne Permezel had died on 7 June. This devastated me as I'd fully expected to see her again when I got back. This unexpected news made me wonder if Barb Anthony was okay as I spent that afternoon writing an obituary for the next *Lesbiana* and crying. It helped when friends wrote and told me about Marianne's final days and how splendid her funeral had been and that I could see the video of it when I got back. And that Barb was okay.

Apart from the three months I spent with Kristi, Dan and Sean in Sweden, I also visited Paris, my sister Marg in Munich for three weeks and my relatives in Belfast, before flying to the United States for the last five weeks of the trip.

I arrived back in Melbourne on a Friday morning. Two days later I caught a bus to Adelaide for the Lesbian ConFest, which started on Monday, 20 September. It was exactly what I needed to do after being away for so long: reconnect with the community and have the support and company of friends for the first anniversary of Maurs' death.

It all worked out as I'd expected. I went to a few workshops. We viewed Deb's video of the scattering of Maurs' ashes. I sat at 6.00 a.m. every morning in the hall. There were any number of lesbians there who knew the significance of this time and responded accordingly.

On the morning of Friday, 24 September, some of us watched the video again before heading outside to hold a candle ceremony in memory of Maurs and to exchange stories of other lesbians and family who had also died. I spent the afternoon on my own. That evening I introduced the acts of the concert I'd organised as well as reading the short story about the day Maurs died.

When I returned, I was so glad to be back in my little house again after six months away that I haven't moved since. The main thing, I figured, was to work out how to live my life on my own now that I was over the most painful part of the grieving for Maurs.

I was mightily relieved that Barb Anthony was still alive when I got back. In fact, I'd rung Jean Ferguson from San Diego to get the latest update because I didn't want to land back in the country to sad news. On the contrary, it seemed Barb was well, although the ravages of the disease were taking their toll.

I began spending as much time with Barb as her busy schedule allowed, sharing her with four grown-up children, a mother and several ex-lovers as well as friends. We had a number of enjoyable lunches together, with me supplying the food, at her Housing Commission flat in Agg Street. "I wish Maurs was here to see this flat," Barb said, "she'd have been pleased for me."

One evening, we watched the video of Maurs' funeral with Deb and Jean Ferguson (because all of them had been overseas on that day) as well as the video of the scattering of Maurs' ashes. Then we watched a video of the previous year's Women's Circus show, *The Soles of Our Feet*.

Barb was pleased for me that Spinifex Press had agreed to

publish *The C-Word*. As it seemed unlikely that Barb would live to see it published, I gave her my copy, asking that she not let anyone else read it as it was still in draft form. She had time to give it a quick look through and to like what she'd read and had no objections to anything I'd written.

Then there was Barb's splendid fiftieth birthday party on 5 November where we put on a circus act for her benefit, "Barb, this is your circus life", and where Barb stayed dancing and socialising till 5.30 a.m. Barb had been determined to make it to her fiftieth, despite medical predictions that she might not. It was a relief to all of us that she not only achieved this but romped it in.

At the opening of the Lesbian Art Works exhibition the following night, Barb sold so many of her drawings she realised she could afford to visit Uluru, a long-held ambition. Barb didn't actually make it to Uluru, but the achievement of being able to afford to do so with her own finances was a satisfaction in itself.

Our last outing together was to the opening night of the Women's Circus show, *Lilith*, on 18 November.

The following day Barb was admitted to the Peter Mac and stayed there for eleven days before returning home to a 24-hour roster of friends and family to care for her.

I was rostered on all day Saturday, 4 December. Barb was in bed, unable to do much more than lie there and take everything in, her wide grin and sense of humour much in evidence. We talked and laughed and reminisced as we'd always done and I was glad to be there with her.

By the time I was leaving to go across to Williamstown for the closing night and bump out party of the Women's Circus show (where I'd been doing a bit of front of house), I was relieved and extremely pleased that we'd had those few hours together.

The following day, I rang to hear that Barb had gone into a coma at about midday. Jean Ferguson rang me just before midnight to let me know that Barb had died peacefully at about 20 to 11 that evening.

Barb's funeral was organised by her family and held on Wednesday at the gay and lesbian Metropolitan Community Church. I was glad to see the self-portrait Barb had painted, showing the butterfly tattoo over the site of the mastectomy, leaning against the coffin when I arrived.

Before Barb's death I went to the Field of Women day at the Melbourne Cricket Ground organised by the Breast Cancer Network. I went partly to be there to support Barb and partly to acknowledge my own grief about losing Maurs to cancer. As there's no comparable public recognition of ovarian cancer this was the next best thing.

A week later, I attended a forum about ovarian cancer at the Mercy Hospital, the first of its kind, organised by a worker at the Mercy. Her mother was having chemotherapy for ovarian cancer and was one of the speakers. Several doctors (all male) also spoke, emphasising how difficult it is to detect ovarian cancer till it is advanced, as the symptoms in the early stages are not distinctive enough for any confirmable diagnosis. As early detection is the main defence against cancer, this confirmed what I already knew, that ovarian cancer is one of the most deadly cancers.

It is likely to remain so for some time because, of course, there's not enough money for research to find a means by which ovarian cancer can be accurately diagnosed as soon as it manifests. Ovarian cancer only affects 1 in 75 womyn (compared to breast cancer's much higher risk of 1 in 15) and the ovaries are not accessible like the breasts and the cervix, both of which have had well publicised early detection campaigns for some time. But "ovarian cancer is still one of the major causes of death from malignancy in women in our community," according to *Mercy Matters*.[1]

I saw the film *In a Savage Land*, set in Papua New Guinea in the late 1930s. Two married white anthropologists have gone to study the behaviour and customs of the Indigenous cultures. Part-way through the film the husband dies and at his funeral, in reference to the local custom for widows to be placed in a cage to grieve, his wife calls out, "Build me a cage."

Before she enters the bamboo cage, bare-breasted and dressed in the traditional grass skirt, the womyn has her head shaved. By this time I was crying. A cage was just what I'd needed after Maurs died. Public acknowledgement that all I wanted and needed was a place where I could grieve to my heart's content. At least, I'd cut off my hair.

On the Wednesday following Barb's funeral, I was still coming to terms with Barb's death—the last few weeks of her life brought up all my grief around Maurs too, of course—when I heard from Pat Rooney that the lump she'd found in her breast, in the lead-up to the Women's Circus show, was malignant. Pat had postponed having the biopsy done till she'd completed playing with the music group in the show, which included her being raised to the ceiling in a harness during the finale.

By the following Thursday, two days before Christmas, Pat was having surgery to remove the lump and a number of lymph nodes in her left armpit (but not her breast). It was recommended that she start chemotherapy as soon as possible. Then radiotherapy. It looks as if Pat will need a great deal of support from the LCSG and the rest of the lesbian community into the new millennium. Whenever I

---

[1] Issue no. 30, September 1999.

ran into Jean Gardner during my visits to Pat at the Peter Mac, I was reminded of all the pain-filled months I'd been through with Maurs, and could appreciate everything Jean was doing to support Pat under similar circumstances.

As for the rest, I'm still not inclined to pick up my activist work where I left off at the end of 1997. But I did call a meeting of interested womyn, to start a campaign to move the Women's Liberation and Lesbian Archives out of my house and to form a committed group to take responsibility for the work that needs to be done.

I'm writing a few short stories and the adventures of Sean Daniel in Sweden, as well as a bit more of the 1970s Women's Liberation Movement activism project I started last year and whatever else takes my fancy. I have drafted an article for the website of the LCSG, and I'm playing with the idea of a film script, *One Day at a Time*.

Today, I'm trying to finalise this book, which has not only had me in thrall now for nearly three years but has been a great source of comfort and support. I'm just back from lunch with Geoff and Anita over at their place. And while there have been several offers of New Year's Eve parties, I'm off soon to catch the free all-night public transport, calling in to visit Pat Rooney at the Peter Mac on the way through, to see in the new year with a few friends.

And above all, to see in the millennium for and with Maurs, who is still very much in my heart.

Afterword

What more can I say?

Maurs and my relationship was not perfect, we didn't always see eye to eye (although we hardly ever argued about anything). We both of us had our own fears and insecurities to contend with and we didn't always deal with the things that needed to be dealt with.

But oh, our love for each other and our togetherness was amazing.

We shared some of the best of the lesbian community times together and in sharing we expanded our awareness and sense of fun.

Maurs gave an altogether different perspective and balance to my otherwise quite narrow and specific views on life. And she kept me up to date with popular culture and world events.

It was a combination of humour, down-to-earth practicality, working-class sensibility, warmth, love, hugs, compassion, kindness, laughter, lesbian sexuality, vulnerability and capacity for enjoyment that made Maurs so lovable.

We had in common our middle age, working-class background and values, Irish-Scottish heritage, and we saw our mothers in each other. We were both members of the Women's Circus and POW Circus. We worked on umpteen events and went to innumerable occasions together. Maurs introduced me to murder mysteries and music and got me painting again. And we danced.

We didn't share my love of writing or travel. However, Maurs encouraged my writing no end; she read (practically) everything I ever wrote and was unstinting in her praise of it. Her confidence in me has helped me get the inevitable rejection slips into perspective so that any ambition I used to have about being a famous writer is now well and truly gone.

Maurs never so much as hinted that I couldn't travel whenever I wanted to, and was always there to see me off and welcome me home again.

Maurs didn't resolve all of her issues before she died. But her capacity for loving and being loved was exceptional.

I miss her.

OTHER BOOKS BY SPINIFEX

Women's Circus: Leaping off the Edge

Adrienne Liebmann, Jen Jordan, Deb Lewis, Louise Radcliffe-Smith, Patricia Sykes and Jean Taylor (Eds.)

This is a big, rowdy, colorful, three-ring circus of a book, packed with death-defying feats and acts that will thrill and amaze— not the least of which is their breathtaking commitment to feminist process. — Carolyn Gage

ISBN: 1-875559-55-8

Voices of the Survivors

Patricia Easteal

Powerful and moving stories from survivors of sexual assault.

ISBN: 1-875559-24-8

Wire Dancing
Patricia Sykes

Circus as drama and risk.
. . . passionate, witty, erudite and ironic . . . the poetry experience of the year. — Bev Roberts

ISBN 1-875559-90-6

Bird
Susan Hawthorne

Many-eyed and many-lived is this poet, as seismologist or lover, bird or newborn child. To the classic figures of Sappho or Eurydice she brings all the Now! Here! sense of discovery that fires her modern girl taking lessons in flight.

— Judith Rodriguez

ISBN: 1-875559-88-4

Kick the Tin
Doris Kartinyeri

When Doris Kartinyeri was a month old, her mother died, and Doris was removed from the hospital and placed in Colebrook Home. A moving testimony from one of the Stolen Generation.

ISBN: 1-875559-95-7

Zelda
Zelda D'Aprano

An essential contribution to the history of the women's movement.

ISBN: 1-875559-30-2

darkness more visible

Finola Moorhead

Fine writing, epic narrative, detective story and a cyber-conspiracy all combine to make this remarkable new novel by one of Australia's most exciting novelists.

ISBN: 1-875559-60-4

Figments of a Murder

Gillian Hanscombe

A rich and robust satire of feminist politics combined with a murder mystery. — Anne Coombs, *The Australian*

ISBN: 1-875559-43-4

Love Upon the Chopping Board
Marou Izumo and Claire Maree

Autobiography, duobiography, love story, cross cultural reflections, lesbian history—*Love Upon the Chopping Board* is all these things and more.

ISBN: 1-875559-82-5

Car Maintenance, Explosives and Love and other contemporary lesbian writings
Susan Hawthorne, Cathie Dunsford and Susan Sayer (Eds.)

An anthology which explores the mechanics of daily life, the explosiveness of relationships, and the geography of love.

ISBN 1-875559-62-0

Photo Kristi Giselsson

Jean Taylor was born in Melbourne in 1944, and raised in country Victoria. Pregnant at 17, married at 18 and with two children by the time she was 19, she came out as a lesbian in 1979.

Jean has worked in a variety of jobs including nursing, waitressing, women's refuge work and tram driving. She has been a member of various feminist activist collectives in the Women's Liberation Movement since the early 1970s, including the Victorian Women's Liberation and Lesbian Feminist Archives, a performer with lesbian theatre groups and the Women's Circus (where she learned how to walk on stilts at age 47) and initiated and directed the Performing Older Women's Circus for womyn over 40.

Jean has written several novels, plays, short stories and some poetry and began self-publishing her books in 1976, including *Sappho's Wild Lesbians* and *Loose Women*, under the pseudonym of Emily George and the logo of Dykebooks.

Jean has recently celebrated her 56th birthday with a croning ceremony and takes great delight in being a grandmother.